ISBN 978-1-331-67486-3
PIBN 10219881

This book is a reproduction of an important historical work. Forgotten Books uses
state-of-the-art technology to digitally reconstruct the work, preserving the original format
whilst repairing imperfections present in the aged copy. In rare cases, an imperfection in
the original, such as a blemish or missing page, may be replicated in our edition. We do,
however, repair the vast majority of imperfections successfully; any imperfections that
remain are intentionally left to preserve the state of such historical works.

1 MONTH OF
FREE
READING

at

www.ForgottenBooks.com

By purchasing this book you are eligible for one month membership to ForgottenBooks.com, giving you unlimited access to our entire collection of over 1,000,000 titles via our web site and mobile apps.

To claim your free month visit:

www.forgottenbooks.com/free219881

English
Français
Deutsche
Italiano
Español
Português

www.forgottenbooks.com

Mythology Photography **Fiction**
Fishing Christianity **Art** Cooking
Essays Buddhism Freemasonry
Medicine **Biology** Music **Ancient
Egypt** Evolution Carpentry Physics
Dance Geology **Mathematics** Fitness
Shakespeare **Folklore** Yoga Marketing
Confidence Immortality Biographies
Poetry **Psychology** Witchcraft
Electronics Chemistry History **Law**
Accounting **Philosophy** Anthropology
Alchemy Drama Quantum Mechanics
Atheism Sexual Health **Ancient History**
Entrepreneurship Languages Sport
Paleontology Needlework Islam
Metaphysics Investment Archaeology
Parenting Statistics Criminology
Motivational

HEART HISTORIES,

SPIRIT LONGINGS, ETC.

By L. B. F.

PUBLISHED BY THE AUTHOR.

MALONE, N. Y.

AND

139 EIGHTH ST., NEW YORK.

1877.

LEAVES FROM THE COUNTRY—FEELINGS AND FANCIES.

———

Go, little book; yet fear I for thee, lest so small and frail a craft, when launched upon a doubtful sea, should ride the sport of the rough winds and waves, till sunk beneath the billows.

May none but gentle gales and zephyrs bland waft thee upon thy untried way shouldst thou once venture from the safer shore.

———

Dedicated to my Aunt Eunice Conant, as a mark of esteem and gratitude.

———

Hoping in God's kind help, I venture forth.

CONTENTS.

LINES WRITTEN WHEN I FIRST THOUGHT OF PUTTING MY EARLY PIECES IN TYPE, IN THE LONG AGO.

Though I am young, in childhood's leisure
I court the Muses for my pleasure,
Fearing, the while, they'll come to shame me
For my presumption, and to blame me
That I so youthful and unwise
Should dare to lift to *them* my eyes.

But if they frown, and slight, and jeer me,
They, sometimes, come so very near me
That I can see the chaplets wreathing
Their fairy brows, and hear their breathing;
And then I screen my blushing face
Lest they deny me, seeking grace.

But though youth's shy, 'twill often venture
To try its wings in spite of censure;
And so do I, a youthful creature—
Who to step safe needs yet a teacher—
Attempt to write a single rhyme,
Hoping I may improve in time.

Then dear friends (if friends I've any—
All have either few or many),
Should these lays, I write in childhood,
Rustic seem, with scent of wildwood,
Or too weak or too pathetic,
Please be, each, my gentle critic ;

For my heart doth faint and falter
Here, before the Muses' altar ;
And my fingers shrink and tremble,
For I cannot well dissemble
That I fear they'll spurn each line,
Though *I* love it, for 'tis mine.
   183–.

THE BURNING OF ST. EUSTACHE, CANADA.

NO FICTION.

Written and spoken at a School Exhibition in my early school days—
1837.

Aurora dawned in beauty on our land—
Skies smiled aloft—the air was fresh and bland;
Morn never shone more lovely, bright, or clear;
But soon a cloud arose—soon dropped the tear—
A darksome doom upon our village fell,
And few were left the horrid tale to tell.
A countless host against the Western sky,
With martial tread and banners streaming high,
Equipped for fight, on our defenseless town,
Like hungry mountain wolves, came rushing down.
And the dark deeds, within that lovely vale,
Will be to-night the burthen of my tale.
The scene, uprising fresh before my sight,
Within my brain seems acted o'er to-night.

"Hark you! th' approaching tramp; the rolling drum;
The 'Tory' hosts draw near! They come! They come!
Haste! to our rescue fly! My son, be brave,
And ne'er return a coward or a slave.
Let 'Death or Freedom' your proud war-cry be;
Fight for our homes, but most our liberty."
Thus says a widowed mother to her son—
Her first-born boy—and quick the deed is done.

He goes, that gallant youth, with eagle eye,
And fervent prayers for him ascend on high.
He joins the " rebel " force, and with his might
He wields his weapons foremost in the fight.
(O ! noble mother of a noble son
Such heroism should the field have won,
E'en though his band, but poorly armed and few,
Wrestled with thousands who the broadsword drew.
But fiends methinks in human shape were there,
And Pity fled the field in blank despair !
Dire carnage and disorder gained the day,
And valiant arms were crushed amid the fray.)
A husband from the scabbard draws his sword,
And turns his face to front th hireling horde.
With dark forebodings in his anxious mind,
He turns from home and dear ones leaves behind ;
Yet looks he back upon the faithful wife
Who long hath shared with him the toils of life.
With gloomy brow, a fond adieu he waves;
Then, speeding swift, o'ertakes the patriot braves.
For her, too hard the test, her woman's heart
Shrinks from the partner of her life to part.
Quick, from the wainscot with her fragile hand
A gun is seized. *She* joins the " rebel " band.
And gray-haired men, far past the prime of life,
With tott'ring steps, haste onward to the strife.
And aged matrons to the battle fly,
Beneath the soldier's tread ere long to lie.
And children, in the hurry and amaze,
Scarce from the parent's knee, their weapons raise.
And mothers, trembling from their couch of pain,
With tiny babes, press to the bloody plain.
    Thus, with a force half puerile, the brave
Push to the confl ct, their loved land to save ;
And, though outnumbered, to the fight impelled,
In honor and in valor they excelled.

Nobly, like men, each battles with his might,
For home and country rush befo·e their sight;
They stagger not before the clashing steel,
Nor the broad claymore's thrusts force them to reel;
But like to savage beasts th' opposing host
Combat, and honor on the field is lost,
While cherished homes and hearths they desecrate
In use for their vile purposes to wait.
 Now serried ranks close on the little band
Which, hot contesting, grapple hand to hand.

    ❖   *

But list! hoarse shouts of victory arise;
'Tis patriot blood the field of carnage dyes;
Dread massacre, with more than brutal mien,
With horrid front, now stalks the dismal scene.
The gasping warriors fly the battle-plain;
In heaps the dying lie; in heaps the slain.
Some, now o'erpowered and fainting, deign to yield;
Some raise the flag of truce—time-hallowed shield;
While women to the house of God repair,
There to invoke the throne of heaven with pray'r.
But all in vain the flag is raised on high,
And ardent prayers ascend the vaulted sky;
Heaven from the carnage turns its mou·nful face,
Lest God, in wrath, should blast the mortal race.
Now, rush the "rebels" to the sacred Fane,
And, in their haste, each nerve and fibre strain;
Still, ruthless murderers their steps pursue,
Thirsting for blood of those whose souls were true
To Peace, to Freedom—not the clanking chains
Of dark Oppression, or a Tyrant's reins.
Quickly o'ertaking those who hither flee—
Unmoved by pity or the suppliant knee—
They thrust through every heart the quiv'ring blade;
The glittering bayonet by no hand is staid;

Not e'en the infant 'neath the fond embrace,
Which anxiously looks up with pleading face;
Nor e'en the pale, consumptive, ghastly form
Of helpless woman can be spared the storm,
Till, desperate, the " rebels " force their way,
And close the portals mid the awful fray.
As heroes brave they now the siege withstand,
And bar each passage with a mighty hand.
Oh, useless effort; life prolonged in vain;
A moment more, they number with the slain.
Sweet Liberty! that name to them most dear
They ne'er can know, ne'er feel its gladd'ning cheer.
Yet Freedom from their dust full-armed shall spring,
And the " proud bird " shall soar with outspread wing.
The foe the sacred temple now defame,
(Methinks a curse hangs o'er their deeds and name,
Despair and anguish shall their pathway wreathe,
And scorpion stings each smitten conscience seethe
As branded Cains upon the face of earth,
No solace to their souls shall life give birth.)
So, nobly, entrance being now denied,
Anger inflames; revenge aloud is cried.
Terrific to behold their mad career—
Thousands 'gainst one—he falls—the brave Chenier!
With back against a pillar of the Fane,
His eye ne'er quailed, nor frenzied reeled his brain;
Boldly he battled, firm and undismay'd,
And slaughtered numbers by his hand were laid.
With more than lion-courage, proud he stood
Till countless saber thrusts spilled his life blood.
Now, 'gainst the temple fiery darts are hurled—
The prisoned soon *must* meet another world—
Before the great Avenger they will stand
To plead their wrongs, that murdered, noble band;
But not as yet—the arrows powerless fall,
Nor bullets pierce the consecrated wall.

Now, to the roof part ply the flaming torch,
And part with firebrands light the sacred porch.
Red flames uprise and crackle in the wind,
And devastation follows fast behind.
The massive walls, now fired, are cleaving through;
The savage monsters raise their shouts anew;
The adamantine souls the trumpet blow;
They raise the cup and drink the crimson flow,
And toast their lives, their wives, their heav'n, their all,
Joying at those foul deeds, which *brave* they call.
Mercy, to them, is as an unknown word,
Its thrilling accents are unheeded heard.
Now, the fierce-raging element within,
Thundering, drowns the ribaldry and din.
Bursting, the scorching flames to heaven ascend;
The earth's foundation shakes; the echoes rend
The air; keen, piercing shrieks, heartrending cries,
Deep, gurgling death-groans from the dying rise;
The ear is stunned; words never can portray
The dreadful scene, nor man the deeds repay.
His soul would faint ere half his work was done;
E'en its foul image he would haste to shun.
Some 'scape the lurid flames through broken sash,
Ere their hot prison-walls around them crash;
They leap upon the graves where sleep the dead
Of earlier days, ere yet the hostile tread
Of British minions had defiled the sod
And drenched the hallowed dust with patriot blood.
Here still pursued?   Oh, whither shall they go?
Followed by hosts who aim the deadly blow,
They dread the massacre they needs must feel,
They dread the mangling of the reeking steel;
A prey to fiends begirt with human form,
They raise alas! the suicidal arm.
Most gloomy fate! that man should spill his blood
To 'scape the vengeance of a demon crowd.

Giroud thus perishes; with his own hands
Stained by his blood, he enters unknown lands.
(One leader he of those few patriot braves
Who courted death rather than live as slaves.)
Thus many fell upon their native soil—
Their late proud home—a prey to fury's spoil.
The foe insatiate still, with rapid haste
The dear, devoted village is laid waste.
(But erst is pillaged every house and hut,
The greedy hirelings' purse with wealth to glut)
Destruction reigns supreme; the burning air
Now drives the rabid soldiery from its lair.
Their work is finished; but the day hastes on
When God will retribute the dark deeds done.

Now turn I back where loved Eustache just stood :
I gaze in anguish on the blood-drenched sod ;
Here lie in heaps the noble warriors slain
Fighting for home and country, but in vain ;
And here the mother, wife and gentle child,
Mangled and to n as by beasts of the wild ;
And there, 'mid smoking ruins where once bowed
The humble souls before a gracious God,
Lie bones and ashes of the bodies doomed
To writhe beneath the flames which them consumed ;
And there, too, fallen homes around whose hearths
The loved ones met ere they had fled from earth.
Oh, sickening sight ! With heart appalled I gaze
Upon the spot beloved of former days.
Havoc of wrath, flames, butchery and death,
Late smiling vales, fouled by war's blasting breath.
Ye weep, kind ladies ! not unpitying, weep ;
Blush not that tear-drops from their fountains creep ;
How could, unmoved, ye view those lone r mains ?
Earth, soaked with crimson gore from mortal veins ?

The noble husband, youth and aged sire
Passed thus from earth to sate a savage ire !
How could, unmoved, ye view your sex enthralled
In war's dire carnage brutally despoiled ?
Unpitying view the nursling innocent,
So harmless, tortured to give vengeance vent ?
Poor little trembling captive, hither led
To writhe beneath the scourge with kindred dead.
The mourning ones (if such their race survive),
Friendless, perchance, upon the earth to live ?
The sight might cause a saint to drop a tear,
To weep with those who still may linger here ;
Might cause the angels who sit round the throne
To heave a sigh for those who thence have flown.
   Ladies, that dreadful day is scarcely past—
The dying embers crackle on the waste—
And while the mournful ta'e to you I tell,
Swine lick the dust where patriot heroes fell.

Oh, tell me, spirits, round the judgment bar—
Ye countless host, who range both near and far—
Oh, tell me, was such doom decreed on High
By Him who reigns beyond the ambient sky ?
Or was it so decreed by hell beneath,
Man should thus perish, thus his life bequeath
To sate a brutal, hireling, ireful foe ?
Here drops the vail—this mortals may not know.

A PROLOGUE.

Written in my early school days.

Kind audience, before you we appear,
With grateful thanks for that indulgent ear
Which you so gently to our voices lent
When last we spake, with fear, so diffident.
And now, again, we beg that same kind ear
To cheer our hearts and calm that youthful fear.
We seek for favor, but ask not applause,
Nor do we think to speak by critic's laws.
Ladies, expect not actresses to come,
With much experience and with glory won ;
But wait us, simple, inexperienced youth,
Whose falt'ring tongues aim to speak only truth,
And while in mimic acts we take a part,
Survey us with a kind and friendly heart;
And should our efforts of this eve be vain
To please or to amuse, dear ladies deign
To judge us gently; all the faults excuse
Of trembling pupils, who are not much used
To speak and act in public on the stage,
To edify an audience of this age.
Mayhap, in course of time, some here will be
As learned and famed as most of those I see ;
Our minds may grow, our faculties expand,
Our knowledge may extend from land to land.
Aye, such as great as Hemans may arise
(In song as gifted, and in lore as wise)
From out these youthful, student ranks of ours,
To show the world their mind's superior powers.
Yes; then some ghosts of writers; long since dead,
May meet superiors soaring in their stead,
And fear their fame eclipsed, come back again,
Revise their musty books—rewield their pen.

AFTER THE NEWS OF LAFAYETTE'S DEATH.

Brave Lafayette! "The nation's guest,"
Who came to bless a land now blest,
Thy noble heart, of heavenly birth,
Revered by all who felt thy worth;
Thy ready true and valiant hand,
Reached forth to aid our struggling land,
Now throbs no more—each pulse is staid,
In the chill tomb thy form is laid;
Yet though from earth has fled thy soul,
Thy fame shall sound while ages roll,
And Lafayette shall ever be
Linked with the name of Liberty.

LAKE CHAMPLAIN.

Written after crossing it in 1835.

Thy waters, beautiful Champlain,
  . Were calm and clear ;
No wave was seen upon thy main—
  Nothing to fear.

But were it always so with thee,
  Lakelet serene ?
Did ne'er man perish 'neath thy waves,
  In tempests keen ?

Have not thy surges swelled and foamed
  An ocean wide ?
And has not man thy billows roamed—
  A dangerous tide ?

Oh, who can tell what thou wert once?
  What thou wilt be ?
Perchance thy waters yet may roll
  A boundless sea.

OUR CLASSIC GREEN.

When in distant, future years,
　We are cast on stranger lands,
Childhood's joys and childhood's tears
　Mem'ry then shall call to mind.
The green on which we oft have met
Shall we ever then forget?

When by time's fast-fleeting breath
　All our locks are silv'ry gray;
When a part lie cold in death,
　Sleeping 'neath their kindred clay,
Then shall those who linger yet
Ere their classic green forget?

Where our halls of science stand,
　Where our happiest days have fled,
Where have oft this youthful band
　Sat beneath their cooling shade;
There upon our classic green
Shall we all e'er meet again?

Land of knowledge—land of fame—
　Land of light and liberty,
Nations, bowing to thy name,
　Envy now thy majesty;
Shall we all e'er meet again
Here upon thy wide domain?

THE BACKSLIDING DRUNKARD.

His name I will not tell.
  He was a man;
But oh, he loved the bowl too well,
And fearful was its fatal spell,
So fearful that the fiends of hell
  Held him in ban.

Kind friends he had and true—
  A sister dear,
A brother and a mother, too,
And anxious prayers ascended new,
And tears were shed that he might rue
  His course with fear.

He tried—in wisdom's plan
  Awhile he lived—
But the foul tempter 'gain began
(A tempter in the form of man)
To burst fair Reason's envied span—
  Again she fled.

And now a drunken sot
  He treads his way;
And prayers and tears of friends forgot,
And friends still dear, he heeds them not,
But better loves the outcast's lot,
  And beggary.

HER JEWELS.

Of a noble and rich lady.

Modesty and virtue were the jewels that she wore,
And, conscious of their beauty, she never asked for more ;
Unmeaning gold and princely gem she felt could not
    adorn
The soul that for Eternity was destined to be born.

Modesty and virtue her every act confest
(No pride of birth or pride of wealth e'er lodged within
    her breast),
And radiant with their purity she shone more sweetly
    bright
Than any earthly diadem beheld by mortal sight.

TO THE SAME.

Since virtue glistens on thy brow,
   A gem so sweetly fair,
Let heaven's grace accompany
   Ever the jewel there.

MUSINGS.

Spoken at school.

Who was not born to die ?   Whose life will never end ?
Whose eye hath never wept ?   Who hath not lost a
    friend ?
Alas ! 'Tis vain to ask, methinks I hear thee say ;
All must in time depart ; all, all must hence away.
    To mansions far beyond these climes immortal souls
      must take their flight,
    Or far beneath ! (Unhappy thought.) Dying, yet
      live through endless night.

Who hath not disappointment felt ?   Whose fond hopes
    ne'er decay ?
Around whom hath adversity ne'er writhed with with-
    'ring sway ?
E'en by the child its grasp is felt—these ills in human
    shape
The infant on its mother's breast can scarce be said to
    'scape.
    Why hope we then for happier days below ?   Since
      hope to us will be of no avail.
    The curtain drops, and lo ! futurity—ah, who can
      read the direful, doleful tale ?

Who hath not heard the warning voice ?   Who hath not
    felt the conscience speak ?
Who hath not watched the pallid brow ?   Who hath not
    marked the hectic cheek ?

Ah, none; none must the answer be; sin causes all a
    pang to feel;
Sorrow and pain here never rest, nor penitence the wound
    can heal.
    But we must look far, far beyond these earthly
        realms to realms unknown;
    There happiness takes its abode; there all that mor-
        tals wish is flown.

ANSWER.

Nay, say not thus, dear friend; that brow was never
    marked with pain;
That eye the tear of sorrow never shed—'tis all in vain
To fix thy thoughts on things so distant, so divine,
When now thy cup o'erflows with bliss—all wished is
    thine.

REPLY.

How little dost thou know of earth, thy youth and inex-
    perience tell;
This heart its anguish cannot speak; 'tis known by none,
    yet 'tis as well;
    And though this brow and eye so gay and tranquil
        may to thee appear,
Know thou that many a smile plays on the lip
When all within would gladly weep,
    And drop the penitential tear.

OLD PICKWAKET, NOW FRYEBURG, ME.

A composition. Fryeburg, Me. Impromptu.

My friends, as all our text doth know
   In rhyme to us was given;
So you will all excuse, I trow
   A rhymy composition.

Please let me then begin my task,
   To tell about a hero;
His name or place you need not ask,
   'Twill soon be all cognito.

In seventeen hundred, twenty-five,
   From Massachusetts came, then,
A hero as gallant as brave,
   And Lovel was his name, ken.

He came up through a forest drear,
   And swamps and bogs and all that,
And quartered at a place quite near,
   Which then they called Pickwaket.

But Lovel came not up alone;
   No, there were others came, too,
With Frye, a chaplain of their own,
   Who—wondrous!—did the same, too.

'Twas on the seventh day of May
   That they arrived here safely,

And on the eighth began a fray,
　At ten o'clock, so gayly.

But ere they did this fray begin,
　They wandered from their course some,
Till they at length two miles had been,
　To meet an Indian's welcome.

'Twas at this time that Lovel spied,
　Upon a neck of land near,
An Indian in all his pride,
　Preparing an escort here.

He cried, at once, "Take heed, my boys;
　We soon shall be gallanted,
By those whom we had rather not,
　If he remains undaunted."

Then all at once they went to work,
　And soon their guns did work, too;
While he—the Indian—quite as quick,
　Two guns did shoot, and run, too.

Yet though he run, 'twas all for naught,
　The English all had feet, too,
And soon he found that he was caught,
　And soon had lost his scalp, too.

But here the fracas ended not—
　Their knapsacks had departed !
They took to heels and left the spot
　Where they had been deserted.

Now, all must know, who use their eyes,
　These heels they must have borrowed;
So these brave men concluded wise
　That they had been discovered.

And hurried, too, they were, I ween,
  For soon, at least, full fourscore
Of the Pickwaket tribe were seen
  To from their ambush forth pour.

Their welcome, to be sure, was hot—
  From hot it hotter grew, though,
Till many Indians were shot—
  Till many of them flew, though.

This battle, as you, doubtless, see,
  Commenced they in the morning,
Nor did they from the contest flee
  Until the sun was setting.

'Twas then that to the water's brink
  A Paugus was escorted,
By one called Chamberlain, I think,
  When one the other challenged.

But which it was I've quite forgot,
  Though Paugus 'twas who paid it;
For there he died upon the spot,
  And none did e'er regret it.

Now, as I once before have said,
  Within this battle, eighty
Of Indians there were, but of
  The English, four and thirty.

Yet, though of Englishmen there were
  But few in point of number,
The loss to them was soon made up
  As they lacked not for valor

They beat the Indians, out and out,
  And ransacked old Pickwaket,

Till not a single soul was left
  To fight for or redeem it.

But, I've before my story got,
  For e'er the battle ended,
'Twas Captain Lovel had been shot,
  And Chaplain Frye been wounded.

And fourteen more there were who found
  That they were tired of fighting,
And prone extended on the ground
  They seemed, in quiet, resting.

And there they rested five days long,
  When they, at length, were buried
(At least, methinks, so says the song),
  And then the rest departed.

[Written running, March, 1841]

TO A SCHOOLMATE IN GORHAM, ME.

Dear friend, like many, we are doomed to part,
   As we, like many, here on earth have met;
But shall the tie that binds a heart to heart
   Perish by time or wither by neglect?
And must we part to meet no more for years—
   To meet, perchance, but in eternity;
Or shall we meet within this vale of tears
   As strangers meet, and pass by silently;
Or shall we meet in friendship's warm embrace,
   Remembered by each other long and well?
Whate'er the time, whate'er the way or place,
   This last fond tale may I be doomed to tell.

ANSWER.

Aye, friend in joy, we here have met,
   Within this earthly vale of tears,
And now in sorrow we must part,
   To meet no more perhaps for years—
To meet (but must it, can it be?)—
To meet but in eternity.

'Tis hard to leave the friends we love,
   With this sad destiny in view;
'Tis hard to sever youthful hearts,
   Enchained by frienship warm and true.
But we can meet on heaven's shore,
Where friends are doomed to part no more.

LOVE.

Love! love! Pray what is love?
Tell me, oh, ye who feel its witchery.
They say that love has charms—
    I do not know—
And that its object of faults disarms—
    An instance show.
I never saw one right in mind and looks;
I've only read the thing in fairy books.

They say, blind are Love's eyes—
    Can this be true?
And that he aims his darts from yon blue skies—
    I wish I knew.
I never saw his arrows cleave the air;
And yet they say it is a thing not rare.

They say that Love is coy—
    I cannot tell;
And yet they say that Cupid is a boy—
    Oh, very well.
Yet still it is a thing to me most strange
That through the world a boy so shy should range.

Oh, naughty little Love!
    Thou art unkind
To reckless aim thy arrows from above,
    When thou art blind.
Poor, silly thing, thou'rt but a name; no more—
Imagination gives thee life and power.

I'LL TAKE IT BACK. TO LOVE.

So, little Mr. Cupid,
You think me very stupid,
And you really do resent it,
And you mean I shall repent it,
Because I called you "silly thing,"
Little boy, with silver wing.

So you aimed at me a dart,
Thinking it would pierce my heart,
Meaning I should make confession
That I did commit transgression
When I called you "silly thing"
Little boy, with silver wing.

But, indeed, you were unkind,
Little boy, though you were blind,
Thus to aim at me love's arrow ;
For I own my 'scape was narrow,
For I almost felt the sting,
Little boy, with silver wing.

And I will take back the word
Which, unluckily, you heard,
Though my heart is safe and sound yet ;
And you needn't think to wound it,
Because I called you "silly thing,"
Little boy, with silver wing.

THE WORDS OF A BROTHER, DYING AT SEA—SHERIDAN.

"Don't leave me—don't leave me—don't leave me," he
  cried,
  "Thus to die here alone on the sea;
Don't leave me—don't leave me, but watch by my side,
  My dear father would were it he.

"My father, my father, oh, father, come near;
  Is this death that is scorching my brain?
How harsh is his touch, how racking and sear,
  Yet, Heaven, I must not complain.

"No, no, I must die on the broad ocean's foam,
  With no friend, with no comforter nigh;
No brother, no sister—far, far from my home;
  But ah! there's a home in the sky.

"Roll on, then, ye waters; roll on, then, ye waves;
  Your proud boast I shall soon cease to care,
That millions now moulder within their deep graves,
  And I, too, must mix with them there.

"Don't leave me—don't leave me," yet once more he
  cried;
  "Oh, my father, my father, come near;"
But ah! no father was there by his side,
  No loved ones his last hour to cheer.

And now in the deep—all unmarked is the spot—
  Doth he sleep 'neath the rough, roaring billow;

But oh ! by his friends he will ne'er be forgot—
  Nor the sailor who watched by his pillow.

And though hard and cruel on earth was his fate
  Yet, dear God, we will strive ne'er to sorrow ;
Though dead—he has gone to a happier state,
  And we'll meet him in some future morrow.

SHERIDAN.

I see him in my dreams, and think he lives;
  And as upon his well-known face I gaze,
I feel him warmly clasp my hand in his,
  While he doth talk to me of bygone days.
I see him in my dreams—my brother dear—
  And as we ramble by some stream or brook,
He points me to the waters bright and clear,
  And then to heaven he casts an upward look.
I see him in my dreams—a vessel lies
  Within a harbor, not far off from land
He tells me there is where the sailor dies,
  And then—too soon—he gives the parting hand.
Again I see my brother—by his side,
  As round his brow a smile of joy doth play,
Upon the foaming, billowy sea I ride,
  Nor deem I there must be a parting day
And then I see him as the deck he walks,
  While loosely o'er his arm doth hang a shroud,
And then I hear him as he whisp'ring talks
  With angels—seemingly an angel-crowd.
And then I see him as he climbs the mast
  (Obeying orders) till he gains its head,
Bedecked in robes of white, on which " 'Tis past "
  In golden letters shines, by angels read.
And then I see him as with them the sky
  He traces till around God's throne they stand.
And then I hear a voice—'tis from on high—
  " Sister, weep not, I came at God's command."
And then, again, a voice like music sweet
  I hear; 'tis his—the strain is silvery clear—

" Sister, weep not, we soon again may meet."
   And then what see I but the funeral bier,
And on it is an open coffin placed,
   Methinks, and by it lies the dismal pall;
And then, methinks that spirits round I trace,
   Who fain me to another world would call.
And then, methinks, I look upon the deep,
   While op'ning yawn its dark and troubled waves;
They tell me there is where I soon must sleep;
   'Tis there the dead at sea must find their graves
" My God !".—'tis now in agony I cry—
   " What meaneth this ?" as quakes my frame with fear.
Again I heard his voice, in soft reply,
   " Sister, why shed you then the sorrowing tear ?
I thought you wept that we had parted been;
   And still you do not wish that we may meet;
Or would you call me back to earth again ?
   Or why refuse in heaven me to greet ?
Or know'st thou not that none can come this way
   Till they have passed the portals of the dead ?
Yet linger if thou wilt; yes, ling'ring, stay
   Till all thou lov'st on earth hath from thee fled.
Linger till time hath furrowed deep thy cheek
   With sorrow, pain and anguish, and thine eye
Hath dull and heavy grown, thy life-blood weak;
   Then we may meet shouldst thou then wish to die.
Yet, sister, hear me, cling not thus to earth;
   There is a poison in its every joy—
Crave not its bliss, 'tis all of little worth;
   And yet how many doth its bliss destroy !
Sister, prepare to meet me soon above—
   Thy mother joins me in this last request.
Here all is happiness and joy and love;
   Here are the loved of God most truly blest."
But now the spell is past, the dream is done;
   While all I have I'd freely, gladly give

Could I but surely know that he had gone
   To where the blest of God triumphant live;
Could I but see, as in my dream I saw,
   Him stand with angels at the Lamb's right hand,
No tears should evermore my eye let flow,
   Save 'twere to meet him in the " better land."

TO ———.

There is a theme on which I'm doomed to dwell
   From night till morn, from rise till set of sun.
I fly in vain the ever-sounding knell,
   And try to shut the imagery of one
From 'neath my heart. But bear with me, my friend,
   For thou ere long may'st know what 'tis to mourn
O'er one whom thou hast loved, and weep his end,
   So unexpected from thy fond heart torn.
And think not I my promise have forgot,
   That "I with scribbling ne'er would vex thee more."
But pardon me for an untruth, and wot
   That when the bosom heaves with sorrow sore,
There is a happiness unknown by all,
   A pleasure pure in breathing out the thoughts
To those whom we esteem and rightly call
   Our friends—those who o'erlook our many faults.
Then let thou me once more my song renew,
Nor chide me though the picture prove untrue.

I woke—'twas morn—no smiling zephyrs played
   Among the blosoms rare of Beauty's bower;
No sportive rills, no airy songsters strayed
   To greet me as I culled a new blown flower.

No; but in sable dressed the heavens frowned,
   And seemed in thunders loud and bold to speak
"A curse on man! Let vengeance heal the wound
   That sin hath made; let God His vengeance wreak."

Then quick athwart the sky the lightnings rushed,
   And all on earth shone as it were one blaze;

Then from beneath their bounds vast torrents gushed
  Impetuously, as 'twere in former days.

Then fierce the howling winds together clashed,
  And seeming, warred with Heaven's elements,
While rocks and mountains huge in twain were dashed;
  And earth was shattered by its million rents.

The oceans rocked and roared and heaved in one;
  The dark above met with the dark below;
They met, but parted—still no rising sun
  Or noonday light dispelled the fear of woe.

'Twas hurrying then ; and many a half-said prayer
  Unheard, was drowned beneath the tumult's roar ;
And thicker, faster, lightnings filled the air,
  And peal on peal of thunder, thunder bore.

I gazed ; but ere the twinkling of an eye
  I heard, I saw, I felt the dead were raised—
'Twas hushed, 'twas calm ; behold ! the sea was dry ;
  The dead of sea the dead of earth amazed.

ENVY AND JEALOUSY.

Envy and Jealousy, two sisters, met,
The one in a stew and the one in a fret;
For as they were viewing the news of the day,
They spied a new piece, in their usual way,
Which troubled them sore, for they were afraid
That credit was due to whom it was laid;
And thus they in confidence quickly began
The piece, with its faults and its virtues, to scan.
They looked first at this part, and then looked at that;
Its faults far exceeded its virtues they thought;
" But who is the authoress, pray can you tell ?
Miss B. it is not; she could ne'er write so well."
" No, not her," now outspake Miss Envy aloud ;
" But I wish those who wrote were not quite so proud,
And those who do not, would cease to lay claim
To what is not theirs, for the gaining of fame.
You doubtless remember a piece, long ago
We heard ; though not good, it was yet something so.
And, too, what eclat the authoress got ;
But yet 'twas half borrowed—do you think it was not ?"
" Indeed 'twas not hers—the piece—I am sure ;
But then if it was, pray who can endure
This writing and rhyming, with all, which of late
The world looks upon as so wonderfully great ?
I wish that Miss B. was as wise as she's witty ;
Yet as she is not, we must scorn her or pity.
Yet we are not all who doubt her, I ween,
For there's Mistress M., who declared she had seen
The very same piece, and had read it before,
Although some one else had for her fixed it o'er.

Now any one might, I should think, if they chose,
Just take an old piece of verse or of prose,
And polish it well with new-fashioned airs,
And then to the world declare that it's theirs."
"Oh, yes," cried Miss Jealousy; " Come, let us try it;
Soon each may be called a great writer or poet."
And now, as she sits with her pen and her books,
The image of Poetry Jealousy looks.
But Envy is still, with her dishevelled hair,
Her serpentine tongue and her maniac air,
With eyes 'neath whose lashes a demon like fire
Lies hidden in part—'tis the murderer's ire—
Engaged in her office-work—peace to her soul;
If peace can be found where has Falsehood her goal.

DEATH'S FLOWERS.

[Written as a small token of respect to the memory of the two cousins and an aged man, all buried in one week in our little village. The two cousins were children of Messrs. C. and T. Briggs.]

Alas! alas! a lovely flower,
   Scarce op'ning on its stem,
Death took, while on his cruel tour,
   To grace his diadem.
And now the parent stock is left
   To droop in sadness o'er
The bud of which it is bereft,
   Till it shall be no more.
And still another blossom rare
   A kindred plant must mourn ;
A blossom precious, more mature,
   Which Death far thence hath borne.
And thus it is the young and good
   Are favorites with all—
Then why should death, in stranger mood,
   Pass those most worth his call ?
Aye, why should Death the prattling sweet,
   That twines so closely round
Its mother's anxious, doting heart,
   Pass by in scorn profound ?
Or why should he, the first-born child,
   Bright with intelligence,
The parent's hope, the fair, the mild,
   Pass by in negligence ?
He never did, he never will
   Neglect the chosen few ;
And though he comes unsought and still,
   His grasp is firm and true.

Yet none but once shall feel his power
   While stay they here below;
The tender " bud," the blooming " flower "
   Death's chill but once must know.
The aged " oak," with palsied breath,
   Fast tottering to the grave,
As his—the boon—but once cold Death,
   With iron hand will crave.
Still all this " once " must yield before,
   His harsh and heavy stroke;
While round their heads his shadows wreath,
   The doom by heaven spoke.
But those most pure he bears away
   To climes more brightly fair,
Where beams in beauty every ray,
   That dares to venture there.
Where streams of living waters glide
   Through beds of pearly sand,
And birds with glitt'ring pinions wide
   Flit o'er the happy land.
Where shines in deep, resplendent hue
   The ruby's dazzling red;
Where " jasper " and the diamond too
   A vast effulgence spread.
Where " emerald " and sapphire bide
   To deck the princely halls;
Where soft luxuriance swells the tide
   And pleasure never palls.
Where " buds " and " blossoms," each a gem,
   And " plants " together glow
And sparkle in the diadem
   That crowns Jehovah's brow.
Where bleeding hearts and pallid cheeks,
   And eyes bedewed with tears,
And quiv'ring lips where anguish speaks,
   And earthly pains and fears;

Where hoary locks and trembling limbs
    Worn out in service long,
And sight that ruthless time fast dims
    With naught but sorrow's wrong,
Are never known ; where joys supreme
    Light with their radiance
The golden streets that richly beam
    With heaven's excellence.

THE STEAMSHIP PRESIDENT.

The first steamship launched on the ocean, and lost in its first and
last trip, in 1841.

They left their native land and home,
To breast the raging ocean's foam,
While many an eye was bathed in tears
That friends might parted be for years,
And many a parent's heart beat wild
As wafted thence a darling child.
They left their native land and home,
And village spire and city dome,
And friends beloved and kindred dear,
And thought their aching hearts to cheer
In foreign climes, 'mid stranger lands;
Perchance to trace the burning sands
Or rocky hills of some far shore,
From all most dear on earth they tore.
And yet within the ship were some
Returning to their childhood's home.
And as they skimmed the deep blue waves
They little knew their destined graves,
But thought ere long again to tread
The land to which they gladly sped.
They wafted on, unwitting harm,
Unmindful of th' impending storm,
While not a single sail in view
Or island saw the jolly crew.
But oh, by Heaven their doom was sealed—
Anon the rolling thunders pealed,

The mighty winds rushed on in power,
Dark clouds did o'er the vessel lower ;
Forked lightnings scorched the lurid air,
Lit the rent sails with vivid glare ;
The ocean rocked, its waves rolled high,
And dashed the ship against the sky ;
The wreathing flames around them raved,
And waters wild the vessel laved,
While all, aghast, in suppliance bent,
Sank with the steamship President.

Days now have passed, and many an eye
Has sought the proud mast towering high,
And many a heart has anxious beat
The proud ship safe arrived to greet ;
But all in vain !   It never more
Alas ! can reach an earth-trod shore.

* * * * * *

Weeks now have passed ; still comes not in
The ship, nor has the wreck been seen.
But daily one fond voice is heard,
" What news ?   What news ?   Again no word !"*
" None, none, my lord !" is sad replied.
" No word !" the mourning father cried.

* * * *

Long, weary months have now passed by,
And still in vain, with sunken eye
And breaking heart, the father dear
Seeks from his long-lost son to hear ;
But oh, no word from him can come ;
He lies beneath the billows' home,

---

* It is said these words were daily uttered by a feeble and almost
frantic lord in England. as he daily went to the Post Office for news
of his lost son.

And not a soul is left to tell
The fate that has to him befell;
Not one of all that vessel bore
Can tread again Old England's shore;
And not as yet one trace appears
To tell what each too rightly fears.

  * * * * *

A year's slow time has now rolled round,
Nor has the vessel's wreck been found.

MY GRANDFATHER.

He was a good old man, but could not stay;
He has been called from earth to heaven away,
And saints have met him with their songs of joy,
And on his breast there leans an angel-boy.*
Grandsire and son have met—I see them now,
While bliss eternal sparkles on each brow;
I see them closely wrapped in fond embrace,
While beams a halo bright round either face;
And saints and angels gaze upon the twain
With holy transport.   God himself doth deign
To call with His loud voice on all the choir
To ring a welcome with the harp and lyre
To the freed soul which late hath conq'ring come
To claim a seat within His heavenly home.
I see the gray-haired man, in robes of white,
In glittering robes too bright for mortal sight;
And on his head I see a diadem
More brilliant than the finest earthly gem;
And on his forehead all the hosts of heaven
Can read the words, " He sinned, but is forgiven."

He was a good old man—I loved him well,
And prized him more than my weak words can tell;
And long methought he seemed too good for earth—
He was my grandsire, and 1 felt his worth.
But he has left us—we no more can hear
Blest counsel from the lips we did revere;
He's gone, and we no more can feel the spell
His holy presence wrought ere yet the knell

* Sheridan.

Of death had sounded, by high heaven's decree,
To bid him to a fairer destiny.
Yes, he has gone; yet we ere long shall meet,
And sit with him around the judgment seat.
Oh, yes, though now the scalding tear-drops start,
And bitter sighs escape our sorrowing heart;
Though he has left an aged bosom friend,
Long cherished and beloved, to weep his end;
Though children far away are doomed to hear
The sad, expected news, and drop the tear
Of silent grief, we know he is at rest
In mansions far above, amid the blest;
We know 'tis vain to mourn, for though in dust
He lowly lies, his soul amid the just,
In sweetest strains of harmony and love,
Is singing praises in the world above.
We know though he a friend hath been to us—
A parent-friend, and deep we feel his loss—
That we may soon with him in concert join
In hallelujahs to the Lamb-Divine.

TO THE MEMORY OF LITTLE GEORGE R——S.

For his mother.

My child ! oh, my child ! why so soon art thou gone
To regions beyond us, to mansions unknown ?
Oh, why, my dear boy, why so young didst thou leave,
In thy childhood's bright morn, thy fond mother to
     grieve ?

'Twere but yesterday, seemingly, thou didst appear
The picture of health ; thou wert ruddy and fair ;
But now in the coffin, with the sods o'er thy head,
They number my boy with the buried and dead.

Aye, low in the earth they thy body have laid,
Yet thy spirit has soared, for thy soul was not staid ;
And over thy grave, thou late joy of my heart,
Thy lone mother weeps, for she cannot depart.

My eldest-born child, oh, my once bright-eyed one,
Pray tell me why set, ere scarce risen, thy sun ?
Oh, why wert thou plucked from thy parent's embrace,
And borne far away an unseen world to grace ?

I mourn thee, and cannot but mourn ; but 'tis vain
I know to regret thee, for my loss is thy gain ;
I know thou hast 'scaped all the dangers below,
And art surer of heaven ; it were best thou shouldst go.

Then my child, oh, my own one ! I'll bid thee farewell
Till I shall be summoned with my lost one to dwell ;
Though my heart-strings would break and my bosom
     would heave,
I'll pray I may cease for thy absence to grieve.

THE DAUGHTER TO HER FATHER.

My father! thou art sad and lone, I know by thy sor-
    rowing sigh,
And by the stealing tear-drop that gathers in thine eye;
I know thy heart is like to break 'neath the chast'ning
    God has given ;
But, father, weep no more, I pray—my mother dwells in
    heaven.

My mother dwells in heaven above; for when the stars
    were bright,
And all below was beautiful beneath their smiling light ;
When evening had her mantle spread, and day from earth
    had driven,
I heard a whisper near—it said, " Thy mother dwells in
    heaven."

And father, if the word is true that they who go before
    us
To that blest land so far beyond the sky that's beaming
    o'er us,
Do ever to this earth return and round the loved ones
    hover,
Our guardian-angel she is now, my mother, oh, my
    mother !

How beautiful and fair a world !
    And yet how lonely, too—
Life is a solitude at best ;
    Its pleasures are but few.

TO A VERY LITTLE CHILD.

Prattle, prattle, little one !
  Tripping light, with tiny feet,
Let that heart beat joyous on,
  And those bright eyes smile, my sweet,
Whilst thou may ; before thou find
Pleasure leaves a sting behind.

Blithesome 'mid the flowers stray,
  Wafting forth their sweet perfume ;
While the gentle breezes play,
  Pluck the fairest ones in bloom ;
But beware lest now thou find
Pleasure leaves a sting behind.

On that flowret's stem, my boy,
  Many a piercing thorn is set ;
Thus in every mortal joy
  Lurks a thorn to pierce ; and yet
Many hope on earth to find
Pleasure leaves no sting behind.

TO A——A.

Think not all thy hopes will be realized here ;
For sadness and sorrow are everywhere near ;
But know thou shalt have thy due share of earth's weal,
If friendship and love can the fountain unseal.

But, dearest, remember that dark hours are nigh,
In the footsteps of sunshine clouds lower the sky—
Thus ever doth sorrow chase pleasure away,
Though the darkness of night oft makes brighter the day.

TO ———.

Though faithless I did seem the while,
   Thou still didst share my he rt ;
'Twas thou first taught me how to love—
   Then act the false one's part.

But oh, a scholar far more apt
   In love than in deceit,
My little art now vanishes
   When we together meet.

And since thou plight'st to me thy troth,
   My heart is thine for aye ;
So love shall light thy path through life,
   Though erst so dark the way.

Then let us don the mask no more
   Which truth has laid aside ;
'Twould ill become a wedded pair,
   Nor grace a happy bride.

TO ——.'

As Adam could not happy bide
  Without companion human,
God took a rib from 'neath his side,
  And made for him a woman.

So every man has one rib less
  Than when at first created,
Unless he seeks some *fair* redress,
  And is by woman mated.

Then take your rib back to your breast,
  Or you are maimed for life, sir;
Man is imperfect at the best
  Until he has a wife, sir.

THE PRESENT—A SOUVENIR QUILT.

A wish for ———. Written upon a block reserved for the purpose.

This souvenir quilt will oft, my dear,
    Full many a friend recall to mind,
Whose every wish of heart sincere
    With love and friendship is combined.

May love's and friendship's sweetest flowers
    Be fondly o'er thy pathway strown ;
While sunbeams bask through joy-winged hours
    Within the cot thou claim'st thine own

Aye, may their garland brightly beam
    Perennial round thy forehead fair,
That all may sip their sweet perfume,
    And feel affection's presence there !

A happy wedded pair may this enshroud,
When winter hovers near in storm and cloud.

ELDER SAFFORD.

A star of our Zion has set;
  'Twill gladden our earth nevermore;
We mourn for its loss with the deepest regret,
  Though it dawns on a happier shore.

It shines 'mid the Zion above,
  Beyond the dark regions of space;
It beams with the rays of peace, glory and love
  Which through the dim vista we trace.

Its beauty will there ne'er decline,
  But brighter and purer will glow;
Then mourn not its exit—'tis wrong to repine—
  'Twere too bright for this drear world below.

A star of our Zion has set—
  O'er the loss of a friend falls a tear;
For the pearl-drops of wisdom we ne'er can forget,
  From the lips we were wont to revere.

A star of our Zion has set;
  A husband and father's no more;
With the dear and departed above he has met,
  And is roaming o'er heaven's fair shore.

OH, WILT THOU EVER THINK OF ME?

Oh, wilt thou ever think of me,
　　When I am far away ?
Aye, when thou minglest in the throng,
　　Amid the glad and gay,
Will memory ever bring to mind
　　One absent from thy side ?
And turning from the festive throng,
　　Wilt thou regret thy bride ?

Oh, wilt thou ever think of me
　　When I am from thee gone ?
When the red daylight fades away,
　　And thou art sad and lone ?
Aye, when thou feel'st the tender spell
　　Of soft'ning twilight power,
Wilt thou not then revert to her
　　Thou woo'd in life's bright hour ?

Oh, wilt thou ever think of me
　　When I am from thee fled ?
Aye, when this form is lowly laid
　　Amid the silent dead,
Will one kind thought anon be found
　　Lurking within thy breast
Of her who loved thee well while yet
　　She was on earth a guest ?

Oh, sometimes, then, pray think of me,
　　My own companion dear,

And o'er my absence deign to drop
   A sad but silent tear.
Aye, may remembrance ever find
   Some glimmering spark is left,
Within thy breast, of love for her
   Of whom thou art bereft.

TO MY CHILD.

My darling, thou wert born to die,
Yet erst to live, hope, smile and sigh—
Wert born to know what 'tis to be
A child of frail mortality.
Sweet! all life's changes thou must learn,
Sunshine and clouds come in their turn—
One moment smiles may deck thy cheek,
Another, grief thy heart may break.
Oh, yes, this little heart of thine
Must oft—full oft, I fear—repine,
And these bright eyes must oft be wet
With tears of sorrow and regret.
And yet for smiles and sighs alone
Thou wert not made, my little one;
Thy hands must ever faithful prove
In works of usefulness and love.
Thy words a healing balm must be,
For thou wert made for sympathy;
And all the wisdom to thee given
Must tend to lead thy way to heaven;
For, dearest child, far, far away
There is a better land, they say;
And when thy work of life is o'er,
And time to thee shall be no more,
An angel-messenger will come
To bear thee to thy spirit home—
To waft thee to those realms of joy,
Where bliss is known without alloy,

Where life is as the sunshine bright,
Where day is never turned to night,
Where love is love unceasing, ever,
And where friends meet no more to sever;
For sin and death and pain and care
And sorrow never enter there.

TO MY LITTLE MARY.

My little Mary, once thy mother, too,
   Had a dear mother, fond and kind as thine,
(E'er sorrow o'er her path its dark wing threw,)
   On whose warm breast she softly did recline.

But oh, those blessed years have long since passed;
   For scarce her tender infant days had fled,
Ere the destroyer smote with blasting breath,
   And laid her dearest mother with the dead.

FOR THE BRIDE.

By her friend of old.

He came, but has gone, yet went not as he came ;
He robbed ere he left us, yet we cannot him blame;
He has taken away from our village its pride,
And the bridegroom hath pressed to his bosom his bride.
He came, but has gone—from the place of her birth,
The place she held dearest of any on earth,
From her kindred and home and the friends that were
    dear,
He has taken our loved one his cottage to cheer.
And he tells her that " there, in their own happy cot,
The words he has spoken will ne'er be forgot—
The promises made to the girl of his heart
Will never be broken till life shall depart."
He says, " Like a blossom or plant that is rare
He will cherish his flower with tenderest care ;
Like a gem that is costly, with price above measure,
He'll wear next his bosom his soul's dearest treasure,
Till the spoiler shall smite with his poisonous breath,
And the ties of their union are severed by death."
He came, and she's left us—the bridal is o'er,
And the friend of our youth we may never see more.
She has left all the scenes to her memory dear,
With a smile in her eye, though it shone through a tear,
And has gone with her mate like a bird to her nest,
And thinks to be happy with him she loves best.
As a friend, then, we wish (though we fear that 'tis vain)
That with him she shall know neither sorrow nor pain ;
May sad disappointment her hopes never blight,
But joy, like the sun, gild her cot with its light,

And friends, never changing, warm hearted and kind,
Where all now are strangers, ere long may she find.
And when, in due time, 'mid her household appear
Nearer claims on her love, her p'otection and care,
With their sweet cherub faces and bright beaming eyes,
May they prove to her blessings not sent in disguise.
With their soft prattling lips and their infantile mirth,
As they sport by her side round their blest cottage-
    hearth,
May they cheer her fond heart ere its spring-time has fled,
And chase from her eyelid the tear it would shed;
And when they have learned from the mother they love
That worth and that wisdom which come from above,
May they glad the lone days of her summer of life,
And lighten the burdens with which it is rife;
And as the chill years of drear autumn shall come,
May they smooth the rough pathway that leads to her
    home.
Oh, may she be happy! May no cloud of sorrow
At the part she has chosen bedim her bright morrow.
Oh, may she be happy! May no tear of woe
Or sigh of regret dim her vision below;
And when she has reached her last haven of rest,
May it be in the land of the good and the blest,
In that far spirit-land, 'mid the angels of light,
And the souls of the saints "who have fought the good
    fight."
Oh, there may the notes from her own harp arise
To join the soft music that rolls through the skies;
Oh, there may she swell with her own voice the strain
That tells of her triumph, her glory, her gain;
And there may I meet with my youth's early friend,
And chant the glad lay that our spirits shall blend,
Where all the sad past will be ever forgiven,
For love is the essence that makes it a heaven.

A MOTHER'S ADDRESS TO HER CHILD.

Suggested by seeing a child admiring the heavenly luminaries.

My pretty one, upturn thine eye
To yonder blue, ethereal sky.
See, countless stars are from it peeping,
Or 'neath its azure folds are sleeping.

And thou, a star as bright as they,
My babe, may shine some future day,
A little silvery star at even,
Thou, too, may'st beam in yonder heaven.

Or when long years have come and gone
And here on earth has set thy sun,
To weary pilgrims, wand'ring far,
Thou yet may'st be the guiding star.

Oh, yes, thy teachings, high and pure,
May bide while time and tide endure;
Thy spirit rays of light may shed,
When thou art numbered with the dead.

TO THE MEMORY OF LITTLE ELIZABETH W——.

Sweet little prattler, gone so soon from earth,
  Too pure, too innocent to linger here,
Thy spirit fled before it scarce had birth,
  Exhaled like dew to some far brighter sphere.

Yet oh, return from thy yon spirit home,
  And soothe, as thou wert wont, with fond caress;
Thy parents' arms are open—dear one, come,
  Thy life-warm cheek we fain again would press.

Sweet little flower, come back—she cannot hear;
  An angel messenger hath borne our love
From us, and we are left with none to cheer,
  Till we shall mingle in the land above.

Fair child, adieu, then!—Oh, too hard the thought;
  It wrings with grief my bosom's very core;
Adieu! With what deep anguish is it fraught,
  For we shall see thee, darling one, no more.

Still, little spirit-star, we beg thy ray
  To softly light us onward to the sky;
Oh, ofttimes, hover near our dreary way,
  Till we shall meet in lovelier realms on high.

Sweet little flower, plucked from thy mother's breast,
  Like a fair bud plucked from its parent tree,
Thou now hast found in Jesus' bosom rest
  As pure and lasting as eternity.

ON THE RECEIPT OF A BIT OF CAKE FROM A NEWLY-WEDDED PAIR.

As fair as their cake
    Be their fortunes through life;
He as goodly a husband—
    She as charming a wife.

They have launched their glad bark, full spread is its
        sail,
    On the sea of life's comforts and cares;
May they never be tempest-tossed—gentle the gale
    That wafts o'er its bed them and theirs.

May ne'er a rough billow nor quicksand appear,
    Nor false lights to allure them astray;
And when to the Eden of Edens they near,
    May it be in the brightness of day.

With a pilot trustworthy to guide at the helm,
    To those moorings above let them ride,
And safely cast anchor in love's brighter realm,
    Where no shipwrecks or dangers betide.

TO ——.

Hymen has claimed another flower,
To grace his garland, deck his bower.

ON THE DEATH OF MY DECEASED BROTHER'S FRIEND.

Is she, too, gone?   Is her last farewell breathed?
Is her young brow by heaven's garland wreathed?
Alas! her friends and kindred now must mourn,
Their fairest flower is from their bosom torn.
Lavinia, my brother's sister-friend,
Did heaven for thy soul an angel send?
Oh, form most beauteous bright, with seraph wing,
Dost thou, too, now a song of glory sing?
And hast thou seen in joy him there above,
With shining face, beaming eternal love?
Speak of thy meeting, fair one—pure one, say,
Was not his welcome sweet in heavenly ray?
Tell to us much of that blest land on high,
Where friends do meet with friends beyond the sky;
Where ne'er a cloud doth flit before the sight,
And noonday brightness never turns to night.
Too, of my mother speak—him thou heard'st tell
That she did in those balmy regions dwell.
Said he aright?   One low, soft answer deign,
Does she amid angelic spirits reign?
Oh, hast thou met her in that joyous band
Which walks the golden streets, the pearly strand?
Oh, hast thou met her in that rapturous choir
Which tunes in harmony the heavenly lyre?
Does she with them in hallelujahs join,
Bedecked in robes of righteousness divine?
Tell me, I pray, if but in whispers low
Thou mayest breathe of weal where sorrows flow.

Tell me, I pray, if but in stillest hour
Thy voice is heard—oh, let me feel its power.
To all thy weeping friends, who mourn thee gone,
Breathe one low word....tell them where thou hast
    flown!
And say who hast thou met in yon blest heaven,
Where dwell earth's lov'd and lost....the Lamb's for-
    given!

A BALLAD OF THE OLDEN TIME.

We met, but soon as lovers parted ;
  He set sail for some far shore ;
I thought that ne'er could prove false-hearted
  He whom then I did adore.
But, list ye maidens fair and pretty,
  Man heeds not the vows he makes:
He will sport with youth and beauty,
  He will spurn the heart he breaks.
He will sport, etc.

Two long, long years flew o'er my head,
  No tidings from him I received,
And many were the tears I shed,
  And many were the hours I grieved.
But in his honor still I trusted,
  Still I thought his love the same,
And though all my hopes seemed blasted,
  Yet him never did I blame.
And though all my, etc.

No, I loved him too sincerely,
  But, alas ! he sought me not;
He has wed a fairer beauty,
  And by him am I forgot.
See my eye grows dull and heavy,
  And my pulse is sinking fast.
Of this life I have grown weary;
  May we meet in heaven at last.
Of this life, etc.

Death ! I hail thee as a blessing,
   Life hath now no charms for me;
Naught on earth is worth possessing,
   To thy cold embrace I flee.
But, once more, ye maidens, hear me,
   Trust not in the vows man makes:
He will sport with youth and beauty,
   Then will spurn the heart he breaks.
He will sport, etc.   1837.

SPRING.

Spring is fretting and blustering, and washing her face,
And making her toilet, to meet us with grace;
And when she's arrayed, with all things to her mind,
Her smiles will be bland, and her greeting be kind.

Haste, then, gentle Spring, cease thy frowns and thy
    tears;
Thy votaries wait thee with welcoming cheers.
Haste, beauty, and don thy fresh mantle of green,
And Nature will crown thee her emerald queen.

MY BIBLE.

Profane not this gift,
   'Tis a gem of rare worth;
The most peerless treasure
   We find on the earth.

A NEW YEAR'S DITTY AND A COUNTRY SLEIGH RIDE AND FEAST.

Huzza l ho, huzza.! let us get in a fix
For a ride, for to-day is indeed forty-six;
Come, come, all ye lovers of frolic and fun,
Lay aside every care, for a new year's begun.

Here we go ! see us go l sober lasses and lads
Stay at home if you will, with your mammas and dads,
While we fly over earth like a bird on the wing,
And the air with the shouts of the merry doth ring.

On we go ! on we go ! swift o'er hill and o'er dale,
Like a vessel at sea, with fair wind and full sail,
And the ladies, God bless them ! all sad thoughts beguile,
Ever ready to offer a word and a smile.

On, on, boys ! delay not, till we're gathered around
The bright blazing hearth where good cheer doth abound.
See ! the table is groaning, the board is full spread;
Who's so soulless he would to life's pleasures be dead?

To the banquet we've come—be seated, do, please,
'Tis but meet that the board of its burden we ease;
Be civil—there's plenty for all—friends, no strife,
Every lad for his lass, every man for his wife.

Will you have some of that ? do be helped, pray, to this;
Nay, be not in haste there, my fun-loving Miss !
The music's not ready—the dance's not begun;
Soon, soon you the laurel of grace shall have won.

The feast is now finished, and dainty we've grown—
'Tis strange that such hunger so soon should have flown;
Where's our glass?   Here's good luck to our friends, aye
    and foes: ˝
Hurra! hip, hurra! will you join?   Here she goes!

Fair lady, start not! this was once from the sky—
Take a draught, it will ne'er cause a tear or a sigh;
From the pure limp d stream may our drink ever come,
'Tis like diamond to dust—'tis like heaven to rum.

Now, on with the dance, 'tis but innocent sport;
Have a polka or jig, and, in fine, every sort;
In joy let the moments fly—for joy they were given—
New Year's comes no more till eighteen forty-seven

THE DESPONDENT MOTHER'S PRAYER.

Drear is the night—the tempest howling, blows
  A chill on all without and all within ;
But drearer yet, alas ! the heart that knows
  No friend, nor has the power a friend to win.

Blow on, ye winds, and all ye storms rage on !
  Ye're but a feint of what my heart doth feel.
There seems no bliss for me below the sun ;
  Dark, gloomy bodings round my spirit steal.

These spectre-visions scarce thy winning face,
  My cherub babe, drives from my darkened soul ;
Wild, wandering thoughts flit through my brain apace,
  And tott'ring reason holds but weak control.

Oh, God forbid my child should ever know
  The dark repinings that have marked my lot !
Alone, unloved, through this broad world to go,
  With scarce the gleaming of one sunny spot.

Renew my heart ; refresh it with thy grace,
  Great Father, let me feel thee kindly near ;
These gloomy phantoms from my spirit chase ;
  For my child's sake, make my dark life less drear.

Oh, make me calm, my precious charge to train ;
  Counsel and comfort fit me her to give—
My twining lamb doth me to life enchain ;
  Cast me not off ; for her oh let me live !

A SONG FOR THE DEMOCRACY.

Before election 1844.

Our country has roused her—her proud bird uncaged ;
On liberty's soil a war has been waged ;
And ne'er will the contest her brave children yield
Till the crestfallen foe shall have fled from the field.

The eagle's broad pinions are spread in the sky,
The gay " stars and stripes" are now waving on high,
While the Democrat ranks, in their glory and might,
All arrayed for the battle, rush on to the fight.

No selfish ambition has goaded them on ;
For no base usurper their swords shall be drawn—
No " high tariff" laws would they palm on the nation ;
But " protection" to all, and a firm " annexation."

" Equal rights to all men " is the war-cry they boast,
Which is echoed from mountain, hill, valley and coast,
As onward advancing, the mighty hosts swell,
Who ere long the news of their triumph shall tell.

By " Young Hickory's "* self is led on the brave band,
To rescue their country from tyranny's hand ;
And with truth for their helmet and right for their
    shield,
The weapons of courage with valor they'll wield.

---

* Polk.

And when they the foemen in battle have met,
And the g ad shouts of victory ring through their set,
The woe egone Whigs, who have hugged the last ray
Of their bubble of hope, shall retreat in dismay.

And Erin's brave sons, who their country have fled,
For the land which our forefathers fought for and bled,
Shall find them a home mid the equal and free,
And the long-promised joys of our liberty see.

Hurra, then, for Polk, he's the man of the nation,
For Oregon, too, and Texas' fleet annexation;
For Dallas hurra! he's a twig of the tree,
Of that staunch-hearted emblem, the " Old Hickory."

And don't let's forget Wright's the man for New York.
We who are in favor of Dallas and Polk;
He's a chief among men, a bright star of our land,
So for him go three cheers from our brave, gallant band.

Now, let's drink a toast to America's daughters,
Our Spartan-like fair ones this side the broad waters,
For though haste they from combat, our glory they'll
         sing,
And thus to true valor an offering bring.

Once more—to sweet freedom let's fill up the cup,
'Tis heaven's own nectar alone that we sup;
Hard cider we'll yield to our sad-visaged foe,*
Lest their spirits should sink when their coon is laid low.

For " three times and out "† is as old as the hills,
And the fowls of the air are now whetting their bills

---

* Hard cider was the pretended Whig drink at that time.
† I think this year was the third time the opposing candidate for the Presidency had been up for the office.

To peck at his dust when his death-knell has rung,
And his dirge by the foes of fair freedom is sung.

Now, to strangers and exiles our goblet we'll drain,
And welcome them home to our own sunny plain;
An asylum to all, their home-country 'twill be,
The " City of Refuge," where thousands may flee.

AFTER ELECTION.

" How are the mighty fallen."

We've conquered !   We've conquered !
  On field and on flood,
The land of our triumphs
  Is deluged in blood.
Yet let us tread light
  On the dust of the dead,
As onward our victors
  From conquest are led.

We've conquered !   We've conquered !
  Again Freedom smiles
On our hills and our vales,
  Our mountains and wilds ;
And glad hearts are gay
  'Neath the lustre she pours
On the land of our fathers,
  Columbia's shores.

We've conquered !   We've conquered !
  And no more is heard
The war-cry which thousands
  Of freemen has stirred.
And " plenty " and " peace "
  In our land again reign,
For the mighty are fallen,
  Their chieftain is slain.

Let the clarion's notes
  Ring the air, as they swell,
On the wings of the wind,
  The glad news let them tell.
Let our hosts lift a shout,
  For our country is saved—
True liberty's heroes
  Her foemen have braved.

Our arms are triumphant!
  Let the cannon's loud roar
Re-echo the sound
  O'er Atlantic's far shore.
Let the voice of her thunders
  Sweep the isles of the sea,
For the mighty are fallen—
  Our country is free!

We've conquered! We've conquered!
  Let the arrogant mourn,
For the down-trodden poor
  From their fetters have torn.
Yet let us tread light
  On the dust of the dead,
As onward our victors
  In triumph are led.

Ayé, let us tread light—
  Yet, freemen, arise!
Let the voice of thanksgiving
  Ascend to the skies.
To heaven alone
  Is our gratitude due;
For heaven has aided
  The honest and true.

TO IRELAND.

Thou gem of the ocean,
   Thou fond home of the brave,
· How long, oh, loved Erin,
   Shall the tyrant enslave ?

Oh, Ireland, sweet Ireland,
   When shall thy sons be free ?
When shall thy fetters fall, and thou
   Hail thy grand Jubilee ?

When shall thy verdant turf be trod
   By freemen of thy soil ?
And they beneath a foreign yoke
   No longer grudging moil ?

When wilt thou shine in freedom's light,
   A nation of the earth,
Whose noble sons shall proudly boast
   Their lineage and birth.

Where honor, valor, science, art,
   Reign o'er thy wave-girt sod,
And Christian hands and Christian hearts
   Pay tithes to none but God ?

Oh, Ireland ! Loved Ireland !
   Near be thy jubilee,
When thou the glorious name shall boast,
   The Island of the Free !

ENNA AND WILLIE ; OR, YOUNG LOVE.

Eight summers scarce had passed o'er her fair head
　When her sick mother's worn and wasted frame
Rested, at length, amid the quiet dead,
　And sorrow to her young and tried heart came.
'Twas her first piercing soul-grief, and she shed
　Such bitter tears a stoic could but feel
Pity for that fair child.　But each one said
　That doubtless soothing Time ere long would heal
The bruiséd spirit of our household pet,
And aid, at least, in part, her to forget.

I turned unto the book of "Holy Writ,"
　And read with her each promise from its page,
Till from her youthful brow the shade would flit
　And she would dry her tears—for, of her age,
She seemed most easily to comprehend
　The meaning of the words to some so blind,
And, daily, we could see our flower mend,
　From the effects of time and truth combined,
Till to her lilied cheek the rose's hue
Returned, and tinged it as it erst did do.

But sorrow came again with lowering cloud :
　The child's remaining parent sickened sore,
Till, by the reaper Death, his head was bowed
　And she could look upon his face no more.
Yet in this second crushing weight of grief
　She turned her dimmed eyes to the Orphan's Friend,
And prayed to him to give her heart relief,
　And resignation to her spirit send.
And, truly, God, methought, her prayer did hear—
No more she murmured, nor did flow the tear.

Yet still I could but mark that passing time,
  No zest for childhood's sports brought to her now ;
She seemed a being of some other clime,
  As slowly thinned her cheek and paled her brow.
And her sweet voice grew tremulous and low,
  Till it was scarcely louder than a breath ;
Each day her blithesome step grew weak and slow,
  And then we knew the seal of all was death.
Longer our flower would have bloomed on earth,
Could she have given voice to her heart's dearth.

We laid her in the churchyard by the graves
  And moldering forms of those she pined to greet ;
And o'er her little form the willow waves,
  And the wild rose and honeysuckle meet,
And gentle winds wake music soft and low,
  As sweep they o'er the turf upon her breast,
And gay birds carol, while the green trees throw
  Their sheltering arms, as if to guard her rest.
There undisturbed and sweetly sleeps our flower,
No more a dark'ning cloud doth o'er her lower.

Still, daily, at the quiet sunset time,
  A dark-eyed youth with noble brow is seen—
Scarce hidden by the dusk, and running vine,
  And willow boughs—to kneel with sober mien,
And scatter flowers, fresh gathered and begemmed
  With crystal drops—not dew, nor from the skies,
But drops that drooping lids awhile have stemmed,
  Lest they should fall before unpitying eyes—
Over her early grave, where every joy
Seems with her buried, to her lover-boy.

From very infancy he was her mate—
  In every childish sport was by her side,
Her champion, if evil lay in wait,
  And bravely fought he for his "little bride."

And he would picture in her willing ear
  Bright scenes of future bliss, when he, a man,
Should, wondrous, make this wicked earthly sphere
  A Paradise after his own wise plan.
Oh, he would be so kind and good, he said,
No tears but those of joy her eyes should shed.

The home he'd build for her would be so grand:
  The finest pictures on its walls be hung,
Gathered from this and from the olden land—
  Of which he'd something read for one so young—
The fairest flowers should in his garden grow,
  And all around should be broad, shady trees,
Where pretty birds would ever come and go;
  And everything he'd have her heart to please.
He'd be so rich when he a man became,
She ne'er should want a thing her lips could name.

And deeper grew his love as years flew by;
  And when dim shadows fell upon her face,
His young heart grieved to see her sunken eye,
  And he would seek her sorrow to efface;
And when, perchance, would lightly flit a smile
  On her fair cheek, caused by his winning words,
And actions kind, his pulse would leap the while,
  And untold joy would thrill its answering chords.
And when time came that she no more could hear
His gentle tones, life lost for him its cheer.

Now, wise ones, claiming no prophetic ken,
  Whisper sad words as he doth pass them by—
Ere long, the wild wind-harp will wake again
  A dirge above the spot where he shall lie;
For daily wanes in his dark eye the light,
  And wasting is his frame with grief's decay;
His brow is paled, his cheek grows thin and white,
  And slower lag his footsteps day by day.

Soon he shall follow where his lost one lies—
His longing soul shall join hers in the skies.

Thus grief may dry the blood in the young heart
  That mourns its idol, and may chill the veins,
And wither for the grave the earthly part
  Of the child-lover, as he scarce retains
The shadow of a wish to longer stay,
  Where hope and joy are banished from the breast;
Till the tired soul, at length, shall flee away
  And soar to mansions where its wings may rest.
There, unremembered of its sorrow here,
How beautiful must youthful love appear.

THE BIRTH OF SLANDER.

For a physician Envy sent,
As she with awful pain was rent;
While her kind helpmate, Jealousy,
Stood looking on in ecstasy.
The doctor came, with greatest speed,
With medicine and tool for need;
And all the neighborhood rushed in,
To learn the cause of such a din.
But, quick as thought—or nearly so—
The company began to grow
As talkative, and happy, too,
As though they did a lost friend view;
While Jealousy, unconscious, stood,
As in a thinking attitude.
" My dearest, you are rather sad
For one who lately was so glad; "
Now Envy said, "but that the child
A fine girl is can't be denied.
Had I have borne a son, my love,

It would not half as faithful prove
As this, for well you know our sex
Can better please, and better vex,
Those whom they choose—you understand
'Twas Eve who got the upper hand,
Not Adam—so, pray do not fear,
We're bless'd in such a daughter dear."

Well, soon the child was passed around,
And all caressed, with love profound,
The little, sprightly "innocent,"
As though they were on pleasure bent,
Save one, who, silent, gazed to see
Proud Envy's darling protegee.

An hour passed by, the child was named,
And through the streets the news was famed
Of youthful *Slander's* name and birth,
A gift so precious here on earth;
When, loud, an agonizing cry
Worse than a death-groan, pierced the sky.
Each turned, to find from whence the shriek,
When each would fain his wonder speak:
" The little sprite has teeth—most strange;
And poison's in the pretty range;
And eyes, like balls of fire they glare;
And, lo ! her head—the snake-like hair;
And hissings fill the sulphured room.
But whence that awful cry; from whom?"
'Twas from the one who gazed to see,
In silence, Envy's protegee.
A friend had bidden her to take
The pretty child, " for friendship's sake,"
And she for friendship's sake obeyed;
When, suddenly, her breath was stayed
And from her bosom clotted gore
In black, thick streams did fearful pour;
While Jealousy and Envy smiled
To see the work of their loved child.

A true friend, passing, heard the sound
And quick rushed in to heal the wound.
But all in vain—too dire, too deep
The poison pierced—she craved death's sleep.

THE TWIN SISTERS : FRIENDSHIP AND LOVE.

Friendship and Love walked, hand in hand,
Over the earth with magic wand;
And where'er their white feet trod,
Sprang sweet flowers from the sod.

Ever going on.   One day
A widow's hut lay in their way.
Grim want within its walls did dwell;
Through many a chink the wind blew chill.
Ragged, freezing, gaunt, and starving;
'Round the dying embers hov'ring,
Sireless babes and once proud wife
Were eking out a cheerless life.
Love and Friendship raised a hand,
And touched the hut with magic wand.
Warmth then cheered the widow's hearth,
And plenty took the place of dearth.

Passing on, they overtook
A maiden with a careworn look.
Sad and sunken was her eye;
From her bosom came a sigh.
Friendless, homeless, weak and weary,
Earth to her was ever dreary.
Love and Friendship raised a hand,
And touched her with their magic wand:
Joy relit her clouded sky;
Gloom no more bedimmed her eye;

But, with home and friendship blest,
Cankering care forsook her breast.

Onward still, upon their road,
Came they to a dark abode.
Low, within, one, racked with pain,
On his tiresome couch was lain.
Love and Friendship raised a hand,
And touched him with their magic wand.
They smoothed his pillow, bathed his brow,
Fanned his cheek, with hectic glow;
Raised to his parched lips the cup
With cooling draught, that he might sup.
His pain was eased; he sank to sleep;
Yet o'er him still they watch did keep,
And nursed him gently day by day,
Till pain and sickness fled away.

Then, again, they onward went.
A man, whose frame with grief was bent,
With withered cheek and hoary head,
Overtook they, as they sped.
Lone, forsaken, broken-hearted;
Wife and children, all, departed,
With none to lean on in old age,
Life to him was one dark page.
Love and Friendship raised a hand,
And touched him with their magic wand.
By cheering word and kindly deed,
From grief's sad thraldom once more freed,
His frame unbent, his eye upraised,
His Maker's goodness 'gain he praised.
Thus, where these two sisters trod,
Sprang sweet flowers from the sod.

LADIES SPEAKING.

We went to hear a lady speak
  In public, 'fore the men,
And, oh, she spoke so very grand
  We thought of our gray hen
That goes a strutting round the yard,
  And then at early morn
Cries, "Cock-a-doodle, doodle-doo !"
  On tip-top of the barn.

The roosters, all, look up aghast
  And wonder what's the matter !   .
But seeing nothing strange about,
  "As mad as hops," they " at her."
And this their conversation is:
  " Dear miss, you'd better lay
Your daily egg, and hatch it out,
  Than crowing in this way.
'Tis very masculine in you
  To crow so bold up there;
We think your common-sense must own
  You're out of hendom's sphere;
No modest hen that's in her wits
  Would get so far astray;
We roosters blush to see your sex
  Made public in this way.
And then, Miss Hen, pray by what right
  Do you presume to dare
Our special honors, years agone,
  Thus nonchalant to share ?"

At this she cocks her little bill
  And ruffles up her breast:
" I'm not a ninny, I can fight!
  Send on your very best:
I've been your servant long enough,
  I'll not lay one more egg.
And why hens may not crow, dear sirs,
  To know I humbly beg."
So down she pounces on the roost—
  The savage little elf—
As though a stealing all her chicks
  Was the old fox himself.

The roosters, 'stonished at her grit,
  Fly off with fallen crest ;
To leave all crowing hens alone,
  (In council) they think best.
Now, gentlemen, take my advice,
  When ladies take to speaking,
Don't " at em" 'bout their " spheres and
    rights,"
  Or you'll go off a sneaking.

[Times have changed since this was written—185-.]

JEALOUSY.

Throw on thy mantle, " Love,"
  And let us walk to-night,
By moonlight, in the pleasant grove,
  The stars are shining bright.

These inner walls, so dull,
  Cast shadows o'er thy heart,
And apathy walks in to lull
  The love I share in part.

Nay, dearest, why so cold;
  Why turn away thy face;
Dost thou esteem a lover bold
  Who in thy heart claims place?

And why withdraw thy hand,
  That soon is to be mine,
By lawful wedlock's silken band,
  By marriage-rite divine?

Dearest, in mercy, deign,
  Within the grove to-night,
This sudden strangeness to explain,
  That puts thy love to flight.

Thou dost not doubt me, "Love,"
  'Tis thee that I adore;
I swear it by the heavens above :
  I'm thine forevermore.

Oh, then, 'tis Mabel Reeve;
  Good gracious ! tell me, pray;
Thou saw us walking yester-eve,
  And now art jealous, " May."

Fie ! cast the frown aside—
  A note for brother "Will,"
To her who soon will be his bride,
  I had for little " Bell."

Just from the post, last eve,
  I overtook her walking,
And that's the way, with Mabel Reeve,
  I happened lonely talking.

Those bright eyes smile again, "Love;"
  Those lips have lost their pout.
Come, let us to the pleasant grove
  While yet the moon is out.

And, prithee, never, "May,"
Be jealous of thy "Ned;"
Do, dearest, set the happy day,
'Tis time that we were wed.

SUNSET.

See, what a glorious sunset !
  Earth's beauteous canopy;
The king of day around us flings
  His gorgeous drapery.

With red, and gold, and purple,
  Each azure cloud is fringed,
And every tree and hilltop gray
  With golden rays is tinged.

No hand of earthly painter
  Can sketch those brilliant dyes;
They more than beggar limner's art,
  Those tintings of the skies.

How glows the burnished steeple;
  Each palace, hut and fane
Is glistening with the golden light
  From gilded window pane.

Such an October's sunset
  Methinks must almost vie
With that far land bright paved with gold—
  With Heaven's canopy.

Oh, is it not a foresight
  Of that fair Paradise
Whose glories beam beyond our ken,
  Too bright for human eyes.

My soul, on such an eve as this,
  Is wild with revery—
It almost bursts its prison-house
  And flies in ecstasy.

Good God, how many beauties here
  Wait on the cheerful heart :
Earth, to the glad adoring one,
  Is as of Heaven a part.

OUR LITTLE RIVER.

Ripple, ripple, little rill;
Always going, never still;
Yet so shallow we can tread
Barefoot o'er thy pebbly bed.

Ripple, ripple, never rest,
Sunbeams dance upon thy breast;
While the spider and the fly
O'er thy crinkled wavelet hie.

Ripple, ripple, pearly stream;
Sportive trout-fish never dream
That the angler drops his line,
In a bosom pure as thine.

Swerving naught, from day to day,
Ripple, ripple, on thy way,
From thy windings, stopping never—
Humming, murmuring, onward ever.

On thy banks the flow'rets blush,
And the birds melodious gush
From the bending trees above thee;
But they tell not how to love thee.

With the home-cot of my childhood.
That stood near thee in the wildwood ;
With the loved ones that have left me,
Of whom Heaven hath bereft me;

With the bright things that ne'er grieved
   · me
(For thou never once deceived me),
Thou art linked, sweet little river:
God preserve thy wavelets ever.

THE HOPE OF OPPRESSED IRELAND.

Hail ! hail the proud day, for our Liberty's nigh;
Nor will freedom's blest ray her twin-sister outvie;
For wherever she sheds her bright beams on a land,
Her sister, twin-sister, is ever at hand.

For her twin-sister, Science, Freedom opens the gate,
And bids proud defiance to tyranny's hate;
For the home of the brave, the noble and free,
Is Science' home-country, wherever it be.

Science withers and dies where a tyrant doth reign,
From his country she flies to her sister's domain,
For with pinions fast fettered she cannot survive ;
Free light and free air she must needs have to thrive.

184—

MA WOULDN'T, ETC.

The twilight shadows fill the vale,
  The flowers drink the dew,
The evening star begins to pale;
  But, dear one, where are you?

You promised you would wait me here,
  Beneath our trysting tree;
Why do your footsteps linger, dear?
  Are you thus false to me?

The moments, leaden-winged, depart;
  The twilight's on the wane,
A darksome pall falls on my heart :
  I list your step in vain.

They told me worthless was your vow;
  I trusted you were true.
I thought you bore a noble brow,
  And eyes of Heaven's own hue.

I'll think so still; I'll not believe
  One of your mien and eye
Could stoop to flatter and deceive
  E'en one as weak as I.

Oh, you have come, my love, at last;
  I almost came to doubt——
"I know the hour, my sweet, is past
  Ma wouldn't let me out."

A DYING AGED LADY AND FRIEND.

When life no longer gives one hope of joy,
 Who would not wish to die?
Who would not pant for bliss without alloy
 Beyond the sky?

With me, dear friends, 'tis meet, then, to rejoice:
 Farewell! let no tear flow.
Hark! hear you not?....'tis His, the Saviour's, voice!
 I gol....I go!

More than "threescore and ten" my years have told,
 Earth's sweets long since have fled;
My pulse is weak, my limbs grow stiff and cold....
 She's with the dead.

Hush!....breathe no word....too holy is the spell....
 In quiet let her soar.
She's gone—in spirit-land her soul will dwell
 Forevermore.

THE LITTLE CHILD-FLOWER.

Sweet little flower, plucked from thy mother's breast,
 Like a fair bud plucked from its parent tree,
Though far more deeply mourned—by Christ caressed,
 Thou now dost sleep—rest, rest, thee, tranquilly.

BOAT SONG.

Row, boys, row!
O'er the waves we go!
As we swiftly glide along,
Let our oars keep time with song—
Row, boys, row!

Sing, boys, sing!
Let your voices ring
Out far o'er the green waves' gleam
Of our proud and noble stream—
Sing, boys, sing!

Chime, boys, chime!
In a pleasant rhyme.
Give us something gay or witty;
Bright eyes, sparkling, wait the ditty—
Chime, girls, chime!

*

Time is passing, land is nearing,
To the shore our skiff is steering—
Grand St. Lawrence!   In thy flow,
Smoothly running, humming low,
Or o'er rocks bound, foaming, rumbling,
From the highlands leaping, tumbling,
Dashing, thundering—bright skies bless thee!
Often may our boat caress thee—
Land, boys, land!

"FORGIVE AND FORGET."

—————

"Forgive and forget"
All the wrongs thou hast met
At the hand of thy brother below—
Those are happiest far
Whom revenge doth not mar
With its spirit of evil and woe.

If thy brother offends thee,
And ne'er makes amends t' thee,
Nor asks thy forgiveness for wrong;
If the trespass be "seven,"
Or "seventy times seven,"
T' avenge doth to Heaven belong.

"Forgive and forget,"
Let the sun never set
O'er thy brow in its nursings of fire;
When thou layest thy head
At night on thy bed,
Sleep not with the demon of ire.

"Forgive and forget;"
Those are happiest yet
Who know nothing of malice or wrath;
There is plenty of trouble
Without making it double
With wicked hate's crossing our path.

AFFLICTION.

Affliction is to faithful woman's heart
  Like to the fire that purifies the gold ;
And tears of grief that from her eyelids start
  Will be reset, as gems of heavenly mold,
Within the crown that waits the chastened one,
Who prays, in penitence, " Thy will be done."

Sorrow, neglect, and poverty and scorn,
  Each one is as a round that doth compose
The ladder she full oft in life's young morn
  Is doomed t' ascend ere end her earthly woes;
But the poor soul, thus in the furnace tried,
Shall rest ere long with Jesus sanctified.

Oh, woman fond, made by affection blind,
  Thy warm and trusting heart too often falls
A prey to selfish man, whose evil mind
  Seeks to entice thee; but the sin recoils
At last upon the tempter—Christ, the Son,
Will " cast the stone" to crush the tempting one.

I THOUGHT, &c.

I thought he came at dewy eve,
　To whisper in my ear;
But now I know, in morn's pale beam,
　My brother lost is near.

I know him by the gentle rap
　Upon the inner door
Of my sad heart, so like the rap
　He used to give of yore.

I know him by the gentle words,
　"Awake, my sister dear,"
So like the gentle words of old,
　My ear was wont to hear.

And, too, my soul discerns the smile
　That lights his pleasant eye,
So like the smile it used to wear
　Ere he ascended high.

And the blest counsels that he breathes,
　I heed with willing ear;
For well I know where wisdom reigns,
　There reigns my brother dear.

"POOR LITTLE THING."

Poor little thing; it never knew
   The blessings of a mother's care;
She died when first its breath it drew,
   And soared beyond the realms of air.

It never laid its downy cheek
   Close on her warm and loving breast;
It never heard the sweet lips speak,
   Or felt them on its temples prest.

It never saw a mother's eyes
   Beaming with love unspeakable—
A mother's love that never dies,
   Deep, holy and unquenchable.

That best and choicest gift of earth,
   Poor little one, from thee hath passed—
Thou ne'er canst know a mother's worth,
   Thy lot in stranger-hands is cast.

But thou wilt miss her, little one,
   As strength and knowledge grow with years;
There'll hang a cloud before thy sun,
   That oft will shower thy face with tears.

An aching void that naught can fill,
   A reaching for a something gone;
A yearning that no joys can still,
   Thou'lt know too well, poor little one.

Thou'lt miss her in the darkling day,
  When sorrow, doubt, disease shall come;
Thou'lt need her hand to guide the way,
  And light the path thy feet must roam.

Thou'lt miss her gentle, soothing tone,
  Her tender care and love-lit eye—
God help and shield thee, little one,
  No mother by thy side is nigh.

Oh, "mother!" "mother!" sweet the name,
  It makes my every heart-string thrill;
It sends a tremor through my frame,
  Big, heavy drops my eyelids fill.

"Mother!" my mother! oh, how much
  I've yearned and pined for love like thine—
I've felt a void which naught could touch,
  For I have missed thee, mother mine.

FOR MR. AND MRS. S——.

Upon their marriage, and referring to his having mourned the death of
a former wife.

We wish thee good cheer, Mrs. S.
Live, love, to be blest and to bless.
   May thy sky be as clear
   As affection's bright tear,
   And thy pathway as fair
   As if Summer were there,
Strewing sweets for thy footstep's caress.

We wish thee good cheer, happy bride!
Smile on in thy walk by his side.
   'M.d thy joy's fleeting hours,
   'Mid thy love's fairy flowers,
   May no thorns lie concealed,
   To be ever revealed—
Serenely through life ever glide.

We wish thee good cheer, happy groom,
With the bride thou hast borne to thy home.
   Let all sorrow surcease,
   And thy heart be at peace;
   For the star in thy sky—
   Woman's love-lighted eye—
Shall chase from thy bosom its gloom.

FOR THE ONE MAN WHO THINKS NO ONE BUT HIS DEARY IS WORTHY OF NOTICE.

He's lost to all but one;
He lives to be her slave;
And when his thread of life is spun,
He'll serve her in his grave.

TO THE LADIES.

Upon being invited to a *Fair* by them at M——.

Had our pen but the power, it should *fairly* portray
All the pleasure imparted on New Year's *fair* day,
All the *fair* things displayed at the *fair* ladies' *Fair*,
All the *fair* viands tasted, so tempting, so rare,
All the *fair* words and greetings from hearts *fairer* still,
As with *fairest* endeavors they swayed all at their will.
But pencil ne'er painted the diamond's bright tints,
Nor the nectarine draughts from Elysian founts;
How, then, when the *fair* sex their efforts unite,
To tickle the palate or dazzle the sight,
Can the charm that enchains in its true light appear?
Oh, we wish we had ever just such a New Year;
Yet our heart's warmest wishes we send in our lay,
And our thanks, gentle ladies, receive them, we pray;
For the kindness ye showed us forget we shall never,
Till the *fair* things of earth from our sight vanish ever.

A CHILD'S IDEA.

"Are the stars the eyes of angels,
  Mamma ?" asked a little son,
Gazing at them from the window,
  As they came out one by one.

"If they are the eyes of angels,
  Then the sun must be God's eye;
For you say that God is greatest,
  And he dwells up in the sky."

"But, my child, God seeth ever,
  And the sun is dark at night."
"Well, I guess he shuts it 'little,'
  And that's why it ain't so light."

THE MEXICAN WAR.

Lines suggested by the motto, " Our Country, right or wrong."

Look ye on yonder battle-field,
  Beneath the southern sky,
Where crimson War's destructive car
  Is rolling fearful by.
List to the bugle's echoing blast,
  The canon's thundering roar,
The sharp, quick clashing of the steel,
  Thirsting for mortal gore l

List! list! as loudly through the ranks
  Thunders each battle cry,
Where great contending armies wave
  Their streaming banners high;
While firmer, bolder, onward press
  Our nation's bravest sons,
Crushing beneath their mighty power
  Opposing myrmidons.

Behold the slaughter! Thick and fast
  The dying strew the ground;
The reeking sword, the fiery ball
  Strikes deep the deadly wound.
And fiercer, fiercer on they rush,
  Each warrior aims the blow,
To haste to an untimely grave
  Some brave, opposing foe.

Oh, few on earth are so forlorn
  That none will mourn their end;
Those dead the sad precursors are
  That grief some heart shall rend.
And ne'er can wealth of lands untold,
  Or golden mines repay·
The pangs that this last hour hath fraught
  With its unholy fray.

See! wilder rages on the fight,
  While grappling thousands fall,
Stretched out upon their earthy bed,
  Heaven's canopy their pall. .
And trampled 'neath the charger's hoof,
  Unheeded lie the slain,
And dying ones, whose welt'ring gore
  Floods o'er the dismal plain.

Hark! hark! those sounds—'tis " Victory!"
  The shoutings pierce the sky—
" They flee! they flee!" triumphantly
  Our conquering soldiers cry.
Some will rejoice—good news it brings—
  Our country's cause is won;
Laurels will grace the victor's brow,
  For carnage he hath done.

Quick, valiant deeds, in triumph proud,
  Are wafted far and near;
Full many a heart ecstatic beats
  The joyous tale to hear.
And every mountain, hill and glen
  Their thankful tribute raise;
For glory crowns our nation's arms—
  Her victor-chief repays.

Now to that sister turn the while,
  As prayerfully she weeps—
Behold that mother lowly knelt,
  Who holy vigils keeps,
Beseeching God to spare her child,
  Her darling, only son,
Nor knows she that 't's vain—e'en now
  His race on earth is run.

There rests in death his pallid brow—
  He was their earthly stay—
A noble intellect there shone,
  Ere he had passed away.
His mother's and his sister's pride,
  He was beloved of all;
But oh, too generous, too brave—
  That form was doomed to fall.

Look on them ! Ah, they know not yet
  The grief for them in store—
They pray ; but that fair, manly form,
  They'll meet on earth no more.
Still "Victory !" proud "Victory !"
  Rings out upon the air ;
But oh, the wounds that they shall feel
  Can victory repair ?

" My country ! 'tis for thee I die,"
  He said with parting breath ;
"A halo let thy glory wreathe
  Around my brow in death.
Heaven support them 'neath this stroke,
  The cherished of my soul ;
Keep, keep, my God ! those dear ones left,
  Within thy kind control."

Turn to the wife—her ear has caught
  The gladsome tale of joy—
Brightens her eye ; she smiles, alas!
  Wists she not of alloy ?
But hopes she soon again to hear
  Her husband's well-known tread ?
Ah, never more will he return—
  He sleeps, too, with the dead.

His clay-cold form on yonder plain
  Lies 'neath the sun's hot ray,
Exposed to every sacrilege
  Of man or beast of prey.
And there, unhonored and unsung,
  Beneath those burning skies,
His fleshless bones for aye shall bleach
  Till Heaven bids him rise.

The child, too, hears of triumph proud-
  " Father will come," she cries;
She waits him on the threshold there,
  And strains her watchful eyes
To catch the first glad glimpse of him,
  Her sire, almost adored ;
But ah, he'll come not there again—
  He fell by war's red sword.

And she is now an orphan child,
  Thrown on the heartless throng,
With no kind friend to take her part,
  Though she should suffer wrong.
Those fragile hands must earn her bread,
  Though poor and mean it be,
Or she must starve, or sink betimes
  To shame and misery.

And see that face so purely sweet,
   Of late bedimmed with care;
She throws aside the cloud of gloom
   That vailed her temples fair,
And listens to achievements brave,
   Heralded near and far—
Ah, fears she not that her betrothed
   Fell on the field of war?

Knows she not that a corpse he lies,
   With sunken, sightless eye,
Where myriads tread the blood-stained sod
   He bathed in agony?
That 'mid unburied heaps he rests,
   All spiritless and still?
Oh, she has yet to bow beneath
   · The mandate of God's will.

Behold that gray-haired man, whose cheek
   Is furrowed deep with care!
Trembles in his dim eye a tear—
   · Upon his lip a prayer,
As bends he down from day to day,
   To beg that God would save
The wild and reckless youth who brings
   Him sorrowing to the grave.

He weens not that already, too,
   He hath been ushered in,
To meet the dread tribunal, where
   All must account for sin—
That now hath passed the sentence just,
   The lasting, firm decree,
Which sends him to his spirit home,
   That must eternal be.

Yet, ah, ere long shall reach their ears
  The story time will bring—
The thorn to pierce the bosom's core
  Is e'en now on the wing;
And frantically their anguished souls
  Shall writhe beneath the smart
Inflicted upon yonder field
  By dire war's poisonous dart.

Oh, can ye soothe their grief when they
  The woeful tale shall hear,
That will their every heart-string break,
  And force the scorching tear?
Or can ye tell of aught on earth
  That can the deep wounds heal?
Or fill, alas! the aching void
  Each stricken breast must feel?

Still " Victory !" glad " Victory !"
  Cleaves with its shou's the air;
" Our country's honor is maintained—
  Scorn now her might who dare !"
Oh, little reck they of the price
  Such truthful words have cost,
The pains, the sighs, the groans, the tears,
  That pay for such proud boast.

They reck not of the helpless ones,
  Upon the cold world driven;
The homeless, friendless wanderers,
  Whose all for it was given,
When death upon that bloody plain
  Asunder burst the ties
That bound them here—that bind them now
  To yonder hallowed skies.

Still every gale is laden fresh
  With conquests bold and new;
Atlantic's and Pacific's shores
  Re-echo valor true.
But oh, what myriads who fall
  Upon that blood-stained sod,
All unawares are ushered in
  To face a righteous God.

Yet, though we sing of war's sad scourge,
  Our cheeks with shame would glow,
If e'en ourself—a woman frail—
  Crouched to our country's foe.
If needed, we the blade would wield,
  Should foes invade the land;
But not " Our country, right or wrong !"
  For " rights " alone we stand.

A WORD FOR THANKSGIVING.

The wished-for day has come at last,
　Young hearts beat wild with glee,
While for God's gifts of kindness past
　We'll bend the grateful knee.

And when beside the sumptuous board
　We eat and drink our fill,
Let us bethink, 'tis Christ the Lord
　Who gives of his good-will.

And though 'tis from his bounteous store
　Our wants are all supplied,
There was a time He hungered sore—
　His own was Him denied.

And let us not forget the poor,
　Who e'en the crumbs would prize
(Which fall upon the banquet floor)
　To soothe their children's cries.

Hail! then in joy let all unite
　The voice of thanks to raise—
The maimed, the poor, the lone invite
　To swell the song of praise.

It is but meet that they should share
　Our nation's* jubilee—
We have enough, and more to spare
　To gladden misery.

---

* I think the year the above was written all the States had the
same day of the year set apart as Thanksgiving day.

WRITTEN FOR M—— H——.

On the death of her mother, and referring to her contemplated departure from her home.

Would some kind angel might draw near to guide
My feeble pen, to speak what woes betide
A stricken heart, so lonely, crushed and sore,
It bleeds with silent grief at every pore.

Oh, who that ne'er hath lost a mother dear
Can feel for her who mourns her absence here—
Who now must tread alone this tearful vale,
With no kind friend to soothe till life shall fail.

Yet I, my friend, can feel for thee in part—
I, too, have seen a mother fond depart—
Have seen death lay on her his icy hand,
As passed she upward to the spirit-land.

I, too, an only daughter, marked the smile
That played around that mother's lip the while,
Ere she was shrouded 'neath the dismal pall
Which vailed the form I would in vain recall.

My sight hath gazed upon the darkened eye
And pulseless frame that stiff and cold did lie;
And oft my steps in sadness trace the spot
Where sleeps her dust—save by her friends forgot.

Yes, I long years have mourned, as thou shalt mourn,
Earth's dearest gift, gone never to return—

And well I know the depths of that dire wound,
Which naught can soothe, save Jesus' grace abound.

My eye, like thine, has wept—of friends bereaved,
My heart, like thine, has bled, and still doth bleed;
For I have missed a fondest mother's love,
And sigh o'er dear ones gone to worlds above.

Yet not for them I grieve—to them 'twas gain
To leave a world where life is linked with pain;
But oh, the dreary path I needs must tread
Oft forces me the bitter tear to shed.

Yet I a father's kindly care was left—
Poor mourner, thou of him too art bereft.
Thy sky is dark—no ray of hope appears.
But " God is love "—He heeds the orphan's tears.

Still, weeping one, it will not dry thy cheek
That one so frail attempt thy grief to speak;
That others may have felt what thou dost feel
Heals not the pangs which none but Christ can heal.

Then bow to Him in prayer—He'll hear thy cry;
On His firm promises in faith rely;
He is the orphan's ever-faithful friend—
His free and loving kindness knows no end.

And though in sorrow from thy childhood's home
And dear paternal roof thou soon must roam,
Let me e'en hope the star of peace will light
In gladd'ning halo round thy spirit's sight.

I can but wish that thou in stranger-land
May find a welcome meet from heart and hand—
That earth shall yield what good it can thee give,
While 'mid its joys thou shalt for heaven live.

Yet should each cherished relic of the past,
On which thine eye ere long must gaze its last,
In fond remembrance cling around thee still—
Like her,* ne'er murmur at thy Father's will.

Then, oh, that blissful port !—thou'lt anchor there,
Where joy is joy unmingled with despair;
Glad will thy meeting be—thou wilt behold
Thy mother smiling in the Lamb's bright fold.

* Her mother.

FOURTH OF JULY.

TOASTS.

Our Unfurling Banner—emblematic of the unfolding power of our nation and its increasing dominion !

Our Country ! The Polar Star to the tempest-tossed kingdoms of the earth.

Our Government ! The sun to which all nations turn, receiving light from its beams even as the planets of the solar system are lighted by their day-king.

> For though a woman, I would boast—
>   Boast of my heirship, wonder ye !
> Was I not born on Freedom's soil—
>   My heritage sweet liberty !
>
> What though no wreath of pearls bedeck,
>   Or diamonds glitter on my brow ;
> Nor costly fabrics beautify
>   My person with their brilliant glow ;
> Nor courses in my veins the blood
>   Of England's proud nobility ;
> Think ye I'd barter for their worth
>   My birthright—priceless liberty ?
>
> Nay, for I'm of a nobler race ;
>   And I am proud, this glorious day,
> That I my lineage may trace
>   To freemen of America.

THE DYING ONE'S ADIEU.

Farewell, father, I must leave you;
   To the realms above I go—
Farewell, brother, do not grieve you;
   Let no tear in sorrow flow.
Farewell, sister, you have loved me—
   Well I know you'll mourn me some—
Seek Christ early—you will meet me
   In a better, dearer home.

Weep not, dear ones! though we sever,
   Wait my voice at even-time;
Oft around you will I hover,
   Oft will leave that blissful clime.
When the flowers are closing nightly,
   Ere the heavy dew-drops fall,
Ere the stars come out too brightly,
   List ye t›my vesper call.

List my whisper! fear me never—
   Spirits harm not those they love—
Heed me gently; I will ever
   Tell of Paradise above.
When ye feel the kind caressing
   Of the breeze at twilight hour,
Know your brows my lips are pressing,
   Ere the skies in darkness lower.

Greet me kindly in my mission—
   Let our loves the hour beguile—
Though ye see no friendly vision,
   Deem my spirit there the while.

I will waft your evening prayer
  To the throne where Jesus waits;
I will be your incense-bearer,
  Till we meet at heaven's gates.

Farewell! farewell! death has bound me,
  Youth's fond dreams of life are o'er;
Angel bands are waiting round me;
  I am on that happy shore.
Clasp me, mother; clasp me, brother;
  All too long we parted were;
Haste! I see the blessed Saviour;
  Let me to his arms repair.

A SONG OF SOLITUDE.

Each heart hath known its own deep woe,
  Too deep for words to tell;
Each eye hath felt the hot tear flow,
  It tried in vain to quell.
Yet fleeting time with some will heal
  Grief's cruel, aching smart;
The bosom soon forgets to feel
  That sorrow there had part.

But one, I ween, there is who finds
  In life no healing cure;
'Tis death alone the chain unbinds,
  She must till then endure;
For in her desolated breast
  A worm is gnawing thére;
And deeper in the soul's unrest
  Is sinking dark despair.

And in her spirit's loneliness,
  No word of soothing power
Essays to cheer life's weariness,
  Or light the darkened hour.
Alone she treads the dreary way
  That sorrow marks her own—
Not even hope's delusive ray
  Hath on her pathway shone.

But why intrude on others' ears
  This drooping heart's sad tale;
Each has enough of earth's dread cares,
  Who treads this gloomy vale.

Each, each has seen the buds of joy
   Lie withered, wasted, strown,
Or felt that even sweets will cloy
   With bitter all their own.

Then let my murmurs be repressed—
   I'll ask of none to share
This lonely waste—woe unexpressed,
   Alone I still will bear.
And when the last slow pulse has ceased,
   The world will never know
The cankering grief within encased,
   That dried life's crimson flow.

Beneath a smile shall hidden lie
   All trace of anguish deep;
Aye, vailed from every human eye
   Shall be the tears I weep.
And when within the grass-grown grave
   This body finds a rest,
The sigh of pity none shall heave
   Above the sleeping breast.

Then when my harp anew is tuned,
   I'll let the strain be glad;
Nor open lay again the wound
   Which makes my spirit sad.
With hope and joy I will inspire
   The songs I yet may sing,
And smother the consuming fire
   Which stains this offering.

ASPIRINGS.

Oh, God, my Father, hear my prayer—
  'Tis Thou alone hast power to grant—
Touch, touch my heart with holy fire;
  For living draughts I thirsting pant.

Let not my spirit vainly strive,
  With higher aims and purpose grand;
But strengthen Thou the drooping wing,
  Till on the towering height I stand.

Bend, bend thine ear, Great God, I pray,
  While humbly at Thy feet I bow;
High, heaven-born thoughts, immortal truths,
  Stamp on my wrestling spirit now.

Let not the "talent" buried lie,
  Which with my being Thou didst blend;
Aid Thou my soul to strike the lyre—
  My Father, to my cry attend.

Let not my being naught avail—
  I fain would sing, to honor Thee,
Songs of Thy deep and endless love,
  Of life and immortality.

Oh, fill my soul with holy zeal,
  And knowledge from the founts of heaven;
Warm Thou my breast, inspire my tongue,
  Till glory to Thy name is given.

With high resolve, unfettered wing,
  Oh, let me soar till I attain.
The summit which I yearn to reach,
  Ere youth and hope are on the wane.

I fain would breathe in willing ears
   The story of the Lamb once slain,
And sing of New Jerusalem,
   Where Christ, the Prince of Peace, shall reign.

I fain would sing of all beyond
   The beauteous skies, high overhead,
And all beneath those azure vaults,
   Which glads the path on earth we tread.

I fain would strike a golden string,
   Whose thrilling melodies should rise
Before Thy throne immaculate,
   Like incense sweet in Paradise.

Oh, would to heaven my God would bless
   The efforts of my feeble pen,
That I might write indelibly
   My soul-thoughts on the hearts of men,

Till every line my hand may trace
   Shall brightly glow with truth divine,
And beaming with its radiance,
   A poet-wreath my brow entwine.

Still to thy praise, my God, alone
   My voice would swell the anthem grand,
Whose music-strains unceasing flow
   From works of Thy creative hand.

Then to Thyself pray consecrate
   (E'en though the offering humble be)
Each verse Thy servant shall indite,
   Ere launched in Thine eternity.

And on the marble at my head,
   When sleeps my dust beneath the sod,
Be this the simple epitaph,
   " She lived to honor Nature's God."

CHRISTIAN.

Christian, safe will sail thy bark,
　While Grace shall guide the helm,
Though tempests rave and skies are dark,
　No dangers shall o'erwhelm.

Be thy companions Faith and Love
　Over life's stormy sea,
And Bethlehem starbeams from above
　Shall light thee to the lea.

FOR MRS. McP——.

Relative to the loss by death of her husband, then child, and then
father.

Does the world seem cheerless to thee ?
  Has the sunlight left thine eye ?
Have the brightest stars departed
  From thy early brilliant sky ?
And is life a weary longing
  For the rest to mourners given ?
Cheer thee, for the loved ones wait thee
  In their blissful home in heaven.

Hear'st thou not their silv'ry voices,
  When the morning zephyrs play ?
Or when stilly twilight lingers
  Round the couch of closing day,
Mark'st thou not the tones ce'estial
  That are wooing thee above ?
Cheer thee, for the lost ones wait thee
  In the land of life and love.

Well I know thy heart, young mourner,
  Pierced hath been, and very sore,
And my words to tell are feeble,
  Of the griefs thou dost endure ;
But the widow and the orphan
  God doth guard with watchful care,
And though 'tis a darksome pathway
  He will guide thy footsteps there,

Where death reigns not, and no partings
  Rend with woe the stricken breast,
Where no more the cloud of sorrow
  On the fair, pale cheek shall rest;
And where all earth's loved and lost ones
  Meet to hold communion sweet,
And in deep and thrilling rapture
  Bow before Christ's mercy seat.

Weeping one, the star of promise
  For thy soul doth brightly beam—
Whom the Lord afflicts most sorely,
  He most worthy doth esteem.
Cheer thee, then, though earth seem lonely,
  Joys await thee in the sky,
And the loved ones gone before thee
  Yet shall waft thy soul on high.

But, sad one, thou still hath left thee
  One who needs thy love-light here;
She, too, mourns her deep afflictions,
  'Reft of one than life more dear.
And in all thy early sorrows
  She hath borne a sacred part—
Cheer thee, then, for she who bare thee
  Claims a share within thy heart.

RELATIVE TO THE DEATH OF LITTLE SARAH.

A sweet little singing child. who followed (in one or two days after
the burial of her sister) her elder sister to the grave.

" Mother, they have laid sweet Sarah
  In the cold and dismal ground—
She, the dearest of my playmates,
  Now can hear no word or sound."

" Nay, my child, but now in heaven
  She is clothed in robes of white,
And she hears the angels singing,
  Where no tear-drop dims the sight.

" Aye, the little cherub-minstrel
  Too hath joined the holy band,
And her songs more sweet than ever
  Tell of joy in Eden land.

" Precious, fairest bud of promise,
  We shall miss her smiling face ;
But we feel she's sweetly blooming
  In her Saviour's fond embrace.

" And in early, glad reunion
  With her angel-sister now
She doth wear the crown immortal
  On her youthful, beauteous brow.

" Still we know fond friends are weeping
  O'er the loved, untimely dead,

Borne away, so sad and lonely,*
   To the churchyard's lowly bed.

" But when this dark vail is riven,
   Which beclouds their spirit-eyes,
They shall look upon the cherished
   In the mansions of the skies.

" Weep not, then, my child, for Sarah,
   She is happy 'mid the blest;
Though no more she shares your pleasures,
   Naught can mar her blissful rest."

---

* Having died of the infectious disease small-pox, few dared accompany her remains to the grave,

FOR THE SORROWING WIFE.

He's gone! his day of life how fleet
  (Too soon, methinks, has set his sun);
And friends bereaved no more may greet,
  This side the grave their absent one.

Then let her weep; the heart would break
  If grief found not relief in tears;
Or reason would its throne forsake,
  And life become a " night of years."

Oh, let her weep—a blight is o'er
  The prospects of her earthly Eden,
For death hath entered love's bright door,
  The " twain in one " his shaft has riven.

Oh, let her weep—chide not, I pray,
  That she for one so dear should mourn;
Naught can on earth her loss repay,
  Or soothe her breast, with anguish torn.

Aye, let her weep—there's One on high
  That marks the stricken bosom's woe;
'Tis He alone can wipe the eye,
  And solace to the soul bestow.

Weep, then, fond one, for Christ hath said
  Comfort to those that mourn he'll give;
And with the loved, lamented dead
  Thou yet in Paradise may'st live.

Weep, then, if tears relief can bring,
  Yet seek in Christ the sovereign balm,
And 'neath the shadow of his wing
  Thy soul will find a heavenly calm.

And when thy spirit soars in flight,
  'Tis he—the early lost—will come,
And bear thee on love's pinions bright
  Up to thy fair celestial home.

TO ———.

Mourn not o'er the dear one's exit,
    For she heeds the tears ye shed,
And your grieving wounds her spirit--
    Well ye know " She is not dead."*

Gently, kindly, oft returning,
    Fain she'd still your rising sighs;
Though on angels' pinions soaring,
    She hath ranged the upper skies.

TWO VERY POOR IMPROMPTU PIECES, A LITTLE RHYMISH, UPON BEING INVITED TO A FESTIVAL.

Dearest ladies, pray allow us
    To return our thanks to all,
For the friendly favors shown us
    At your New Year's festival.

'Twas delightful, ladies, surely;
    But indeed 'twas not our due,
To o'erflow our hearts so truly
    With such gratitude to you.

Dainty viands, music heavenly,
    Tableaux lovely to the sight;
Ah, we thank you very kindly
    For that happy New Year's night.

* "She is not dead, but sleepeth."—TESTAMENT.

TO MR. H——TH, UPON THE PRESENT OF A ROSY CAKE OF SOAP.

Thank you, Mr. H——,
  For the sweet, rosy cake
Of soap that you sent;
  'Twas not soft—do you take?

And since I well know
  It can ne'er make me pretty;.
If it can't make me neat,
  Why the more is the pity.

Then if you should meet me
  Ere 'tis gone, sir, I ween,
(If 'tis not unexpected,).
  My face shall be clean.

OUR COTTAGE.

Lonely looks our little cottage,
  When stern winter holds her reign;
All alone adown the meadow,
  Skirted round by hill and plain.

Each tall tree, hard by, is leafless;
  Not a shrub its verdure wears;
And the greensward on earth's bosom
  Now a snowy mantle bears.

Not a songster from the green bough
  Warbles forth its silver strain;
Never bird now save the snow-bird
  Taps at Mary's window pane.

Never now the lowing cattle
  Graze before the open door,
Waiting for sweet Ann, the milk-maid,
  Till her day's-work spinning's o'er.

Never now the cheerful farmer
  Comes from labors of the field,
While earth drapes in sheening mantle,
  Or night's shades their sceptre wield.

Yet though all without seems cheerless,
  In our cot bright love-beams shine;
And with grateful hearts and happy
  Much we taste of bliss divine.

And as by the glowing hearth-stone
  We partake our simple cheer,
Naught to us seems half so pleasant
  As this lonely cottage here.

A PUFF.

In return for a beautiful book.

Friends, listen a moment to truth—nothing more—
If you wish to be charmed, go to * * fine store;
There are visions of beauty! such pictures! such vol-
    umes!
The which, if half told, would fill newspaper columns!
There are books filled with science, and books to amuse—
Walk in—you will find just whatever you choose.
More splendid gilt pages, or more handsomely bound,
Or lovelier plates, you'll ne'er meet the world round.
Say, is't not a fairy sight? Who can but linger
To turn the neat leaves with the tip of love's finger?
Each taste is here catered to, from warriors to lovers,
Statesmen, poets, divines, or the sea's gallant rovers;
'Tis a sight for the eye and a feast for the soul—
Ye spirits that hunger, sip from this " golden bowl;"
On Elysian draughts ye may here safely count,
Or nepenthes more soothing than the Lethean fount
In short, if you're seeking for knowledge or pleasure,
At this beautiful book-store 'tis found without measure.

CAN IT BE WE KNOW SO LITTLE OF ETERNITY?

When Time and Tide shall roll no more
Along this evil, earthly shore—
When day and night have passed away
To mingle in eternal day—
When pain and sorrow shall have fled
To dwell in regions where the dead—
And yet not dead, but dying—lie,
Wishing, in vain, that they might die—
When sun and moon have turned to blood,
And drowned the wicked in the flood—
When man no more shall curse the name
Of the eternal great " I Am "—
Oh, then, and not till then, shall rest
The ransomed spirits of the blest—
Oh, then, and not till then, shall we
Have tasted of eternity.

UPON OUR CHURCH BEING TORN DOWN TO GIVE PLACE TO A NEW AND MORE STYLISH ONE.

Farewell, old church !

Farewell, old, cherished church, farewell !
  We now can look on thee no more—
Thy walls are leveled to the earth ;
  Thy holy mission here is o'er.

Oh ruthless hands and hearts of stone,
  The heavenward spire how could ye fell ?
And raze the sacred temple low,
  Where Christian spirits loved to dwell ?

Alas ! we never more may tread
  Those hallowed aisles we oft have trod ;
Nor prayer nor praise from contrite hearts
  Within those courts shall rise to God.

Nor from that consecrated desk
  Our pastor's voice shall we e'er hear,
Breathing the gospel-tidings glad,
  The sin-sick soul and sad to cheer.

Farewell, old, cherished church, farewell !
  Another fane may point above ;
But who of us again may trace
  The temple of our early love ?

LINES SUGGESTED BY THE APPROACHING DEDICATION OF OUR NEW CHURCH, JANUARY, 1852.

An impromptu, almost.

Our Father in heaven !
We hither are come,
To pray Thee to hallow
This temple, Thy home.

In kindness, dear Saviour,
Look down from above,
And sanctify to Thee
This mark of our love.

Here, Lord, let our voices,
In union upraised,
By love pure and holy,
Resound to Thy praise.

Oh, here let us drink
From life's welling spring,
As we list to the words
Of our Shepherd and King.

Oh, here, in contrition
With heart-worship meet,
Let us bow in Thy presence—
With our " tears wash Thy feet."

Here, here let the sinner,
    Repentant and sad,
Be cleansed by Thy blood—
    By forgiveness made glad.

And here let the mourner,
    In affliction bowed low,
Find a balm for each sorrow,
    A cure for each woe.

Our Father in heaven !
    Consecrate, we entreat,
This temple on earth,
    For Thy worship made meet.

May seraphs and angels
    O'er its portals keep ward,
That naught may defile
    This true house of our Lord.

LINES SUGGESTED BY A VISIT IN JAIL TO THE UNFORTUNATE PRISONER BICKFORD, CONFINED ON A CHARGE OF THE MURDER OF SECOR.

But little more than one score years have passed
   Since lay an infant on its mother's breast;
Her cherub babe the mother fondly clasped—
   Loved, tiny form!—how sweet its nestling rest!
'Twas a fair child—that mother's earthly joy—
No sadness brooded o'er the baby-boy.

Few years had sped—I saw a child at play
   Within the garden gate; with lightsome feet
'Twas tripping happily the hours away,
   Gazing at insects bright and flow'rets sweet—
Fair innocent! none would have dreamed the stain
Of guilt would ever light upon its name.

A few years more—I saw a stripling boy
   Wand'ring o'er fields or by the running brook,
With loaded gun, the birdling to destroy,
   Or bait to lure the fish unto his hook.
But those were trifles—so the truant thought—
And older boys the wicked lesson taught.

Again time sped—confined within a cell
   Of narrow, darksome walls and iron grate,
Behold the youth! 'Tis useless to rebel,
   Or curse, or mourn, alas! his dismal fate.
A crime too dire for one so young to dare—
A woeful crime had brought the prisoner there.

I gazed on him where no glad sunlight beams,
   Nor flow'r's perfume, nor wildwood minstrelsy,
Nor aught of nature cheers the spirit's dreams—
   Sad bodings of its coming destiny—
A dread, a rayless passage to the tomb!
A shrinking of the soul to meet its doom!

'Twas then methought of that fond mother's grief,
   And cruel agony that bowed her frame;
No bitter tears can bring her soul relief,
   Nor kind words soothe the anguish of her pain,
Unless she deem him guiltless of the blow
That laid a mortal, all unthinking, low.

Then, too, methought of that young sister* dear,
   That climbed so lovingly upon his knee—
Must she, the darling of his heart, e'er hear
   A felon's sentence—deemed a just decree—
Upon the brother she in innocence
Had counted guiltless of the least offense?

Father, forefend! if guilt, indeed, hath stained
   The soul of him within that prison drear;
If trusting friends with this sad truth are pained,
   And naught below their sinking hearts can cheer,
Oh, let them look above, where mercies wait—
If penitent, they'll meet at heaven's gate.

Or if, perchance, fair justice yet shall tell
   Him blameless of that deed in forest wild;
If by another's hand the murdered fell,
   Restore, then, doubly blest, the injured child.
Let noble acts attend his upward way,
And, Father, all his wrongs in love repay.

---

* A little sister that sat upon his knee, with arms twined around
his neck, in court, previous to his regular trial.

LINES.

———

Embodying a wish reported to have been made by the mother of the prisoner Bickford, after his conviction, and a few days before the execution of his sentence of death.

———

"Jailor, be not over cruel—
   This one boon pray grant to me—
Listen to a mother's pleading,
   As she bows to thee the knee.

"He is still beloved—my first-born—
   Of my life the dearer part;
Grant, in pity grant this favor—
   Bless this once my aching heart.

"On my dear one's precious forehead
   I my loving lips would press;
I would seal a mother's pardon
   With a fond, a last caress.

"Take me to him, human jailor;
   I will use no art to free
Him from suff'ring his just penance,
   E'en though hard his doom must be.

"Dost thou doubt me?—bind and guard me,
   Every needful caution take;
Bind my boy, my child, my darling—
   Heed me lest my heart-strings break!

"I would know him once more near me,
   Feel his breath upon my brow;

Would to God that I might clasp him
  To this yearning bosom now!

"But so blest a boon I ask not—
  'Tis to press his pallid cheek
Ere he leaves this world of sorrow,
  This the priceless gift I seek.

"Do not chide me nor refuse me—
  'Tis his mother cries to thee—
Hear me; heed me; God reward thee,
  When thou bend'st to Him the knee."

Thus, with tears, the stricken woman
  Wildly, earnestly did plead.
Didst thou yield to her entreaty—
  Of her simple wish take heed?

Man, bethink thee of thy mother,
  Ere thou left thy parent's care;
Had fell death come nigh unto thee,
  And had one thus spurned her prayer!

Or bethink thee of thy darlings,
  Were one doomed a felon's end;
Wouldst thou deem a being mortal
  Who would not such prayer attend?

Weeping, broken-hearted woman,
  Thou may'st clasp thy child above—
God can pity! God can pardon!
  He'll regad a mother's love.

There thy erring one may greet thee,
  Washed and every sin forgiven.
Trust in Jesus—He'll sustain thee
  Till ye meet again—in heaven.

HOW MUCH I SIN.

How much I sin !
  How oft misstep and slip !
When most I would do right,
  How sadly trip !

In closet* oft,
  Bowed low in earnest prayer,
Why do I fail so much,
  If God be there ?

Can tempter come,
  When I my soul uplift,
With greater power to try
  My faith to sift ?

Oh, when shall I
  O'er sin a victory gain ?
Through Jesus' blood alone
  I can attain.

* "Enter into thy closet," &c.—TESTAMENT.

GOD PITY THE POOR.

God pity the poor,
Without shelter secure;
For the cold wind of winter is biting and sore;
'Tis whistling and tapping,
And lustily rapping,
To be ushered in at each casement and door.

Close tightly the shutters;
The wind rattles and mutters,
And boldly creeps in through each crevice and pore.
To the fire draw nigher,
Pile the faggots on higher;
God pity and shelter the suffering poor.

Give each one a heart,
Who has plenty, to part
With a small share, at least, of their provident store.
All the wealthy possess
Is the gift of thy grace—
God soften their hearts to the suffering poor.

The cold wind is howling
Round the poor man's frail dwelling,
And shrieking and blowing through casement and door;
Without food, without fuel,
Though the storm rages cruel—
God pity and shield and provide for the poor.

SNOWING.

Little snow-flake, comi·g down,
While the skies above us frown,
(Lighter than the downy feather,)
Thou dost tell of wintry weather.

On the door-sill, in the casement,
On the street and on the pavement,
On the pretty silver lake,
Thou art falling, little flake.

Little wee thing, everywhere,
On the earth or in the air,
Thou art resting or art flying,
While the wintry winds are sighing.

Covered is each hill-'op's brow
With thy mantle, feathery snow ;
Thither urchins in their glee,
With their sleds and shoutings, flee.

Upward drawing, upward riding,
Boys hurrahing !—downward sliding ;
Oh, such sport on earth was never
As boys have this wintry weather.

Hark ! the sleigh-bells' tinkle. jingle,
With the merry voices mingle ;
Scarcely has the snow-flake rested,
Ere its slippery virtue's tested.

Little snow flake, thou dost cheer us,
When cold winter hovers near us;
While to loving youth and maiden
Thou with joyousness art laden.

Never was such time for courting—
Cupid with his arrows sporting.
Naughty elf, makes young hearts tingle,
Chiming with the sleigh-bells' jingle.

Ho! hurra! what joyous riding,
Chatting, laughing, gaily sliding.
Other seasons bring us pleasure—
Winter, thou bring'st fullest measure.

OUR CANARY, "WILLIE."

Written for my little girl, "Nelly."

Dear Mr. Yellow coat,
With your sweet, pretty note,
   How you do charm me !
Singing the whole day long
Such a nice little song--
   Oh, who would harm thee ?

Now, little " Willie," sir,
Don't get so vexed at her—
   Nell is a pet, too—
Pointing her finger there,
Should not our " birdie" scar
   Nor should it fret you.

She is but playing, "Will,"
So do not whet your bill,
   Harder to bite, sir;
But from your little throat
Give her a pretty note—
   Birds should not fight, sir.

Fold up your little wing,
Pray, little " birdie," sing
   Songs that are charming—
Just let her see your eye—
Don't peep around so sly—
   There's naught alarming !

Please let her pat your breast—
Don't ruff your tiny crest—
  Flit not so weary ;
Soon I will let you out,
Then you may fly about,
  Lightsome and cheery.

And when you're tired, then
You may go back again
  In your snug nest, sir—
Then you may whet your bill,
That you may eat your fill,
  Or you may rest, sir.

That's the way—chirp again,
Warble a silver strain—
  Oh, how you charm me !
Sing on the whole day long—
'Tis a sweet, pretty song—
  Oh, who would harm thee ?

DEATH OF BIRDIE CANARY.

Sweet birdie, why liest thou so low ?
  What ails thee, little one ?
Hop up again upon thy perch,
  And trill in merry tone.

Birdie, sweet Birdie, dost thou hear ?
  Why, Nellie, Birdie's dead !
Darling, how came it all about ?
  Was't sick, or not been fed ?

Poor little thing !   I am afraid
  It suffered much, indeed ;
And then to suffer all unhelped—
  None near it e'en to heed.

Hush, Nellie, hush !   I know 'tis hard.
  To lose your birdie dear ;
But grieving thus will make you sick,
  Nor make sweet birdie hear.

Try, darling, try to dry your tears—
  We'll put him in the ground,
Under a shady tree, near by,
  And cover o'er the mound

With pretty, twining, flowering vines ;
  And each fair summer day
My Nellie there may sew and sing,
  And while the hours away.

Try, darling, try to dry your tears—
  "Why, m i, your eyes are wet."
We all loved birdie very mu h—
  We'll miss our little pet.

We'll miss his pretty morning song,
  His warblings day by day—
Ah! Nellie, mother's heart is weak—
  We'll put the cage away.

And then, when birdie's buried there,
  Out in the garden near,
We may not think of him so much—
  Ah! birdie, thou wert dear.

MY COUNTRY HOME.

My heart is in my country home ;
  The spot where I was reared
Is still the brightest spot on earth,
  The most to me endeared.
To childhood's haunts and childhood's friends
  My memory closest clings,
And round the dear paternal roof
  A beauteous halo flings.

My heart is in my country home;
  That pretty little cot,
Nestled so snug between the hills,
  Will never be forgot.
The winding, rippling, singing rill,
  That runs before the door,
Within the chambers of my heart
  Will wander evermore.

My heart is in my country home ;
  Each flower and bird and tree
Upon the tablet of my soul
  Is stamped indelibly—
Where father, mother, ever kind,
  Three brothers—noble boys—
And sister round the hearth-stone met,
  And shared our household joys.

My heart is in my country home,
  Though I am far away ;

In other haunts my footsteps roam,
   In scenes where life is gay;
But to my childhood's happy home
   My memory fondest clings,
And round the dear paternal roof
   A heavenly halo flings.

TO A SISTER ABOUT TO LEAVE HOME.

Sweet sister, must it, can it be
  That we are doomed to sever;
That all our days of mingled bliss
  Are past and gone forever?
Those days in which were fondly linked
  Our hearts and souls in one—
Tell me, sweet sister, tell me true,
  Have they forever gone?

Yet, sister, breathe it not again—
  I know " we must be parted "—
But sing for me a joyous strain,
  'Twill soothe the broken-hearted.
Oh, once more let me hear that voice,
  While yet thou ling'rest near;
None other e'er will charm like thine,
  For none were half so dear.

Sweet sister, should we meet no more
  This side of death's dark river,
Our souls will often mingle here,
  Till called from earth to sever.
And shouldst thou first be called above,
  Oh, then, sweet sister, come
And woo me with thy seraph songs
  Up to thy spirit-home.

TO THE SEA.

After the sinking of the Arctic.

Tell me, dark sea, thy mission here;
  Why ceaseless roll thy troubled waves?
For what avail that thou dost rear
  Thy billows high o'er ocean graves?

Who bade thee thus, thou restless deep,
  To yawning ope thy billowy crest,
And low within thy bosom keep
  The loved and lost ones gone to rest?

"Who bade me? Ask thy God above;
  I answer but His firm decree;
And those who on my waters rove
  Must bow to destiny the knee.

"What though my surges swell and foam,
  And now and then are yawning wide;
Am I not still the trav'ler's home?
  Am I not still the trav'ler's pride?

" What though I oft present a snare,
  To turn man's weary feet astray;
And in my bosom treasures rare,
  And untold secrets hidden lay?

" What though I oft man's life doth end,
  And make my bed his early grave;
Still, am I not the trav'ler's friend?
  Dost still his vessel plow my wave?"

Thou deep, unconquerable deep,
   Roll on, then, roll thy billowy waves,
Though millions thou dost cause to sleep,
   And moulder in their watery graves.

Roll on, nor cease thy raging moan,
   Though wild and fearful it may be;
Roll on, yet there is One alone
   At last shall deign to conquer thee.

Though once thou burst thine iron band,
   And overwhelmed creation's bound,
Yet there is One by whose command,
   Thou, too, shalt feel the deadly wound.

Roll on, then; roll till time shall end,
   Unheedful of man's piercing cries;
Roll on, and rage, though thou dost rend
   Millions of hearts in sacrifice.

THE BLACK-SEALED LETTER.

Friends, did you e'er, when far from home,
   Await a letter, and with joy
Clap your young hands when you espied
   One brought you by the good post-boy ?

Away from early friends, at school,
   One day, at recess, blithe and fleet
My young feet er the common ran,
   Thus joyously, a line to greet.

I took it, turned it o'er to break
   The seal—'twas black ! my palsied hand
Dropped by my side; like marble cold
   I stood, as changed by magic wand.

At length my life-blood coursed again—
   I took the letter and I read,
My brother, far away at sea,
   That brother dear, it said, " was dead."

O God ! that none may ever know
   Such hour of woe as then I knew ;
Though sorrow since has marked my brow,
   That seal is fresh before my view.

MY GRANDMOTHER.

I love my good old grandmother,
  That feeble, quiet dame,
As helpless as an infant child
  That scarce can lisp its name.

She is so very hard to hear,
  And, too, so very blind;
Her body paralyzed in part,
  She's as a child in mind.

Her constant friend, the ticking clock,
  Four times an hour each day
She asks the time; and, sitting, rocks
  The lagging hours away;

Save when, in curious mood, she wheels
  About her easy chair,
To learn, by feeling round the room,
  The strange things lying there.

I pity my good grandmother;
  She bears her lot so meek—
And can but press with loving lips
  Her paled and withered cheek.

So nearly deaf and nearly blind,
  And crippled, too, withal,
Methinks she, longing, waits to hear
  Her heavenly Father's call.

Ninety years old that grand-dame is,
  In second infancy,
No trace of firmer years is left
  Save early memory.

Oh, memory is a blessed light
  That shines within the breast
Of good old earthly wanderers,
  To cheer their path to rest.

OUR LITTLE " MAY."

My babe was sleeping on my breast,
   So sweetly, yester-eve,
I kissed its life-warm lips in joy,
   Nor thought so soon to grieve.
But oh, an angel from the skies
   Has borne our love away,
And we are left to weep o'er her,
   Our darling little " May."

Her tiny form, now cold in death,
   Is gathered for the grave ;
No tears will bring our jewel back,
   Though they her body lave.
But friends will lay her in the earth,
   Beneath the willow trees,
Whose pliant branches, bending low,
   Sigh to the summer breeze.

There birds will sing their matin songs,
   And we at evening hour
Will kneel beside her precious dust,
   And breathe our vesper prayer.
And daily to her little grave
   Our silent steps will stray,
Till we are called in heaven to meet
   Our own sweet angel May.

PLAIN WORK AND PLAIN WORDS.

The useful life.

He has spaded and plowed,
And the ground has been sowed
With seed, an abundance to yield;
As he planted with care,
The crops promise fair
In garden and meadow and field.

The corn now is hoed,
The grass has been mowed,
Nor rest you, good farmer, from toil;
But at it again,
You must cradle the grain,
Ere the over-ripe kernel shall spoil.

The reapers are gone,
The harvesting's done,
Now garner up safely the wheat,
Lest dew or lest rain
Should smut the cut grain,
And nothing be left us to eat.

Now, fall winds are sighing,
The flowers are dying,
The hoar-frost is nipping the leaves;
'Tis time to be thrashing,
The flail should be crashing—
Haste, farmer, and riddle the sheaves.

The apples now fall,
Come, boys, girls and all,
With baskets, and gather the fruit.
When come snow and ice,
'Twill then taste so nice;
Let's with it our cellar recruit.

Then comes the potato,
(The cabbages ditto,)
The onion, turnip, carrot and beet—
Put part into the ground,
And heap on them a mound,
And in spring there'll be something to eat.

Now ceases the digging,
And comes on the killing—
The farmer is hard at his work;
With scraping and scalding,
With cutting and salting,
He lays down his beef and his pork.

Then comes on the snow—
To the woods he must go,
To fell the birch, maple and oak;
Through felling and cording,
The sled he is loading,
And the oxen must tug in the yoke.

Now, with plenty of wood,
And plenty of food,
He sits by his bright blazing hearth;
Blest with peace and good health,
Contentment and wealth,
What knows the good farmer of dearth?

Oh, a farmer's life,
Free from turmoil and strife,
Is the chosen life I lead;
With the sweat on my brow
I handle the plow,
And put in the earth the good seed.

Then I weed and I hoe,
And the waving grass mow,
And cradle and garner my wheat;
Then with threshing and digging,
And fatting and killing,
I've abundance to spare and to eat.

ON THE DEATH OF WILLIAM H. SAFFORD—1846.

The wife of his bosom mourned over the dead,
As she thought of the gloom of his cold narrow bed.
She had wept till the fountain of tears was dried up,
O'er the sorrow just tasted from life's bitter cup;
While the deep-breathing sigh she heaved from her
    breast,
Told the anguish that still her sad spirit oppressed.
The eyelids drooped heavy o'er the pale check of woe,
And the pulse, aching, throbbed, though no tear-drop
    could flow,
As she turned from the grave to the days that were gone,
With the soul of the loved, that could never return.
She thought of the time when he wooed her his bride,
And the sweet happy hours she then spent by his side.
She looked back on the day when he claimed her his
    own,
While the smile of affection on his countenance shone,
And felt how true-hearted, and noble and kind,
Was the bosom on which she in fondnesss reclined;
And she smiled mid her grief when she thought how he
    pressed
Their first nursling babe to his own manly breast—
How his eye beamed in pride as years brought, one by
    one,
A fair loving daughter, and two darling sons;
And how, as time sped, when each eve's twilight came,
He would join in their play as they echoed his name,
Till, weary of sporting, they lisped their short prayers,
And nestled in sleep, free from infancy's cares.
Aye, she saw him again by their glad, social hearth,
As the three frolicked round him in innocent mirth;

And she heard their sweet prattle as they sat on his knee,
And his softly breathed, "Hush!" at their too noisy
    glee;
Then the warm kiss of love that he pressed on each
    cheek,
As they lisped their " good-night," ere they scarce learned
    to speak.
And she knew, as she thought of the scenes of the past,
That such moments of joy were too blissful to last;
And deep on the tablet of mem'ry she traced
His last dying look, which can ne'er be effaced;
While her heart bled afresh as she turned to the day
When the loved of her bosom was passing away.

      *   *   *   *   *   *

The young, widowed mother sat cheerless and lone
Again by the hearth where the glad light once shone.
Long she silently gazed on the tenantless chair
That still stood by her side, as if waiting him there,
And, listening, longed for the voice that was dear,
For the words of affection she once used to hear;
But in vain, for he came not, the hours dreary sped,
Her husband was laid mid the buried and dead,
And she sighed as she thought she should see him no
    more,
Till she met him, alas! on Eternity's shore.
A step caught her ear—two fair, bright-eyed boys,
The hope of their father, the life of his joys,
With the daughter on whom he had scarce breathed a
    breath
To grieve her young heart ere he sank down in death,
Gently entering, sought her, and, hand clasped in hand,
Sadly asked for their father—that fond little band.
Then she wept for the dear, helpless babes he had left,
Of a father's kind care in their childhood bereft;
And she lifted a prayer—'t was "O, God! look from
    Heaven,
Be a father to them Thou in wisdom hast given."
She wept, though she knew they should meet him again

Where the eye is not dimmed and the heart is not
    pained;
Though she knew he had soared where the weary ones
    rest,
And was leaning in love on his good Savior's breast—
She wept for herself, so forsaken, forlorn,
But grieved more in her heart for the babes she had
    borne ;
And her cry rose anew to the Father of Love—
"Oh ! in mercy, in mercy look down from above."
A calm rested on her, the tear-drop was dry—
" My promise* is firm," was the Father's reply.

* "I will be a Father to the fatherless."

VENUS.

Bright, sweet little Venus !
    Pet star of the sky !
Thou look'st down so mild
    With thy clear, silvery eye,
That methinks some kind angel,
    Which from earth winged its flight,
Gazes lovingly on me
    From thy heavenward height.

Had I wings that would waft me,
    I'd try, lovely star,
If thou wert the realm
    Of some soul wandered far
From this dark vale of sorrow!—
    Perchance some I love,
From earth-scenes departed,
    Await me above,
On yon shining sphere
    Which my gaze now doth meet....

Perchance on yon star
  Is our Lord's " Mercy-seat."

Perchance—aye, perchance—
  With what dreams has the mind,
While here by the weight
  Of earth's fetters confined,
Been fraught, as the eye
  Ranged the far ether blue,
And drank in the light
  Of the orbs shining through !
Oh ! shall we, then, know,
  When the soul bursts its bars,
The glories that burn
  On the radiant stars !

Shall we, then, hear the song
  Of the spheres as they roll
In musical chime
  To their Maker's control !—
The jubilant song,
  That the morning stars sang,
When the news through Heaven's hosts
  Of creation's birth rang!
Perchance—aye, perchance!....
  How the soul gropes its way,
All wingless and blind,
  To the light of Life's Day!

WORDLESS.

How, all unworded, in me burns
  The incense of my soul's deep fires !
And vain my spirit strangely yearns
  To pour it forth from mortal lyres

IN MEMORY OF MY BROTHER WILLIAM, WHO DIED JULY 20, 1846.

And has another much loved brother gone !
  Gone, gone, O God ! far from our mortal view.
Has he, so soon, been summoned to Thy throne,
  There to be judged ! Is night of darkest hue,
Or bright, soul-cheering day his lasting doom !
  Dear brother, would to heaven that thou might tell
If there is bliss in thy eternal home.
  Oh, could'st thou say to us that all is well,
We feel, whate'er *our* lot below should be,
  We would rejoice that *thou* wert spirit free.

I know that *once* the passage dismal seemed
  Through which thy soul must wing its way to God ;
No cheering ray on thy dread vision beamed,
  To light the path by mortal never trod.
I know, full well, thou shrank from that dark hour,
  When cruel Death should seize thy helpless clay;
When thy poor, weakened frame should feel his power,
  Though thou didst patient wait the coming day.
But now, 't is passed, are not thy troubles o'er !
  Glad would I know thou art on heaven's shore.

Yet still my selfish heart could naught but weep
  At the now sick'ning loneliness of earth,
Unless it knew that thou didst vigils keep,
  Ofttimes, around our home and native hearth.
Oh! did'st thou know how longs mine ear to hear
  Thy cherished voice, in nature's tones, once more ;
How much I wish thy company, to cheer
  This bosom, that is sick, and sorrow-sore :

Thou wouldst entreat, at least, that thou mightst tell
  Thy sister if with thee all things were well.

O William! shall we never meet again,
  As we so often here before have met !
While I shall linger must I feel the pain
  That here below thy sun has ever set !
Can I ne'er more e'en clasp thy clay-cold hand,
  Nor on thy fair, pale forehead press a kiss !—
I gladly would, though death has broke the band,
  Which bound thy spirit to a world like this.
And yet I could not sorrow if by thee
  A harp is tuned mid heaven's minstrelsy.

Nay, I ne'er more shall see thee. Low in dust
  Thy youthful form fast moulders to decay;
While where, methinks, dwell the redeemed and just,
  Angels have wafted thy glad soul away.
Yet, oh, 'tis hard to breathe the word " farewell;"
  Fain would I think thee wont to hover near;
Thy holy presence would with rapture swell
  The stricken breast with hopes so crushed and sere.
We grieve, alas! that thou art from us fled,
  So early laid within thy lowly bed.

But why weep thus ! I am not all alone,
  One brother still is left for me to love ;
Together we may sympathize and mourn,
  Till one of us shall be called home above.
Yes, one of all the three is left me still,
  One link in that rent chain remains the same ;
One dear, last link till our great Father's will
  From our fraternal band one more shall claim ;
Then the lone lingerer glad will follow, where
  Death reigns no more, nor hopeless, black despair.

Then, dearest brother here, and only one,
  Let us prepare to meet the loved in heaven,

For soon on earth, I know, will set our sun,
　E'en though long days may yet to us be given.
Our mother dear and brothers there we'll find,
　And Jesus, our bless'd Savior, we shall see,
Whose words of sweet compassion, ever kind,
　Will cause for us a gladsome jubilee.
Come, dry these tears, though God awhile shall sever
　Us from the dead, we'll meet in joy forever.

Aye, our dear William, there we'll fondly meet
　In rapturous joy, known by the blest alone ;
In converse, face to face, we him will greet
　In that fair land where all of bliss has flown ;
Our heartstrings, then, no more with grief shall break,
　Nor sadness longer dim the tearful eye ;
For then to bliss eternal we shall wake,
　When from these bodies our freed spirits fly.
Seraphs and angels then will constant be
　Companions with us through eternity.

July 31, 1846.

"FATHER, HAVE YOU NO HOPE FOR ME ?"

WORDS OF WILLIAM, WHO DIED OF CONSUMPTION, JULY 20, 1846.

" Father, have you *no hope* for me ?"
　In anxious tone, he said,
As on his frail, decaying form
　His saddened eye was laid.
" Father, have you *no hope* for me ?"
　Is youth's fond promise fled ?
Must I so soon in earth's cold grave
　Sleep with the silent dead ?

" Father, have you *no hope* for me ?"
　Must I ascend to heaven,
There to appear before the Judge,

Who has the summons given,
  To render up my dread account,
    And hear the sentence just?
Dear father, strengthen my weak faith,
    Learn me in Christ to trust.

The way of death is dark and drear,
    No ray of heavenly light
Beams on my lonely path, to bless
    Or cheer my upward flight.
Pray, father, that in *slumber* sweet
    Death's portals I may tread,
And wake in realms of happiness,
    Where no sad tear is shed.

.

" Father, have you *no hope* for me ?"
    In trembling voice he cried,
While the fond parent's deep distress
    The father fain would hide ;
" I dread to feel Death's cruel smart,
    While youth's hopes buried lie,
And all their fair, bright visions crushed
    Within my breast must die."

But oh! the father could not speak;
    He shunned the searching gaze;
For well he knew that soon must cease
    On earth his length of days.
His tongue refused him utterance,
    He could not feel to quell
The glimmering spark of hope still left
    In his sad soul to dwell.

But now 'tis o'er....he's gone to worlds
    Of bliss beyond the sky;
He left at last the joys of earth
    Without a groan or sigh.
The prayer was heard, he " slept " away,

The pangs of death unfelt....
'Twas not in vain that friends for him
  Before his Maker knelt.

Though *once* he feared the soul's release,
  None heard him more repine;
But oft he spake of cherished ones
  Who in Christ's kingdom shine;
With eyes of faith he saw the Lamb
  Who cleanseth us from sin,
And the abodes of righteousness
  He sought to enter in.

Yet oh! those words, so piercing keen,
  Still ring within mine ear....
"Father, have you no hope for me?"
  Methinks I still can hear:
The quivering lip, the anxious eye,
  The sad, expressive tone,
Within my heart's deep core shall live,
  Till I from earth have flown.

Sleep on, now, sacred dust, sleep on,
  Let naught disturb thy rest,
Till the last trumpet bids thee rise
  To meet the ransomed blest.
Sleep, dearest boy, guarded from harm
  By God's protecting hand,
Till we shall mingle, soul with soul,
  In Heaven, the Better Land.

I LONG TO GO HOME.

There was music afloat in the air,
   'Twas the song of the *spirits redeemed ;*
Angels' notes with such cannot compare,
   Though 'twas heard as in slumber I dream.

Oh, who would not sigh for the bright Eden shore
   Where the spirit may bask in the sunshine of love!
Oh, who does not pant that fair land to explore,
   And mingle in joy with the loved ones above!
Can the soul love the fetters earth binds on it here,
   Where briers and thorns choke the pathway we tread?
I fain would go home to that yon happy sphere,
   Though my body should slumber awhile with the dead.

Fair, fair land of beauty and raptures untold,
   I fain wou'd my barque might be launched on thy sea;
Bright isle of the joyous, thy treasures unfold,
   Let heaven in kindness my spirit set free.
Why should I now cling to life's sorrows and cares,
   When nought but a void drear and dark fills my breast,
Why longer caress its temptations and snares—
   Oh, soon let me go to the Home of the Blest.

I have wandered in dreams o'er the green banks of
     Jordan,
   As the smooth, crystal waves glided silent along,
And I felt that my soul was released of the burden
   That here clogged its flight to the angelic throng.
I have walked, hand in hand, with the cherished
     departed,
   In valleys all glittering with the dew-drop of pearl,

And methought I should never return broken-hearted
  Where sin o'er my barque should its sorrows unfurl.

I have bathed in the waters of Siloah's fountain,
  While the smiles of the Savior have brightened the
    scene,
And have viewed from the summit of Sion's loved
    mountain
  The glories that in New Jerusalem beam.
I have heard the rejoicing o'er the soul that repented,
  And sought for salvation in Christ's precious blood,
And have marked the freed spirit as it upward ascended
  To join in the praise of its Maker and God.

In dreams I have sipped the perfume of the flowers
  That fragrantly bloom in the regions of bliss;
I have found me repose in their emerald bowers
  While the spirit-bird warbled its carols of peace.
I have drank in the strains of the seraphs' glad lyre,
  And the clear, thrilling tones of earth's lost and
    redeemed:
But, alas! I awoke, though my soul was on fire,
  My vision no longer in ecstasy beamed.

Earth desolate seemed, not a sound caught my ear,
  Save the harsh, jarring notes of the passion-stirred lip;
Glad music no more did my sad spirit cheer
  Nor the nectarine draughts could I still fondly sip;
But I thought of the griefs and the woes of the heart
  Which naught but the hopes of a heaven could cure.
Though I tried to be calm, yet I sighed to depart,
  And I prayed to be mingled soon, soon with the pure.

Oh, who would not sigh for the mansions of rest,
  Where beings celestial from sorrow are free;
I fain now would sail o'er the bright water's crest
  And leave the rough billows of life's raging sea.

Is there aught to entice the soul longer to cling
　　Where shipwreck and death is the destiny given ?
I long to go home, and with myriads sing,
　　And join in the joys of the dwellers of Heaven.

I long to go Home! aye, I long to go Home!
　　Are angels in waiting to bear me away?
In Eden's fair gardens, oh, when may I roam !
　　Oh, when shall my spirit be freed from its clay !
When shall I behold all the glories that blaze
　　In majesty round the Eternal's high throne,
And the voice of thanksgiving and gratitude raise
　　In loud-swelling anthems, where sin is unknown?

August, 1846.

I STOOD BESIDE HIS PILLOWED HEAD.

I stood beside his pillowed head,
　　And wiped the death damp from his brow;
My brother, deeply, dearly loved,
　　Before my eyes was dying now.

His youthful form, week after week,
　　Had wasted with a slow decay;
While racking cough and fevered cheek,
　　Kept warning of the dreaded day.

But, his last days, his patient mind
　　Shone mildly through his o'er bright eyes;
And well we knew by every sign,
　　His soul was fitting for the skies.

The dreaded day at length had come,
　　The parting moment fast drew near,
When I would gladly died to save
　　From that dark hour my brother dear.

Each short'ning brea th reached my heart's core,
 Tearing its fibers till they bled,
When, looking up, " 'T will soon be o'er;
 Death conquers all!" he meekly said.

And then between each breath he'd point
 To something that he saw above:
" 'T is beautiful, though hard the path;
 'T is beautiful, that Land of Love."

Then in a clear, ecstatic tone,
 " They come," he cried, " in robes of white;
I see the Lamb, with star-gemmed crown"....
 He slept....his soul had taken flight.

I stood beside his pillowed head,
 And wiped the death damp from his brow;
But though he, dying, suffered then,
 'T is those he left who suffer now.

IF HOPE, ETC.

If Hope were Faith, how those we love
 Would come and soothe the hearts bereft;
But oh! when Hope—the Angel-dove—
 Droops her white wings, the heart is cleft.

COME, COME TO ME, BROTHER.

Come, come to me, brother, when twilight is o'er us;
　Come to me gently, arouse not a fear;
Tell me, oh, tell me of heaven's bright glories;
　Whisper them softly—the spirit can hear.

Come when the stars all above us are shining,
　Tell me on which thou hast fixed thine abode;
Come thou and hush all this evil repining,
　Calm the grief-stricken soul, wipe the tear that has
　　flowed.

Come, tell of our brother who left us before thee—
　Oh, say didst thou know him, so long from thy side?
Tell of our mother departed who bore thee—
　Do they with thee now in eternity bide?

Come, come when the moonbeams are falling around us,
　And the dew the fair leaflet is gemming the while,
And soothe in soft numbers the woe that has bound us,
　In telling the tales of that far, sunny isle.

Aye, come to me, brother, at even's still hour,
　When man from his labor sinks down to repose;
Leave, leave for a season thy love-lighted bower—
　Tell me all, ere night-slumber my eyelids shall close.

Aye, come to us when the red daylight is waning,
　And the musical spheres in sweet harmony chime;
Bring with thee a lyre of the seraphims' tuning,
　And sing us a song of their beauteous clime.

Come when we're waking, and come when we're sleep-
  ing,
  In dreams thou canst bring thee so plain to our eyes
The vision will make us forget we were weeping,
  And drive in thy presence the clouds from our skies.

Come, brother, come oft—be our guardian-spirit,
  While here we are waiting from sin a release;
And when life is over, with thee we'll inherit
  And joyfully enter the haven of peace.

SORROW.

Leaden-winged sorrow, shall I never
  Shut the door upon thy back?
Wilt thou haunt my pathway ever,
  Casting shadows o'er my track?

Dost thou guard my spirit's portal,
  Lest some joy may enter in,
And I should forget that mortal
  Suffer must to punish sin?

Oh, could I strike an angel's string,
  And sing a song from heaven,
It were but faint the offering,
  To tell of Christ's forgiven.

"HE'LL KNOW ME WHEN I MEET HIM."

William.

He'll know me when I meet him—
    Has he forgot me now?
He'll know me and will greet me,
    Where heaven's beauties glow;
He'll lead me to my mother,
    All radiant with joy,
As round her twine the spirit-arms
    Of her first angel-boy.

And with him, all I dearly loved
    Will know me when I come,
And kindly they will welcome me
    In gladness to their home;
And smiling in their joyousness,
    Their tale of bliss they'll tell,
'Mid all the beaming glories
    Where saints immortal dwell.

And there in that blest circle,
    Surrounding Jesus' feet,
All time unheeded by shall flit,
    While hearts ecstatic beat;
And all my soul has longed to know,
    'Twill learn in that glad hour,
When love and wisdom joined in one,
    Show forth the spirit's power.

E'en now I sometimes dare to wish
    That death would haste the time
To free me from this earthly coil
    For that celestial clime.

For oh, my spirit's longings,
  They almost burst the band
That fetters this sad, yearning heart
  From that fair fatherland.

And yet again I turn me back
  To all the dear ones here,
And ever with the living-loved
  I fain would linger near.
My darling child, thy prattlings sweet
  Recall my thoughts from heaven;
For should that tender tie be broke,
  My hope of joy is riven.

He'll know me when I meet him—
  Has he forgot me now?
Doth never he in shining realms
  On me a thought bestow?
Do I ne'er feel the holy spell
  His presence round me flings,
When ofttimes sunk in sorrow's night
  I soar from earthly things?

Do I ne'er hear his gentle voice,
  Sweeter than seraph tone,
When all around is hushed and still,
  Breathing of loved ones gone?
So softly soothing to mine ear,
  1 deem my soul away,
Where kindred spirits twined in love
  Meet in eternal day.

He'll know me when 1 meet him—
  The time is drawing near
When I shall join the cherished one
  Beyond the starry sphere.
And oh, what bliss unspeakable,
  We'll meet to part no more;

For parted friends were never known
   On heaven's happy shore.

He'll know us all—the kindred dear
   Who mourn him here below;
And warmer will our greeting be,
   Since we are severed now;
And joying, he will lead us forth,
   And point us to the throne
Where waits the Saviour, merciful,
   To claim us for his own.

He'll know me—hush! he's coming now—
   That soul-entrancing strain!
Methinks that all the kindred choir
   Are following in his train.
List! they have gone—on angel-wings
   I see them soar afar!
Ah, knew I not he sometimes came,
   My spirit's guiding star!

List! list again! melodious notes
   Are wafted back on air;
Zephyrs have caught the thrilling song
   For my enravished ear.
Those tones are like the tones that cheered
   My father's household hearth
In days now gone, but sweeter far—
   They are of heavenly birth.

That song was like the simple lays
   My mother used to sing,
When with her joined her eldest born*
   Praising their righteous King!

      * Sheridan.

Though purer, higher, holier,
   Yet brings it back to mind
My childhood's early, happy home,
   Where friendship was enshrined.

My childhood's home! O God! what spot
   On earth can fill its place?
What charms can from my aching heart
   Its memory erase?
There love did all its seeming prove,
   Cherished within each breast;
Now, onward, upward I must look,
   Till comes my final rest.

My childhood's home! My mother's love!
   What music in the words!
Sweet as the silv'ry strains that come
   From angels' golden chords.
'Twas she that tauᵧht my lisping tongue
   Its first and infant prayer;
'Twas there I knew a parent's worth,
   And felt a parent's care.

But kinder, dearer, more divine
   Will be our Jesus' love;
More happy still our dwelling-place,
   When all have met above.
There death and all the woes he brings
   Will never enter in;
But ever-living, reigning joy,
   Free from the stains of sin.

He'll know me—ah! he's with me now;
   He's left those sunny climes,
And guides my pencil while I trace
   The hopes of future times;

Yet tells me, as was told before,
   That man can ne'er conceive
The glories of bright Paradise
   For those who Christ believe.

She'll know me—can a mother e'er
   Forget the child she bare ?
Are not her shelt'ring wings oft spread
   O'er me in watchful care ?
Doth she not still before the throne
   For me in meekness pray ?
Aye, she will wrestle for her child
   Till she, too, flee away.

And he, my elder brother,
   Who died on ocean's wave,
With no friend near to soothe his pain,
   His burning brow to lave;
To breathe for him a cheering word,
   Or smoothe his sailor-bed ;
Oh, he will clasp his sister dear,
   When she hath thither fled.

And he, my aged grandsire,
   Who oft did wipe the tears
Of grief from off my youthful cheek,
   And calmed my childhood's fears—
He, too, will swell the chorus grand
   That through the vaulted sky
Tells of another ransomed child
   Borne up to worlds on high.

[Having alluded in the foregoing poem to a mother's
singing, please permit me to annex a short extract from

a prose piece written by my brother S. a year or two previous to his death.]

"With unutterable emotions I review many scenes of other days, but memory revives nothing in my heart more melting than a mother's voice in a mother's song. Not the rural airs of the shepherd's flute, nor the deep tones of the majestic organ, nor the rolling blast of the matchless bugle could ever awaken in my soul such thrilling interest as that voice.

"Not even the music of Nature's favorites—the murmurs of purling streams, the pensive strains of the Æolian harp, nor the lauded carols of summer birds ever breathed half the sweetness that fell from a mother's lips.

"But the best of voices has long since ceased to yield its melody on earth. They say that in heaven the good sing to God and the Lamb. If so, there breathes in that chorus the voice of one who was dear to me."—SHERIDAN F. B.

MARY, JESUS' MOTHER.

Sinner, didst thou e'er bethink thee
  Of the crucifying smart,
When our Saviour bled and suffered,
  That did wring His mother's heart

Thus to see her son—her Jesus—
  Crucified upon the tree;
Pure and gentle, sinless – groaning
  In the depths of agony.

Thus to see the huge nails driven
  In His guileless feet and hands,
And to hear the heartless jeering
  Of the throng that round Him stands.

Thus to hear Him, dying, pleading,
  (While the blood sweat doth bedew
Every pore upon His body,)
  " For they know not what they do."

Thus to see them pierce Him, hanging
  Lifeless, drooping from the cross—
Spilling blood, unsullied, holy,
  From His side, as 'twere but dross.

Sinner, 'twas for thee that Mary
  And her Jesus felt each smart,
And their throes of pain and anguish
  Should subdue thy wayward heart.

'Twas to gain thy sins a pardon
  That the Son of God came down
From His home of bliss, to suffer
  And obtain for thee a crown;

Not of " platted thorns," to pierce thee,
  But a crown of glory bright;
Not a " purple robe," to mock thee,
  But an angel-robe of white;

Not to smite and bind and scourge thee
  Then thy hapless state deride;
But to cleanse thee from pollution,
  Bled His hands and feet and side.

Mother, bending o'er the death-couch,
  While thy grief-wrung heart beats wild,
Think of Mary at Mount Calv'ry,
  Bowed before her dying child.

Not upon an easy pillow,
  Or upon a downy bed,
But long hours upon the gibbet,
  Drooped our Saviour's weary head.

Mother, when thy heart would murmur,
  Saying not, " Thy will be done,"
Turn thine eyes to Calv'ry's mountain,
  Think of Mary and her Son.

OUR BABE.

Angel bands are flitting near us,
  Hark ! the rustle of the wing;
Oftentimes they come to cheer us,
  And in heavenly accents sing.

Nearer, nearer, then retreating,
  Farther dies the sound away ;
Then again we feel the pinion
  Softly round our tresses play.

With the angels, bright and shining,
  Comes a little birdling-dove,
And we hear her sweetly hymning,
  Hymning of her nest above.

Little strains, so soft and soothing,
  Lisps the angel birdling near;
Tones so winning, tones so wooing—
  'Tis our darling one we hear.

Ah ! we knew our pretty birdling
  Would with angels come again;
And we knew she would be hymning
  In our ear a silver strain.

And we knew her little pinion,
  Softer than a wing of down,
Would be flitting, near us flitting,
  'Neath her little golden crown.

I have felt its gentle brushing
   On my sorrow-moistened cheek,
And it dried the fountain gushing
   With the grief I could not speak.

Pretty little heavenly nestling !
   Angels guard our birdling dove;
For I hear their kind caressing,
   And their lullabys of love.

And I see with spirit vision
   Where they lay my babe to rest,
Folded in the wings of angels—
   Cradled on an angel's breast.

Thou art blesséd, sweetest birdling,
   Sin can never mar thy lot;
Thou art now the Saviour's nursling,
   And thy mother clasps thee not.

But she hears thy gentle cooing,
   And she feels thy little wings,
And she knows that thou art wooing,
   Wooing her from earthly things.

THE DYING MOTHER; OR, ALMA'S FLOOD.

"My mother, did you call?" "I did, my dear—
Come, love, and sit beside thy mother here;
I have somewhat to say before I die—
Hush, darling, do not o'er thy mother cry.
Sit close; in thy warm hand take mine, 'tis chill;
My daughter, weep not at thy Father's will.
Though thou art young, in patience learn to bear
Thy early grief—kind Father, hear my prayer;
Temper to my shorn lamb the winds in love,
And guide her here, till we shall meet above.
My child, far, far away from Alma's flood,
Whose waves are red and swollen with the blood
Of human beings, comes a wailing cry,
Though faintly in its wake comes victory.
A Christian nation, for religious rights,
Against a sister Christian nation fights.
Not such a precept taught by Christians' God,
To thus surcharge the waters, drench the sod.
There, by that stream, thy father sleeps to-night—
Love, move the lamp, its bright rays dim my sight—
Or if he sleeps in death—some water, child,
My throat is dry, my pulse is throbbing wild.
There, that will do; but if thy father's gone,
Thou wilt indeed be friendless, darling one.
Father, again, oh, heed a mother's prayer,
Keep Thou my darling in Thy fost'ring care.
My love, the room is dark; take back the lamp-
I cannot feel thy hand—wipe off this damp,
It chills my brow—I faint, I gasp for breath;
Quick, raise the sash—O God! can this be death?"
That very hour from far-off Alma's flood
The father, too, ascended to his God.

THE WOODS.

'Tis mine to range the grand old woods,
　While gently blows the rustling breeze,
And pluck the wild-flower and the fruit,
　And list the music of the leaves.

'Tis mine in sultry summer's heat
　To muse within the shadowy glade—
There sit for hours in pensive mood,
　Till twilight skies begin to fade.

'Tis there in morning time I turn
　My steps to hear melodious lays;
Each tree is vocal then with birds,
　Which, warbling, hymn their Maker's praise.

And oh, 'tis in that temple grand,
　Of God's own handiwork, I kneel,
And pray to the Eternal One
　To cleanse my heart, its wounds to heal.

I feel Him nearer to my soul,
　Where naught but nature's works are near;
There loving angels wait to waft
　The prayer, and wipe away the tear.

A LITTLE PIECE OF PROSE.

My pen is destined still to write of the departed,
To cheer, well as I may, the grieving, stricken-hearted.

Relative to Mercy Elizabeth, infant daughter of Wm. and E. S——.

Oh, what a tender tie now binds our souls to heaven!
We see our darling there. Sweet little cherub, how her
bright wings shine! How radiant that little face with
bliss! Angels have decked her. Round her fair young
brow is twined a wreath of never-fading flowers, fresh
gathered for our angel-child in heaven's fair, perennial
bowers. And see that dainty robe of spotless white, in
shining folds so crystal clear, falling around the little
seraph form in which her sinless soul is clad. She
blooms in beauty now, too beautiful for mortal eyes to
scan. And see that little, smiling band of countless
cherubs round her wait, waving bright palms and sing-
ing sweetest songs of gladdest welcome to the new-flown
lamb! Behold how carefully her Saviour takes and
clasps our precious one within his arms! How innocent
she nestles there, as rests her downy cheek on Jesus'
breast! How trustingly her bright eyes gaze upon the
countenance divine of Him who saith, while yet on earth,
of such pure innocents His holy kingdom did consist.
And see what love He doth on her bestow! More than
a mother's love is His. More than a father's care she now
shall know. Passing description is His kindness shown.
How priceless, too, the lessons of true wisdom He to her

shall teach! E'en now, could she return, earth's wise ones might of her a lesson learn. Then should we not rejoice that she, our darling one, has gone, though she doth all so closely cling in twining tendrils round our loving hearts. Is it not sin to drop o'er her a tear? Jesus, to Thee in meekness let us bow, and kiss the chastening rod with which thou didst, in thine unerring wisdom, smite our sinful, earth-bound hearts.

THE RAINBOW.

"Mamma," said a little girl-of two years, as she came running in from the garden, after the cessation of a fine April shower, with eyes big and shining like two brilliants—"Mamma, dere be great wibbon in de sky ; come, mamma, see ; 'tis such pitty." I fol owed my little one, as she desired, and, true enough, a beautiful "ribbon" spanned the heavens. The wee thing had never before seen the glorious " bow of promise," and in her child's head she compared it to things she had seen.

And so, thought I, is it with us children of larger growth. Our ideas of heavenly things are but a reflection in our minds of the beautiful things of earth.

POETRY—WHAT IS IT?

And what is poetry? Is it but rhythmic verse and jingling sounds, unhallowed by a holy touch, accessible to all?

And what is poetry? Come forth, my muse, and tell. Is it the golden spring from the Invisible which opens egress to the soul, that it may pour forth utterance in deep, harmonious strains that will enchant the ear while it gives vent to unpent longings for the spiritual of the vast Unknown? Is it the dialect in which the angels converse hold, and chant sweet praises as they bow around the throne of Him the "Great I Am?" Is it the language Eve addressed to Adam, father of the human race, ere yet by sin they fell? Or is it but the plaint from the poor love-sick heart of disappointed maid or swain? Or is't the siren's witching voice of love, polluted love, as man doth oft declare? Oh, shameless man. Or is it something indescribable, so precious and so rare that few obtain the glittering gem, more famed than is Golconda's shore, more prized than Eastern diadem? And what is poetry? Who shall to me make known? Where is it found? Is it obtained from musty books and college halls; from rocky steep, or woody glen? Or from the water's brink, or flowery mead? Come forth, my muse; direct me to the spot; give me the key that doth unlock the hidden mystery. Where shall I search, oh, whither turn to find? Cometh it down in twilight's hush, or in the moon's pale beam? Or is it wafted in the perfumed gale? Tell me, oh ye, its votaries. Where is it found, and where may I obtain? I've sought it long, and sought in vain; it shuns and 'scapes my grasp.

WHEN THE SOUL.

When the soul is worn and weary,
　Drooping low with broken wing,
Turn the eyes to sad Mount Calvary:
　Look on Christ the sorrowing.

See Him in His throes of anguish!
　Suffering more than man can feel;
That thou, sinner, might not languish,
　For He died thy wounds to heal.

Mourner, is thy burden heavy?
　Does thick darkness round thee bide,
Turn thine eyes to Jesus, dying:
　Look on Him the crucified.

He will bear thy weight of sorrow,
　He will lighten every care.
Bright thy sky will shine to-morrow,
　If thou bow'st to-day in prayer.

He can raise thy fainting spirit,
　Groping in a starless night,
And on Faith's white pinions waft it
　Till it basks in Heaven's pure light.

THE WORD "MOTHER."

How sweet is the sound of the simple word "mother,"
  When lisped by the lips of the child of our heart!
Oh, breathe, if you can, in the ear such another
  That to woman's warm bosom like joy will impart.

With thrilling delight I drink in the soft cooings
  Of a dear little dove nestled close to my breast,
And when it essays, in its infantine wooings,
  To utter *that name*, was e'er mortal more blest!

Oh, when years have vanished, and life has grown older,
  And the circlet of womanhood rests on her brow,
To a fond, noble bosom may a loved one enfold her,
  And she list to " mother " as I listen now.

HAVE WE FLOWERS ?

Have we flowers ? fair lady ; oh, yes ; we have flowers,
  That we rear with the tenderest care;
We would not exchange them for all your gay bowers,
  Blooming fresh with the choice and the rare.

We have two little sunny-sweets, fair as the morning
  That wakens the blossoms of Spring,
With loveliest beauty our cottage adorning,
  While round, sweet soul-fragrance they fling.

Oh, yes, we have flowers that we lovingly cherish,
  More prized than the gems of the mine;
We train, we watch over, and tenderly nourish,
  These immortals, these flowrets divine.

Oh, yes, we have flowers, two bright, rosy blossoms,
  That bloom by our own cottage hearth;
And we clasp them, in happiness, close to our bosoms,
  Giving thanks for their being on earth.

Oh, yes, we have flowers, two sweet little creatures,
  Perennials that spring to our arms;
They have eyes bright as dew-drops and love-tinted
    features;
  Naught else hath for us half their charms.

Our flowers ne'er will perish, though the vases that hold
    them
  May fall into dust in the tomb,
For then our dear Jesus to His bosom will fold them—
  Eternal our blossoms shall bloom.

IS THERE NOT ROOM?

Is there not room for me, too, Lord,
  Before Thy throne to stand,
And sing a song and wave a palm
  Amid the angel band?

May not I bask within the beams
  Thy glory sheds around,
All cleansed from my pollution, Lord,
  And in Thy grace abound?

Let my soul soar on wings of faith,
   Enrobed in righteousness,
Till it is closely folded in
   Thy loving blessedness.

LOVE.

Awake, my soul, to joyous strains,
   No more let sorrow's plaint be heard;
Earth is all fair and beautiful,
   When *love* the soul's deep fount has stirred.

And love has found its way within
   This heart of mine, erst sad and lone,
And, oh, how bright all things appear,
   Which seemed so dim ere love's light shone.

Love is the guerdon God has given
   To those who, patient, walk the road,
Mantled in faith and charity,
   That leads up to His blest abode.

Then evermore, my soul, o'erflow
   With love that emanates from heaven,
And clearer will my pathway glow,
   Till rest is to my footsteps given.

MY LOVE'S RETURN; OR, MY LOVE SONG.

The sun shines again through the cloud,
   For my Love smiles upon me once more,
And the heart that of late was low bowed,
   On pinions ecstatic doth soar.

The sun shines again through the cloud,
   And the pearl-drops of joy fill my eyes;
Nature now hath put off its dark shroud,
   And laughs in the light of the skies.

When the light of love shines in the heart,
   Dark shades from our path flee away;
On life's stage we no more walk our part,
   But skip, like young lambkins at play.

The sun shines again through the cloud,
   My lover no more looks askance;
And my heart that lay chilled in its shroud
   Is aglow with the thrill of love's glance.

The words now his loving lips speak
   Are sweeter than dewdrops to flowers,
And the breath of his kiss on my cheek
   Is like perfume from Eden's fair bowers.

His melody fills all the air,
   Over mountain and valley it floats;
No tones with my Love's can compare,
   As he trilleth his musical notes.

The sun shines again through the cloud,
   Nature joins in the voice of my mirth;

When the soul with love's light is endowed,
  A roseate hue gilds the earth.

Do you wish my Love's name, friend, to know?
  If I tell will you give me your hand?
He groaned on the cross years ago,
  But reigns now in the Beautiful Land.

LET THE LITTLE STAR SHINE.

Let the little star shine;
  Its light may be sweet,
To somebody straying
  With bruised, bleeding feet.
It may be to some poor heart,
  Dearer by far,
Than the clear, twinkling light,
  Of the large, brilliant star.

Let the little star shine,
  Dear Lord, though 't is small;
Let no cloudlet come o'er it,
  Its faint beams to pall.
Its soft, silvery ray
  May light to its goal
Some longing, and fainting,
  And earth-wearied soul.

Let my feeble pen write,
  Dear Lord, though 't is weak;
A thought or a feeling
  It aids me to speak,
May be to some lone one,
  As sweet as the light

Of the dear little star
  That I gaze on to-night.

Let my feeble pen write;
  Though of " talents " but " one "
Thou hast given me, Lord,
  Let my work be well done;
If wisely I use it,
  Some good it may do,
To *some* poor soul wandering
  Life's wilderness through.

I fain would prove faithful,
  Be the " trust " e'er so small;
I care not to hide it,
  Though it pleaseth not all.
Some weak, simple soul,
  Near akin to my own,
Good harvest may reap
  From the seed I have sown.

Oh, the weak, simple soul
  Is of just as much worth
As the proudest and wisest
  And greatest of earth
" Inasmuch as ye 've done it,
  To one of these ye,"
Dear Lord, thou hast said,
  " Have done it to me."

Let the little star shine,
  Though away and afar,
And smallest mid thousands,
  It may be the star
That shall guide *one* to port,
  On life's ocean-waves driven;
It *may* be the star
  That shall lead *one* to Heaven.

THE SICK CHILD.

Poor little suff'rer, keen is thy distress,
  Fain would thy mother bear for thee thy pain.
Father above, our every effort bless
  To bring our dear one back to health again.

The rosebud lips, to us now doubly sweet,
  Are parched and dry, and scalding is her breath;
The tender flesh is scorched with fever heat....
  Dear Father ! save our cherub child from death.

Bid cooling draughts allay her burning thirst,
  And bathing check the pulse's rapid throb;
Those swollen veins above her brow must burst;
  Oh, let not Death us of our fondling rob!

She is the darling of our little band,
  Our precious lamb, for whom our prayers arise;
Stretch forth, dear Father ! Thy all-healing hand,
  And bless once more with joy our weeping eyes!

      *   *   *   *

My babe looks up....a smile illumes her face,
  The burning glow has left her fevered cheek....
To Thee, kind Father, we this blessing trace;
  Our depth of gratitude no words can speak.

OUR HOUSEHOLD LAMBS.

———

Our household lambs are rich,
  For God is very kind!
He's given to each a gift worth more
  Than all earth's wealth combined—
A thinking, joyous soul,
  Shining through love-lit eyes;
More sweetly beaming than the worlds
  That light the evening skies.

We parents, too, are rich;
  These lambkins in our fold
Earth's richest monarch could not buy,
  Nor wealth of worlds untold.
These jewels that are ours,
  We hope will shine on high,
When sun, and moon, and stars, no more
  Hang in the vaulted sky.

———

OUR YOUNGEST CHERUB.

———

We 've a bright little cherub, with wings not yet grown,
Who pats round with tiny feet—she is our own.
Hands fat and chubby, cheeks dimpled and chin;
Fairer than any flower earth's vale within.
Flossy curls, golden-hued, circling the brow,
In its sweet purity, white as the snow;
Eyes blue as sapphire, outsparkling the same!
Nectar-dewed lips that the ruby's red shame!—
The prattle of which is like music from Heaven.
Oh, will she e'er from our fond arms be riven ?
Our sunbeam, our birdling, our precious, our own—
We know *from our hearts* thou canst never be flown.

A BABY RHYME. OUR SUNBEAM.

A little "morning sunbeam" bright,
　　She shines within our nest;
As prattling every morn she springs
　　From her sweet cradle-rest.

"I love you, mamma—let me kiss—
　　Papa and sister, too;
And little 'Birdie'....but I can't—
　　But, Birdie, I *love you.*

" So I will say, good morning, sir;
　　And put a lump that's sweet,
Between the bars for dearie bird,
　　To peck at and to eat.

"See 'Prinny' wag his tail ! mamma;
　　I love my 'doggy,' too;
Just see him lick my face ! I guess
　　He loves *me, too, don't you ?*

"I love poor pussy, too; I love
　　To stroke her soft fur skin,
And hear her hum and purr so nice—
　　Please, may I let her in ?

"I love the pretty skies and flowers,
　　And all the birds that sing,
And the green grass, and God who made
　　The earth and everything."

Thus always prattling as she springs
  From her sweet cradle-rest,
Our little "morning sunbeam" shines
  Within our little nest.

And all the day with winning words,
  And happy heart and light,
And pleasant eye, she seems to us
  A streak of sunshine bright.

And when at eve she sinks to rest,
  Like starlight in a flower,
She smiles a little heavenly ray
  Within our little bower.

THE CHILD-DREAM.

It chanced to me to overhear the words I now may tell,
Of childish faith and innocence that from the sweet lips
    fell,
Of a little girl, scarce five years old, sitting on papa's
    knee,
Gazing into his loving eyes earnest and tenderly:
"Mamma is gone to Heaven, you said, where there's no
    grief nor pain,
But don't she want to see *us* there? can she come back
    again?
The days are very lonely here, and when 't is dark at
    night,
I wish that I might wake in Heaven before 't is morning-
    light;
For there mamma would speak to me when I'm afraid
    and weep,
And fold me closely in her arms till I should go to sleep.

And, O papa, last night I thought, when I'd been long in
    bed,
That dear mamma came back and bathed my little,
    aching head,
And asked of you to let her take me to her happy home !
'T was for her little girl, she said, that God had bid her
    come.
But you were loth to let me go, and begged that I might
    stay;
Till mamma caught me in her arms and bore me far
    away,
Where there are lovely birds and flowers and many pret-
    ty things,
And angels like my dear mamma, with bright and downy
    wings,
And music sweet as any song my mamma used to sing,
Before she slept so very sound that morning in the
    spring—
But, dear papa, what makes you cry? it was a dream,
    may be ?
For here your little girl is now, sitting upon your knee.
I'll kiss those sorry tears away....I think I would not go,
If dear mamma *should* come for me, I know you'd miss
    me so."
Thus prattled in her father's arms, a fair-haired, bright-
    eyed child;
And looked up sweetly in his face with loving eyes, and
    smiled.
But when the sun again looked o'er the little eastern hill,
Her eyes were rayless, and her form lay waxen, cold,
    and still.

ANOTHER BABY RHYME.

"Call me 'Darling-blessèd,' mamma;
  Call me 'Lamb,' and 'Love-bird,' too;
Call me everything that's pretty;
  Call me 'pet names,' mamma, do;

"Kiss your little Darling-blessèd,
  Fold your 'Lamby' to your breast,
Softly pat your little Love-bird;
  Make my little heart be blest."

Thus, our little "Chubby" pleadeth,
  Pressing kisses on my cheeks,
On my lips, and eyes, and forehead,
  Between every word she speaks.

Oh, what loving, sweet-lipped kisses!
  Innocent and pure as heaven!
And what gentle, fond caresses,
  By our "Baby-bird" are given!

"MAMMA, IS IT JESUS SMILING?"

Mamma, is it Jesus smiling,
  Makes the Summer-time so bright?
Oh, my little heart beats happy,
  When the pretty world's so bright!

But when it is dark and cloudy,
   And the rain comes from the skies,
Then is Jesus very sorry?
   Does the rain come from His eyes?

And, dear mamma, when the thunders
   In the black sky roll along,
Then is Jesus very angry,
   Because I've done something wrong?

Does he surely see, dear mamma,
   Every thought that is not right?
Can he look into my bosom,
   When it's very dark at night?

Oh, I'm sure I'll try, and never
   Think a naughty thought again;
For I love the pleasant sunshine,
   Better than dark clouds and rain.

THE CHILD'S WISH TO PRAY

'T was a dark and rainy evening,
   And the wind was moaning wild,
While anear a bright fire sitting
   Were I and our darling child.

"Dear mamma," she sweetly asked me,
   Looking up with earnest eye;
"May I kneel and thank 'our Father'
   For this home so warm and dry?

"May I tell Him, too, I thank Him
   That I'm no poor *orphan* child?

Do you think that He can hear me
   Through the rain and wind so wild?"

" Yes," I answered, " and will love thee
   For thy thankful little heart ;
Ever be thus truly grateful, .
   Choosing, ' Sweet,' the ' better part.'

"And remember, too, when kneeling,
   To entreat our Father kind
For all homeless, friendless children,
   Shelterless from rain and wind;

" Who, in poverty and sorrow,
   Through grim want, so poor and pale,
Tread a thorny, weary pathway,
   Where temptations oft prevail.

"Ask Him, from His bounteous storehouse,
   To supply each needy one;
Kindly feeding, shelt'ring, guiding—
   Ending with ' Thy will be done.' "

Then our darling knelt beside me,
   With hands folded on my knee,
Raising her blue eyes to heaven,
   A sweet bud of piety.

I SAT, ETC.

I sat me down weeping
   Beside a small mound,
Where my baby lay sleeping,
   Low hid in the ground;

For I missed the soft lovelight
  Of her star-beaming eye,
And I thought I would gladly
  Lie down, too, and die;

And be laid by the sweet one
  That slumbered so still,
In the moonlighted churchyard
  On side of the hill.

A CHILD'S PRAYER.

How beautiful the morn, serene and bright;
Dear Lord, how good to guard us through the night
From evil prowler, angry storm and fire,
From sorrow's wakeful plaint and sickness dire!

Dear Lord, how loving must Thou be to keep
Watch over us while we are lost in sleep!
How sweetly kind is Thy forgiving power,
To shield our heads in such a helpless hour!

And when, dear Lord, we take our final rest,
And our frail forms lie deep in earth's cold breast,
Withdraw not, then, Thy loving, guardian hand,
But lead us safely up to " Fatherland."

A BEGGAR'S PETITION; OR, KIND WORDS.

Kind words! oh, more than gold are they; they thrill
　　Through my poor heart;
They touch, so tenderly, my eyelids fill—
　　For tears will start.

When such for me vibrate within mine ear,
　　They leave a spot—
A blesséd little sunny spot to cheer
　　My hapless lot.

Kind words, they say, are plenty and are cheap,
　　But not for me;
Nothing 's so plenty as the tears I weep
　　Through beggary.

I meet the rich and crave a trifling boon;
　　With angry face,
Harsh words and cruel, in a cutting tone,
　　They give in place.

Kind words, my friends, oh, give the needy some!
　　'T will do them good;
'T will make less cheerless the hard path they roam,
　　Crying for food.

CORNELIA.

Sweet, only sister, fare her well.

Consumption seized upon her frame—
  Our sister wasted, day by day
Drooped like a lily, from its stem
  Borne by the blast away.

So her frail body perished here;
  But from its precious dust arose
A being bright and beautiful,
  In Eden's blest repose.

And thus the fairest flower that bloomed
  Upon our stricken household tree,
By its Creator's hand was plucked,
  To grace eternity.

OUR DARLINGS.

We had a little visitor,
  A pretty, fairy thing—
She came to us one morning
  Just at the close of spring;
Oh, she was such a darling,
  The little, wee, wee thing.

She had the roundest, brightest eyes,
  Of just the sweetest blue;
Her lips were like fresh rosebuds
  Her skin carnation hue.
She was the plumpest, prettiest babe
  I'm sure I ever knew.

But this young tiny creature
  Was not the first sweet bird
That had visited our household
  And our depths of love had stirred,
For just about six years before,
  A like wee voice was heard.

Oh, such a perfect picture
  Of innocent delight
Was now our six-year birdling,
  She danced from morn till night
Around the little lump of love,
  Dressed in its robe of white.

And as our nestling flourished,
  And grew from day to day,

The elder sister birdling
  Scarce from her side would stray,
Not even with her former mates
  To spend a time in play.

But she would sit beside her,
  And each fair feature trace,
Or hold her on her little lap,
  In fondest, close embrace,
And thinking her so beautiful,
  Resolved to call her Grace.

Thus lovingly she tended
  The pretty, winsome thing,
Till she began unfolding,
  As 'twere, her little wing,
And tottered timidly about
  When came the early spring.

Nor ceased her tender care e'en then,
  For closely by its side
In all its fragile wanderings
  She strayed a patient guide,
Lest something evil might befall
  Her darling pet and pride.

Oh, 'twas a very pleasant sight
  To see that loving child,
Scarce out of babyhood herself,
  So patient, tender, mild,
In all her daily watchings
  Over our infant child.

And then when first its tiny lips
  Essayed to lisp a word,
Her glad eyes sparkling danced with joy,
  And gleesome voice was heard,

" Oh, never on this earth," she said,
 " Was such another bird."

Which care the little nursling
  Did seemingly requite,
Throwing her arms round sister's neck,
  The loving little wight,
Pressing warm lips upon her cheek,
  With honied dew bedight.

Thus " Nellie " watched our " Gracie,"
  And in her joyous pride
Would prattle of her budding charms,
  Which daily she espied ;
Nor ever lagged her loving care,
  Whatever did betide.

Till suddenly our Father,
  When spring came round once more,
Recalled our youngest birdling
  To the celestial shore,
And she was hidden from our view
  On earth forevermore.

Oh, then the change 'twas piteous
  That o'er our " Nellie " came ;
She, in her bitter sorrow,
  No more appeared the same ;
But moped about in silent grief
  That wore away her frame.

And few, too few, the golden days
  Ere borne by angel bands,
Another precious darling
  Entered the unknown lands ;
And there, methinks, are happy clasped
  Our cherub babies' hands.

LINES.

Sorrow's Music Strains.

Oh, would you stiike a thrilling chord,
  Whose music strains should pierce the soul,
Play on the quiv'ring heart-strings where
  Sorrow awhile hath held control.

Aye, let the poet's magic wand
  But touch the bruised and bleeding lyre,
And sweeter melodies shall rise
  Than all the joys of earth inspire.

For when the soul is sorest tried,
  The o'erstrained heart-strings almost riven,
Will not earth's purest notes ascend
  And plaintive vibrate nearer heaven?

God doth not purposeless afflict
  The children of his loving care;
But wrings with grief the bosom's core,
  To gain a fitter dwelling there.

To buoy the soul on wings of faith,
  And raise its best aspirings higher;
To waft its sweetest incense forth,
  He probes the heart with sword of fire.

Then, poet, would you strike a chord
  Whose notes should penetrate the soul,
Play on the quiv'ring heart-strings where
  Sorrow awhi'e hath held control.

"SHE IS NOT DEAD, BUT SLEEPETH."

"She is not dead, but sleepeth,"
Though thou, loi e mother weepeth
    Above her head ;
Her body, fast decaying,
Keeps not the spirit staying
    In earth's cold bed.

"She is not dead, but sleepeth,"
Though Death, the reaper, reapeth
    The lov'd forms here ;
Her soul, unscathed, adoring
Its Maker, now is soaring
    Where falls no tear.

"She is not dead, but sleepeth,"
Though the sky vigil keepeth
    Above her breast;
She has passed o'er death's dark river
To the bosom of her Giver,
    There sweet her rest.

"She is not dead, but sleepeth,"
Though now the zephyr sweepeth
    Around her bed ;
Thine eyes ere long shall greet her,
For in heaven thou shalt meet her,
    When life has fled.

Thy child hath upward risen,
She has burst her clayey prison—
    Thy faith gird on ;
"She is not dead, but sleepeth,"
For Christ, the Saviour, keepeth
    The spirit gone.

THE DYING PAUPER CHILD'S ADIEU.

It is growing dark, dear sister,
  But I know it is not night,
For I see the sun go upward,
  And the clouds of pearly white ;
But the light around is fading,
  And my limbs are growing cold,
And I hear the Savior calling,
  " Little lamb, come to my fold !"

Do not weep for me, dear sister,
  I am very glad to go
Where no hunger-pain is gnawing,
  And no shiv'ring winds do blow.
Up in Heaven, they say, " there's plenty,
  No poor children dwell up there,
And that Jesus loves the orphan,"
  And I know He's heard my prayer;

For the other day I begged him,
  When we'd nothing left to eat,
And the people did not heed us
  When we asked for bread or meat—
Then I begged that He would take me
  To His Home up in the sky;
And I'm going now, dear sister,
  And you'll come, too, by-and-by.

You will come, for when I see Him,
  I will tell our Savior dear
Of our cold and of our hunger,

And of every bitter tear;
He'll pity you, dear sister,
　　You'll not have long to stay;
I'll ask dear Lord to call you soon,
　　He'll hear, *there*, when I pray.

And then when we have entered,
　　We'll search that Happy Land
Until we find our mother,
　　For she's mid the angel band;
I'm sure that I shall know her
　　By her eye so mild and blue,
And her hair so soft and shining,
　　And she looks so much like you.

And I'm sure that she will know us,
　　For when she was going away
She laid her thin hands on our heads,
　　That on her bosom lay;
And said she would watch over us,
　　If Christ would let her come,
Till she should meet her children
　　Up in her other Home.

And father, too, he may be there,
　　For mother used to pray,
"That God would turn his erring steps,
　　Nor cast his soul away."
And, while upon his dying bed,
　　I heard him cry to Heaven,
"To grant, if it were possible,
　　His sins to be forgiven."

And there, too, we shall see her—
　　Sweet "Baby-bird" that died;
For when I fell asleep, last night,
　　Within a palace wide,
And prettier than you can think,

A thousand children played,
And " Baby " there looked very sweet,
In shining robes arrayed.

Then do not weep, dear sister,
  You'll not have long to stay;
I'll ask dear Lord to call you soon,
  He'll hear, *there*, when I pray;
And when you come, those golden streets
  We'll happy, happy roam....
Hark! Mother calls her little boy....
  Good-by! I'm going Home.

—1858.

I have thought best to change a part of two stanzas in this piece, for they have apparently been purloined from me, and are quite common in some of the " songs of the day " for the children. It was written eighteen or twenty years ago for *The American Union*, Boston. " Are the Stars the Eyes of Angels ? " was printed in a New York city paper several months after I had it inserted in Grace Greenwood's *Little Pilgrim*, and another name attached to it. I wrote to the publisher at the time that it was purloined, but he paid no regard to me, supposing the piece was not worth the trouble, I presume.

TO MY BROWN-EYED ONE.

Darling, those dark-brown eyes of thine
   Are beautiful to me,
I prophesy thought in their depths,
   And poet minstrelsy.

No crime shall e'er pollute thy hand,
   No taint of meanness stain
Thy noble heart—upon thy brow
   Sweet chastity shall reign.

And charity and love shall blend
   To make thee Christian here;
Within those windows of thy soul
   I read thy mission clear.

Those lustrous star-beams light the page
   Whereon we read thy life—
A child obedient, trusty friend,
   A Christian, honored wife.

A LETTER TO MARGARET VERNE,

A contributor to the " American Union." Published in Boston, 1859.

Please to tell me, " Maggie Verne "—
For I do so wish to learn
Just precisely all about you,
Since earth's stars were less without you—
Is your figure tall and graceful,
Or petite, yet neat and tasteful ?
Is your skin of lilied whiteness—
Eyes of dark, or azure brightness ?
Are your lips like roses budded—
Chin and cheeks with dimples studded ?
Have you golden hair or jetty ?
Are you plain or are you pretty ?
Tell me, Maggie, Maggie Verne,
For I so much wish to learn.

Please to tell me, Maggie Verne—
For I do so wish to learn—
Are you young, or, growing older
Do your pulses throb the colder ?
Are your skies with pleasure glowing—
Fortune's rich gifts round you flowing ?
Does your heart enfold another,
Dearer than a friend or brother ?
Or if maiden, or if married,
Have health's blessings round you tarried ?
Are your manners mild or queenly—
On your brow sits fame serenely ?
Tell me, Maggie, Maggie Verne,
For I so much wish to learn.

Please to tell me, Maggie Verne—
For I do so wish to learn—
Which or earth or heaven seems nearest—
To your soul vhich clings the dearest ?
Do bright angels' soft wings fan you,
And their love-arms gently span you ?
Do earth's love-beams dance around you,
Till their halo quite confounds you ?
Doubly blest in mind and graces,
Has care left on you no traces ?
Have life's rough winds ne'er blown o'er you,
Strewing hopes like leaves before you ?
Tell me, darling Maggie Verne,
For I so much wish to learn.

Maggie's answer to my questions has been lost, not by myself, but by the carelessness of another. I intended to insert it directly following the above letter, because it was so very beautiful, and because it seemed appropriate so to do, before I recorded my reply.

A RESPONSE TO MARGARET VERNE.

Dear, delightful, lovely starling,
All things bless thee, Maggie darling,
For thy words such music ringing;
Oh, methought 'twas some one singing
Who had strayed from skies above me—
Some one who I thought did love me,
And would fain my soul waft lightly
To the stars that shine so brightly—
To the heaven smiling o'er us—
To the friends who've gone before us.
Sure, some angel standing near thee
Moved thy pencil, Maggie dearie,
To the music-strain you sung,
Though a part were sorrow-wrung.

Dear, melodious warbler, charming
All my being, sweetly warming
Every vein; with rapture thrilling
Every heart-string; dew distilling
From my eyes, my eyelids filling;
Scarcely dared I hope you'd deem me—
Since my words were so unseemly—
Worthy of your least attention,
Though I'd dared your name to mention
In our prized and model " Union,"
Wishing I might hold communion
With a gentle sister-spirit,
Whose heart beats the Loves inherit;
And to thank you now I write you,
Hoping thus far to requite you
For your kindly, beauteous favor,
Which so much of love did savor.

With my thanks, I pray you, please
Accept the heart of plain Louise;
'Tis a heart somewhat like thine,
Thinks all beauty is divine—
Is in goodness a believer,
Firm in friendship, non-deceiver;
'Tis a heart that's joyed and sorrowed,
Warms to love, yet oft been harrowed
By the cold, unfeeling crowd—
Often bled when death's pale shroud
Closely folded some departed
Friend, and left me broken-hearted—
Mother, brothers, sister dearest—
This it is makes heaven nearest,
All my musings upward turning,
All my bosom skyward yearning,
Groping in the gloaming shadow
Till my feet shall press Lile's meadow.
But a truce, the while, to sadness,
Turn thee, pen, again to gladness.
Well, dear Maggie, by the blue
That's above us, I with you
Wish that you were married, madam,
To some noble son of Adam;
And in time that cherub love-ties,
Prattling sweet, might peep with dove-eyes
Into yours all-thankful, smiling,
For the precious, care-beguiling
Charmers, whose soft arms and faces
Nestle 'mid your bosom's graces.
Now good-by, melodious starling,
Though I wish your music, darling,
In my ears vibrated ever,
Till the Fates my li'e's thread sever.
In joy and sorrow, your most truly
Ever-faithful, loving Lulie.

THE BEAUTIFUL COQUETTE.

Her jeweled fingers touch the keys so lightly,
While from her ruby lips come words so sprightly;
Or, as her sparkling eye to you she raises
As, airy, floats she in the dance's mazes—
You almost deem her come from fairy dell,
A fairy queen, she knows to charm so well.

Her skin so fair, her cheeks so tinged with roses,
While o'er her polished brow soft hair reposes,
Her form so sylph-like!   Perfect, every feature;
Manners so naivete, the lovely creature;
You wonder if she is of mortal mold,
Or has escaped from some angelic fold!

But should you chance to spy her in the morning,
Ere she has donned her outward fair adorning,
Ere pearl-white teeth are set within their places,
And the false raven hair her forehead graces,
You'd deem you looked upon some haggard being,
That e'en with paint could scarce be worth the see-
     ing;
And wonder if the metamorphosed elf,
So graceless seeming, really *knew* herself !

APPLICATION.

Then, noble sex, *that never dost dissemble*,
Of *beautiful coquettes* beware and tremble;
For ever since fair Eve did eat the apple,
You've found it hard with woman's wits to grapple.
And as a friend has given you fair warning
That *sometimes* " belles " appear in false adorning,
If e'er *your true* hearts are by them deceived,
She feels her hands of all the guilt relieved.

TO THE "LOUNGER" OF HARPER'S WEEKLY.

I wish I were a little bird
    That could face wild wintry weather,
I know where I would fly just now
    And wait and watch together.

I'd fly with all my little might
    Straight off to your great city,
And light upon your window-sill
    And sing my sweetest ditty.

And then when you should look around
    To spy the saucy stranger,
I'd take a sly peep in your face—
    This prying little ranger.

And when I'd looked about enough,
    Back to my forest dwelling
I'd fly; and to my woodland mates
    Such tales as I'd be telling!*

                        Feb., 1858.

* I had not seen New York when I wrote this, and did wish for wings to go there.

A WISH.

For Mr. " Lounger," of " Harper's Weekly. '

Heaven bless thee, dear Lounger !
   Preserve thy kind heart—
May love-buds blooming round thee
   Sweet fragrance impart.
May bright birds singing near thee,
   With magic control,
Cheat time of the wrinkles
   It would print on thy soul.

And when the worn casket
   That has lock-bound thee here.
Lies broken and shattered,
   May bright angels be near,
Blooming fairer than flowers,
   Singing sweeter notes still
Than the loveliest songsters
   Of earth ever trill.

Heaven bless thee, dear Lounger !
   May'st thou stay with us long,
And oft listen kindly
   To the would-be bird's song ;
And if Harper or no now,
   May thy harp by and by
Swell the anthems of glory
   That roll through the sky.

FRIENDSHIP.

How soothing to grief and how oft a relief
    Is sweet sympathy's token—
    The word kindly spoken—
Oh, 'tis heaven to know we have true friends below,
Who would fain ease our burdens and soothe every woe

When thy innermost heart has been pierced by the dart
    Of soul-sinking sorrow,
    With no hope-beaming morrow,
Hast thou ne'er felt the worth of that blessing of earth,
The sweet-savored blossom to which friendship gives
    birth ?

Blest Friendship and Love, ye come down from above,
    Joy-tastes to us giving
    Of the purified living—
By both rich and poor sought, yet too pure to be bought,
To the warm-hearted being life without you were naught.

Oh, 'tis heaven to know we've a friend here below
    Who would 'suage to-day sorrow,
    And with bliss gild to-morrow ;
But alas many learn 'tis in vain that they yearn
For so priceless a boon, save to Jesus they turn.

THEY THINK ME COLD.

They think me " cold "; ah, me, they little know
  The wellings of affection in my heart;
How, often, they their confines overflow,
  Though curbed with all the force life doth impart.

They think me " cold "; ah, me, they little ween
  The fires of love that burn within my breast;
With proud reserve these fires from view I screen,
  Though rob they my whole being of its rest.

They think me " cold "; ah, none with skillful hand,
  And chords responsive in his bosom strung,
Plays on my quiv'ring heartstrings—no sweet wand
  Hath love's deep echoes from my bosom wrung.

Yet love burns all aglow there, though well masked
  By all my strength of reason and of art;
Oh, would you have me yield my love unasked!
  More dearly do I prize this yearning heart.

They think me " cold "; they do misjudge so much;
  They cannot read me, since I'm unlike them;
The herd around me never felt a touch
  Of the warm heart-throbs which I scarce can stem.

They think me " cold "; they whose loves are to mine
  Like frozen raindrops to the summer shower;
The reaching tendrils of my heart *would* twine
  Gladly around some loving, sheltering power.

CHARLEY FLINN.

Heir to his grandsire's spacious farm,
  Within a "stone front," brown,
There dwelleth handsome Charley Flinn,
  The smartest lad in town.
His manly brow is broad and high,
  His hair as black as jet ;
And then he's such a pleasant look,
  One cannot soon forget.

The girls around their eyes would give,
  (To him) if they could win
The tender tones and loving smiles
  Of handsome Charley Flinn.
They say his heart is cold as ice
  And harder than a stone;
They really fear a bachelor
  He'll live and die alone.

But little "Nell" could tell a tale
  They wouldn't like to hear:
Some morning in the month of June—
  (Oh, are n't it very queer)
That he should choose me for his wife,
  (Plain little Nelly Stiles),
When there is queenly "Polly Ann,"
  With her bewitching wiles!

Now Charley Flinn, without his shoes,
  Is over six feet tall,
And when I hang upon his arm
  I feel so very small!

But since I'm seventeen to-day,
  My gaiter boots within
This lump of " four-feet-ten " will make
  A *stately* Mrs. Flinn.

Mamma pretends to think 't is strange
  The choice that some men make;
But, on the whole, I rather think
  They know who 's best to take.
Charles says he'd rather have a wife
  Can perch upon his knee,
Than forty such great, bouncing girls
  As " Polly Anna " Lee.

Poor Polly Ann, I pity her,
  And have my secret fears,
'T will break her heart to *lose that farm*—
  The cherished hope of years.
And then to miss of Charley, too,
  The dearest man alive;
But who, pray tell, could want a wife
  As old as twenty-five!"

"JULIET."

Do ye mourn for her yet ?
   Years have now passed away
Since your eyes rested on her,
   The beautiful clay !
Since the star of your household—
   The bird of your nest—
Lay drooping and fading,
   And sinking to rest.

Do you mourn for her yet ?
   In the deep hush of night
Comes she now in your dreams
   Like a star to your sight ?
And with tones still so dear
   Does she, long laid to sleep,
Glad your hearts sad and lone,
   Till you waken to weep ?

Do ye mourn for her yet ?
   Oh, how oft have I thought
Of the dark, lustrous eyes,
   With the love-light inwrought—
Of the fair, smiling face,
   And the sweet, bird like voice,
That in years long agone
   Made your household rejoice.

Sweet spirit of beauty !
   Like a bird on the wing

Thou flutteredst round us
  In thy fresh, early spring ;
But alas ! in thy earth-home
  The bird-star went down,
And the Holiest seized thee
  For a gem in His crown.

OUR COTTAGE.

Very pleasant looks our cottage,
　In the meadow by the rill,
While the summer sun is setting
　Slow behind the western hill.

Emma goes to milk old brindle
　Grazing by the open door;
While sweet Anna makes the supper,
　For her day's work spinning's o'er.

Mother calls the smaller children
　From their frolic on the grass—
Quick they run to wash their faces
　In the wavelets as they pass.

Then with hands all clean and chubby,
　Eating bread and milk they sit
On the freshly-scoured door-step,
　Their young eyes with pleasure lit.

Father now is coming homeward
　From his labor in the field ;
But he stops him at the well-curb,
　To the oaken bucket wield,

Which, c'ear-dripping from the fountain,
　He the cooling draught surveys,
And with grateful heart and humble,
　Glad his burning thirst allays.

Then he sits him at his table,
  Laden with a housewife's care,
And in meekness asks a blessing,
  Ere he tastes the frugal fare.

And when supper time is over,
  And has set the summer sun,
Then the farmer and his household
  Rest them from their labors done.

And the quiet cottage, watched o'er
  By the angels from above,
Charms the gazer in the moonlight,
  For 'tis guarded round by love.

KINDLY WORDS.

Patter, patter on the roof
  Falls the gentle rain;
Patter, patter on the ground,
  And on the window-pane.

Such gentle rain-drops deeper sink
  Into the thirsty earth;
So gently, gently drop reproof,
  'Twill prove of greater worth.

Harsh words rebound, nor penetrate
  Into the wayward heart;
But kind rebuke, in kindly tone,
  Will rouse the better part.

So gentle words, in counsels wise,
  Will well repay the toil,
As summer's gentle showers refresh
  The hot and thirsty soil.

LOVE AND THE MAIDEN.

By a sunny, rippling river,
Cupid strayed with bow and quiver,
Gazing at a little maiden
With her bosom flower-laden.

Like a gleesome fairy tripping,
Sweet as blossoms she was nipping,
Happy as a bee in clover,
She spied not the wily rover.

But when Cupid, by the river,
Shot the arrow from his quiver,
Coy and blushing stooped the maiden,
With her flutt'ring heart love-laden.

Vain she tried t' extract the arrow—-
Helpless as a little sparrow—
From her wounded, timid heart,
But the more she felt the smart.

Then beware !—by life's fair river
Cupid strays with bow and quiver—
Lest thy bosom, happy maiden,
Be, too, with love's arrow laden.

ETTY VALE.

Found dead upon her mother's grave.

Oh, Etty Vale, sweet Etty Vale,
  The burning tears my eyelids lave,
When memory brings thee, cold and pale,
  In death upon thy mother's grave.

To think that no one near thee bent
  To press with loving lips thy cheek;
To feel thy soul unheeded went,
  None near a kindly word to speak.

To know the slanderous tongue of man
  Had caused to shorten thus thy days,
And see the wretch without a ban,
  Who virtue's self in spite betrays,

Still fawned upon and flattered by
  The very sex he so defames;
Oh, 'tis enough to drench the eye
  And scorch the heart with anger-flames.

Oh, Etty Vale, sweet Etty Vale,
  The day will come when thou wilt be
Avenged, for Christ has heard thy tale
  Of wrong—and just is Deity.

DRESS.

That lady-folks love dress men say—
　　I say men love it dearest;
And if you'll let me, in my way
　　I'll prove my case the clearest.

Pray, for whose eye do ladies dress
　　In jewels, silks and laces?
Now, men, be honest, and confess
　　'Tis for your lordly graces.

And why do men don plain attire,
　　If not to please fair woman?
For well they know that we admire
　　The noble, plain-clad human.

Pray what observer has not seen
　　That flounced and jeweled maiden　.
Is mostly worshiped by the men?
　　With their love-glances laden?

And he who notices will mark
　　The beauty, gaudy seeming,
Will oftener choose the plain-clad spark,
　　Whose eye with truth is beaming.

Now, gentlemen, be it confest,
　　I've proved my case most clearly;
You love the dress-y sex the best—
　　We love the plain most dearly.

THE DEPARTED MOTHER.

I am lonely, lonely, lonely,
   For the loved one is not here;
And I weep, but weeping never
   Will recall my mother dear.

Oh, my friends, who ne'er have listened
   For a mother's voice in vain,
Can ye blame me if I miss her
   Whom I ne'er shall see again?

Little know ye who ne'er felt it
   Of the anguish in my heart;
Clouds take now the place of sunshine,
   Hot tears from my eyes will start.

Motherless! how can I say it?
   Motherless! take back the word,
Twine thine arms around me, mother;
   Let thy loving voice be heard.

Mother! mother! list—no answer—
   Must I see her face no more;
No more clasp the hand that led me
   Till my saddened life is o'er?

No more wait the coming footsteps
   Of the form I loved so well;
No more hear her words of counsel?
   Oh, let not my soul rebel.

But, dear, sainted, best of mothers,
Oftentimes, in spirit, come;
With thy spirit-arms entwine us,
Till at last we meet at Home.

Written as a simple offering of affection to the bereaved daughters of our friend Rev. Mr. Treadway.

THE LOST SHEEP.

Who knows but this world is the hundredth sheep,
Of worlds upon worlds through the endless sweep,
That has gone astray from the Father's Fold,
Lost in the fogs as her centuries rolled!

The hundredth sheep! so "the ninety and nine"
He left in the care of His shepherds divine,
And, with loving heart bleeding, down the thorny path
    came,
This sheep wand'ring lone with His blood to reclaim.

Oh, the world is full of beauty,
    When the heart is full of love,
But when swell the fiercer passions
    Sadly flees the stricken dove.

KITTY LE GRAVE.

Over the meadow and over the hill
And over the river there stands a mill,
And Geoffrey, the miller, is handsome and brave,
And I know 'mong the lassies the one he would crave,
To 'tend to his cottage and wait at his door,
To welcome his coming when his day's work is o'er;
But though he is handsome and though he is brave,
He'll sue yet awhile for young Kitty Le Grave.

Over the river and over the hill
And over the meadow he comes from the mill,
In his " Sunday-best " drest, two evenings each week,
And I know by his eyes 't is of love he would speak;
But I'll laugh at his wooing and keep him " at bay "
Till 't is no longer safe with his feelings to play;
For though he is handsome and though he is brave,
He shall sue yet awhile for young Kitty Le Grave.

Over the meadow and over the hill
And over the river my heart 's in the mill
Where Geoffrey is grinding six days out of seven,
But he shan't find it out when he comes here at even;
For I'll laugh at his wooings and keep him " at bay,"
Till 't is no longer safe with his feelings to play;
For though he is handsome and though he is brave,
She shall not seem won lightly, young Kitty Le Grave.

Over the meadow and over the hill
And over the river, not far from the mill,
Stands a neat little cottage, so white and so new,
That Geoffrey has built for his Lady-love true.
But the harder the winning, more valued when won,
And I would be prized when his wooing is done;
For though he is handsome and though he is brave,
His cottage must wait for young Kitty Le Grave.

IN A LITTLE COTTAGE; OR, DOUBTING.

In a little cottage, near a little rill,
Is a little maiden, sitting very still;
For she's deeply thinking of the little word,
Said to Kitty Comely, she had overheard,
As she passed the hedge-row near the garden gate,
Home, last eve, returning, lone and rather late.

" Was he quite in earnest, did he mean it true,
That she was the dearest girl he ever knew ?
Did I hear it rightly, 't was his heart's desire,
She should be his wife, instead of little Letty Hyre ?"
Thus she sits a thinking till the moon is set,
And sleepy stars are blinking, with her eyelids wet.

Pretty little Letty, fair as any flower,
Go rest your little golden head, 't is near the morning
    hour;
Let no more a thought of him becloud your sunny brow,
He's not worth a single tear from such a one as thou;
The roses on your cheeks, the glintings in your hair
Are gins will catch a better "fish" than Elverton St.
    Clair.

QUESTION AND ANSWER.

HE.

You're tired of the dancing, Kate;
　Come in the garden walk;
With none to listen but the flowers,
　We'll have a little talk.

I gave my heart so long ago
　Entirely to thee;
I dare to ask a fair return—
　Wilt thou give thine to me?

Just say me one short word, fair girl,
　While no one is about,
One easy, sweet, consenting word,
　Three letters spell it out.

Your lips are silent, dear—is't then
　To say so hard a thing?
May I not on your finger place
　This little pearl-drop ring?

SHE.

Bold sir! a word of letters two
　Is quite as easy spoken;
But since 'tis you, dear Will, I'll wear
　In pledge of troth the token.

THE SWAN.

[Suggested by seeing the beautiful Swans in Central Park, said to have been brought from England.]

Bird of the snowy plume! fairy-like creature!
  Daintily cleaving this miniature lake,
Graceful in motion and graceful in feature,
  Light on the wave as the snow's tiny flake,

Often I've read of thy plaintive song-singing,
  Sweeter than woman's when sweetest and best—
Sing me a bar while the lakelet thou'rt skimming,
  Or when thy white wings on the bright waters rest.

Bird of the snowy plume! come here a stranger,
  Away from thy kindred far over the sea,
Thy heart must turn homeward, thou dear little ranger,
  Sing of thy home, then, wherever it be.

I wait me—I listen—no song is forthcoming,
  No musical trills from the fairy-like throat;
The birds of the air their sweet strains are humming—
  From the bird of the waters no notelet's afloat.

Is it a fable, then?   Sings the swan never?
  Or with her last breath comes the plaintive refrain?
Or here for her native home sighing forever,
  Dies in her bosom the musical strain?

Bird of the snowy plume! here let thy home be;
  We'll cherish and love thee—from danger will save;
With thy dear, pretty nestling-brood merrily roam free
  On this sweet silver lake as on Albion's wave.

THE VISION.

Once upon a moonlit even,
Like to those of ancient Eden,
As I sat with heart o'erflowing,
Thankful for the beauties glowing
    On that sublunary night,
Heard I something humming, humming,
On the stilly moonbeams coming,
Floating to me lower, nearer,
Ever sounding sweeter, clearer,
    Till I saw a form alight.

'Twas more beauteous than a fairy,
Bright and shining, yet so airy
That I knew it was not mortal,
Standing in my chamber portal,
    Standing in the open door;
But methought it was a spirit
From the land the good inherit,
From our Father-land above us,
Where have gone the friends who love us,
    There to dwell forevermore.

And I mutely sat and listened,
And my eyes enraptured glistened,
And with soul entranced, confounded,
Every pulse within me bounded
    At the fair, unearthly scene;
And my heart's ecstatic beating,
Sounding like great waters meeting,
As I viewed the glorious vision
That had come from fields elysian,
    From its ken I failed to screen.

Then outspoke the fairy creature,
Sweetly beaming every feature,
Lips with heaven's dew a-dripping,
As the silver tones came slipping
    From the pearly portals twain—
Spoke she, and all ceased her singing,
Though her voice, like soft bells ringing,
Lost for me no sound enchanted,
But my heart throbbed, no more daunted,
    As she spoke in mortal strain :

" Fear me not, on heavenly mission
Come I from the land elysian,
Where joy ceases never, never,
But where those we love live ever,
    Come I from that happy shore;
Come I with my Father's message,
'Tis for thee a blissful presage
Of thy doom when life has left thee,
When death of thy form hath reft thee,
    That thy soul may freely soar.

" This the message that He sent thee,
'Tis a heavenly nepenthe,
Coming only from high heaven,
To God's children freely given,
    To the souls who Him adore ;
Those who in His works behold Him,
And in grateful hearts enfold him,
Shall surcease for them each sorrow,
Brighter beaming every morrow."
    This she said and nothing more.

Then she waved her downy pinions,
And she fled from earth's dominions

Like a meteor-flash, far shining,
Till she passed the moonlit lining
 Of the starry dome on high ;
And I started as from dreaming
Of a something more than seeming,
Though I found no sign nor vestige
Of the beauteous, heavenly prestige
 That I lost beyond the sky.

But I do believe a vision
Came to me from realms elysian,
For I know it was not mortal,
Standing in my chamber portal,
 Standing in the open door ;
And I know I was not dreaming,
For 'twas something more than seeming,
Music strains that so enchanted,
And the vision that so daunted
 Every sense of my heart's core.

But methinks a shining spirit
From the land the good inherit
Really came to give monition
Of beatified condition,
 Of the loved ones gone to rest;
And I patient wait my going
To the land with bliss o'erflowing,
Where I never more shall sorrow,
But where brighter beams each morrow,
 For the pure and heaven-blest.

Oh, blest land of The Forever
Shall one mortal see thee never,
Never look upon thy glories,
Spoken of in olden stories,
 Talked of in the Book divine ?

Is there *one* of earthly number
Who can in his sins so slumber,
And neglect his soul's well-being,
Never from his sinning fleeing
  Till Death's arms his form entwines!

Pray, forbid it, Gracious Father!
Let the sinner sorrow rather,
And repent him of his doings,
While he hears the Spirit's wooings
  And its warnings of his fate;
Turn him with thy admonition—
Let him feel his sad condition,
And look humbly to his Maker,
That in Christ he be partaker,
  Ere it be for him too late.

Let him, thankful, feel Thy presence,
Glorying in Thy Ommiscience;
And to Thee give glad oblation
For the beauties of creation—
  For Thy ever watchful care;
And when Death has disencumbered
His tried soul, let him be numbered
With the beings like the vision
That I saw from Fields Elysian—
  To thy courts may he repair.

WHEN EVENING PUTS, ETC.

When evening puts her curtains down
  With silent, shadowy finger,
And stars like diamond circlets shine,
  And on her dark brow linger,
I put my hat upon my head,
  My tartan on my shoulder,
And turn my steps to Jenny Grant's,
  One short hour to behold her;
For Jenny is a winsome lass,
  · So gentle and so tender,
I mean with my strong arm through life
  From each ill to defend her.

Her heart, I know, is warm and true,
  I think she loves me dearly;
For in her blushing, tell-tale face
  I'm sure I read it clearly....
But who, alack! with steps so bold,
  Dares, there, before me enter?
Now, by my troth, 't is Alec Mac,
  'T was he that letter sent her:
Oh, fickle, false, and soulless sex!
  While I'm a being human,
I never will put trust again
  In any living woman.

Hist! Jemmy Gregory, you're too fast,
  Made quite too easy jealous;
Within that little parlor sit
  Two maidens fair, they tell us;

And one is pretty Jenny Grant,
   And one sweet Nelly Campbell—
There's room beside the parlor hearth
   For you and Alec, ample.
'T was of her coming Nelly wrote
   To Jenny in that letter;
And Alec Mac is Nell's betrothed....
   I hope you 're feeling better.

Now Alec's arm clasps Nelly's waist,
   Warm lips, in love, are meeting;
With honest, frank, and noble heart,
   Full trustful is his greeting.
From every ill of life he'll raise
   His manly arm to shield her;
Till, some day, he to death's embrace
   Shall be obliged to yield her;
But woe! to winsome Jenny Grant,
   So gentle and so tender,
If such a jealous *booby's* arms
   Through life are to defend her.

OUR ANNIE.

On the banks of the smooth-flowing Salmon
   Stands the cot where our Annie was born;
She was fair as the stars in the heavens,
   Ere pale they in midsummer's morn.

Each day did our fresh little blossom
   Unfold some new charm to our view;
And we strained her in love to our bosom,
   More dear as in beauty she grew.

Her eyes than the blue skies were bluer,
   And bright in their merrisome beams;
Her voice in its music was sweeter
   Than angel-tones heard in our dreams.

Her ringlets were sunny and golden,
   Her cheeks with rose-blushes were tinged,
Blooming soft in the mellowing shadow
   Of the lakelets above silken-fringed.

Her form was as lithe as a fairy's,
   More graceful than wood nymph or fawn,
And her footsteps came ringing with gladness,
   Like bird-notes at early day dawn.

But early one spring-time came sorrow,
   With wings dark and heavy as night,
Straight into our erst happy cottage,
   And she pass'd away from our sight.

And now, in my desolate chamber,
  W·herc phantom-baiks glide on the wall,
I wait to pass over the river,
  When Death. the pale boatman, shall call.

And another, who woo'd her, stands watching
  The boat from the dimly-lit shore ;
By mourning worn most to a shadow,
  He soon the dark waves will pass o'er.

A STAR IN THE NORTH.

There shines in the North a bright, beautiful star,
   I wish I had wings and could scan it;
Though sweetly it twinkles and glistens afar—
   Pray is it a sun or a planet?

Do beings immortal, like angels, there dwell,
   All sinless and sorrowless, holy?
Nor was there an Eve to ring happiness' knell,
   That earth might not reek in sin solely?

Bright star of the North! I'll believe thou art blest;
   That beings pure, beautiful, shining,
Rove in thy fair gardens, with soft verdure drest,
   Love's garlands their sweet brows entwining.

Who knows, lovely star, but some soul once earth-bound,
   On thee tells its earth-sadden'd story?
Perhaps one I lov'd has his heaven there found,
   And basks in thy day-beams of glory.

Bright star of the North! when my spirit takes flight
   From the dim shores of death's troublous river,
Perchance on thy beauteous plains it may light,
   As it wends on its way to its Giver.

SABBATH EVENING

This is a holy eve;
   Angels breathe around us;
And sweetly soothing is the spell
   With which their love hath bound us.

This is a holy eve;
   Our Father-God is nearer
Than in the turmoil days of life,
   And earth to Him is dearer.

This is a holy eve;
   In such a twilight hour
May my freed spirit take its wings,
   And soar to Eden's bower.

SUNSET.

My soul is in love with the sunset skies,
When they shine in their beautiful, brilliant dyes,
When the soft-winged gales fan my hot brow at eve,
Bringing sweet scent from the flowers they leave,
And the vespers of birds are afloat on the air,
As off to their nests for the night they repair;
When the day-king, retreating, is bidding good-night,
Passing behind the red clouds out of sight,
Hugging the horizon close to his breast,
As if loth to leave earth a while to its rest;
While the army of stars are a-donning their dress,
To march through the skies while our pillows we press;
Oh, then 'tis I feast my glad soul on the grand
Paintings wrought out by the great Painter's hand

THE DYING ONE.

Come, stand beside my bed, Willie,
  My breath comes faint and slow,
I feel that I am dying, Willie,
  One word before I go.

You've loved me long and well, Willie,
  And kindly cared for me ;
You'll grieve when I am dead, Willie,
  When Marv's gone from thee.

Then, when I'm lying down, Willie,
  Beneath the new-made mound,
You'll come to my lone grave, Willie,
  And plant sweet flowers around.

The lily and the rose, Willie,
  And pale forget-me-not,
Are flowers that I'd love, Willie,
  All o'er that little spot.

And you will plant some trees, Willie,
  A-near my feet and head,
That birds may come and sing, Willie,
  Above my lowly bed.

And when your tears shall fall, Willie,
  Like rain upon the sod,
Remember that my soul, Willie,
  Hath upward soared to God.

Then by my grave you'll wait Willie,
    When sorrows round thee bide,
And think of her there laid, Willie,
    You wooed, a happy bride.

And there you'll sometimes kneel, Willie,
    And lift your heart above,
And I will waft your prayer, Willie,
    Where all is peace and love.

Now kiss me a good-by, Willie,
    A long, a last adieu,
Till we shall meet again, Willie,
    In the home I'm going to.

SMILES.

How love we to look on a sweet smiling face,
To young one or old one it addeth a grace—
The red laughing lip and the bright cheery eye
Give the homeliest visage a beauty thereby.

Have a smile for the stranger as well as the friend,
To a desolate heart it may be a " Godsend,"
As the rays of the morn when she flashes her lights,
Make the pulsing earth leap after darkest of nights.

Have a smile for the rich, have a smile for the poor,
The purse may not buy what the heart would procure;
The soul of the rich may sometimes send a cry
For a sweet-sounding voice and a bright smiling eye.

The poor we know ever will catch at the light
Of a word and a smile, if we mean it aright;
Tis our duty to God and our duty to man
To be pleasing to all if, unsinning, we can.

MY VISION; OR, THE SOUL'S TRIUMPH.

On the wings of my spirit I rise,
   From darkness and doubt evermore,
Away to the beautiful skies,
   To regions of happiness soar.

Ho! angels, archangels, I come,
   And tap at your heavenly gates;
Outside your beatified home
   A young fledgling anxiously waits.

Haste! lead me to Jesus the Lord,
   To Him I obeisance would make;
My soul on the strength of His word
   Has risen your joys to partake.

He found me lost, beggared and blind,
   Begrimed with the dust of the earth;
He opened the eyes of my mind,
   And I came from my chrysalis forth.

All washed from pollution and sin
   By the blood of the Lamb that was slain;
Your courts I would fain enter in—
   My garments are free from a stain.

You open! I enter! Hosanna!
   My feet walk the streets' golden pave;
My soul feeds on heavenly manna—
   In Siloa's waters I lave.

I drink at the fountain of life—
   No more shall I hunger and thirst.

I've fled from all turmoil and strife,
   And left all earth's fetters accursed.

Hosanna! hosanna! I cry,
   All glory to Him who was slain;
I bask in the realms of the sky,
   And roam o'er the emerald plain.

I shout, with the angelic throng,
   The triumphs from Jesus' blood wrung;
I sing with redeemed ones the song—
   Golden harps to the music-strains strung.

Hosanna! hosanna to God!
   High heaven's broad arches loud ring;
Hosanna to Jesus the Lord!
   Triumphant, cherubic hosts sing.

(Hosanna! those who would be good,
   And humbly repent them of sin,
Will be washed and redeemed by Christ's blood;
   And through heaven's gates enter in.)

Hosanna! the victory's won!
   I'll grovel in darkness no more—
My sands from earth's hour-glass have run,
   I tread on the seraphim's shore.

I wear on my head a bright crown,
   And wave heaven's palms in my hand;
My garments are softer than down,
   And shine in the beautiful land.

My censer no more burneth out,
   Nor pales in the light of the sun;
Hosanna! all hail! do I shout,
   I've fought, and the victory's won.

With pinions unfettered forever,
    No s'riving, nor sorrow, nor pain ;
Earth's sunlight shall shine on me never,
    Here the Sun of the Godhead doth reign.

The beams of His righteousness lighten
    The concave of heaven's high blue ;
No candle or moonlight to brighten
    The holy Jerusalem new.

Hosanna! hosanna! hosanna !
    I cast my crown low at Thy feet ;
I feed upon heavenly manna,
    And walk on the golden-paved street.

Hosanna ! hosanna ! eternal
    The wings of my spirit are free ;
I fly in the regions supernal,
    By blood shed on Calvary's tree.

I rest in the smile of the Giver ;
    I roam at His loving command ;
I float o'er the crystalline river—
    Regale me where zephyrs are bland.

I walk in the gardens celestial ;
    My soul in its heavenly flights,
Unclogged by the fetters terrestrial,
    Soars o'er the empyreal heights.

Hosanna ! hosanna ! with angels
    I worship, I love, I adore !
With angels, archangels, evangels,
    And Jesus I'll live evermore !

WILLIE WOOER.

Willie Wooer stands tapping,
A-calling and rapping,
　To enter my warm, cozy heart;
He is chilly and lonely,
And says, "If I only
　Will bid him walk in—not depart,
He'll reward me most handsome,
Give his own heart as ransom "—
　Declaring 'tis faithful and fond—
"I shall share in his pottage,
His purse and his cottage,
　And his hand shall go into the bond."

But my heart's door shuts tightly,
Nor opens it lightly
　To wooer, tho' constant and bold;
I'm afraid if a lover
Should walk under its cover,
　Sweet peace would escape from its fold.
So, Willie, stop rapping,
I fain would be napping,
　While Cupid storms some other fort;
Some softer heart enter,
Walk into its center—
　At the altar your conquest report.

A SONG OF THE SEA.

Off, off and away o'er the white sea-foam,
With sails all unfurled, doth our proud ship roam;
No sombre cloud in our sky is seen,
But the silver sheen of our nightly queen,
While the stars look out in their prettiest dress,
And smile in their sparkling loveliness.

Off, off and away o'er the deep blue sea
Floats our gallant bark right merrily,
And every eye on its deck to-night
Laughs in its glee as the winds blow light,
And every heart is as glad and gay
As a soaring bird in a midsummer's day.

Give, give me the sea when the breeze is fair,
And the sky is clear and the stars shine there,
With the water's flash as the vessel rides,
And light o'er its mirroring surface glides;
Oh, I glory then in the boundless deep,
On whose peerless bosom the wild waves sleep.

And give me the sea when the waves run high,
And the billows clash with the raging sky;
When the thunders peal 'mid the lightning's glare,
And the vessel sports like a thing of air,
And the foam-caps mad in mountains tower—
Oh, I glory then in its mighty power.

Hurra for the sea! I'm a sailor bold,
But I kneel to Him who the sea doth hold;

And when it boils in its mighty wrath,
And the wild winds sweep the vessel's path,
I bow me in awe to the Potent Will,
Who saith to the winds and waves, " Be still."

And hurra for the bark like mine to-night,
That leaps the waves in her joyous flight;
Or that fearless rocks when the tempest raves,
And the storm-king howls in old ocean's caves;
Oh, she is dear as my heart's life-blood—
'Tis she o'er my destiny reigns next to God.

Then give me the sea, the glorious sea,
In storm or in calm, whiche'er it may be,
And the friendly hand of the brave, g.llant tar,
Who faces the dangers when fierce tempests war,
And the proud bark that safe o'er the wild waves doth
    leap—
Oh, the joy of my heart is a life on the deep.

BEAUTIFUL BIRD.

Beautiful bird, come hither to me—
Never a harm will I do to thee—
Thou shalt partake of my daintiest fare;
Come, and I'll feed thee with lovingest care,
                    Beautiful bird !

Beautiful bird, fly into my bower,
Perch on my sweetest and prettiest flower;
Come, and I'll give thee some down for a nest
In shrub or in tree that thou lovest the best,
                    Beautiful bird !

Beautiful bird, do not flutter and start,
Come, and I'll hold thee so close to my heart;
Fold in my bosom thy soft little wing,
Rest thee and chirp there and prettily sing !
                    Beautiful bird !

Beautiful bird, wilt thou leave me so soon,
Never once stopping to sing me a tune ?
Off to the green-wood away, out of sight,
Never once waiting to warble good-night ?
                    Beautiful bird !

Beautiful bird, wilt thou never return ?
Have I nothing will lure the from forest and fern ?
But true to thy home and thy mate wilt thou prove ?
Thus teaching a lesson of dutiful love,
                    Beautiful bird !

THE MAIDEN'S CONFESSION.

Those eyes, they pierce my very soul ;
　In vain I strive to break the spell;
But over me they 've such control,
　I hardly dare, confessing, tell.

So deep the penetrating gaze
　They turn upon me, that they start
The early loves of bygone days,
　Not dead, but sleeping in my heart.

I know 't is wrong for me to feel,
　So exquisitely, all their power;
And I essay each art to steel
　My bosom in the tempting hour.

Yet when within mine ear his case
　He pleads, so warm and earnestly,
I list, though on his soul I trace
　A sad, a dark deformity.

Another lovelier, fairer one,
　An innocent and trusting heart,
He sought and won with loving tone,
　With all a truthful lover's art.

But soon he sickened of the prize,
　And from that pure heart faithless turned;
Her bruiséd spirit sought the skies,
　And found the rest for which it yearned.

Oh, if man, once inconstant, spurns
　The virtuous love for which he sought,
His fond gaze on another turns,
　With warm and earnest pleadings fraught;

Shall not the sister-woman shun
  The spell he fain would o'er her cast,
And thus revenge the injured one,
  With broken heart, who sleeps at last;

But who forgave the cruel wrong,
  As she would wish to be forgiven,
And with his Maker wrestled long,
  That he might share her rest in Heaven?

Alas! with shame I can but own,
  Not lost is all his suasive art;
Too deeply sinks the anxious tone
  Into my weak and wayward heart.

Those eyes, so meaning in their gaze,
  Have, o'er my spirit, such control,
They wake the loves of early days,
  Long buried in my inmost soul;

They peer upon me in my sleep—
  In dreams I try to fly their power;
But all in vain th' attempt, I weep,
  And, wearied, wake in night's still hour.

Oh, help me Heaven! to school my mind,
  To feel indifference or disgust
Toward the man who, thus unkind,
  Wins, then betrays, the sacred trust.

THE SONG I LOVE.

Sung in Former Times by a Sister Now Dead.

Dear Mary, sing for me the song
   I so delight to hear,
And when I die, let the ref. ain
   Linger within mine ear.

Methinks 'twould ease the pangs of death,
   And waft my soul above
On lighter wings, if from thy lips
   Was breathed the song I love.

Dear Mary, didst thou ever deem
   It was an echo come
Floating on wings of seraphim
   From their celestial home?

Oh, often when mine eyes are closed
   In slumber's happy spell,
Have angels b eathed the self-same song,
   I knew the numbers well.

Then Mary, when I'm dying, sing
   The song to me so dear—
My soul will wait the sweet refrain
   Its upward path to cheer.

And wouldst thou sometimes lure me back,
   When I have passed death's portal,
Then sing that more than seraph song
   To charm mine ear immortal.

HEARTH AND HOME.

Gone ! Gone ! Alas, 'tis vanished now
   The Hearth of other years.
Gone with the purer hopes and loves,
   The heartfelt smiles and tears.
Gone ! and the angels looking down
   Miss the best joy of earth—
The happy family sitting round
   The cheerful household hearth.

I see with memory's wistful eye
   A hearth of other days
Where father, mother, children, friends
   Begirt the evening blaze
Speeding the time with youthful chat,
   Or tales of soberer age,
Of bygone joys, or bygone woes
   Gleaned from experience' page.

I see with memory's wistful eye,
   A happy cottage home—
Ere mother journeyed to the skies
   Or brother sought to roam—
Where dropped the purest, kindest tones
   That children ever heard.
The softest, sweetest lullaby—
   The gentlest chiding word.

Gone is the cot of earlier years,
   And that fair family tree.
Long sorely smitten by the blast
   Has bowed to destiny.
But naught, to me, can ever fill
   That vacant spot on earth,
Or half compare in blessedness
   To the old Home and Hearth.

PLEADINGS.

Take me to thy manly bosom,
  Clasp me in thine arms once more,
Let my heart 'gainst thine be beating,
  As it beat in days of yore.
Let me feel thy b'eath upon me,
  While thine eyes with love-beams shine
With the same magnetic lustre
  As when erst they gazed in mine.
Let thy manners speak thou lov'st me,
  By thine actions may I know
Thou still prizest me the dearest
  Of all beings here below.

Speak again sweet words of fondness;
  For thy love my soul's athirst;
Press thy warm lips on my forehead,
  Breathing vows thou breathedst first,
Ere thou plightedst at the altar
  To me thine eternal troth,
When my trembling lips did falter
  "Yes," though naught was my heart loth
To be given to thy keeping,
  To exchanged be for thine own,
And if I have thee offended,
  Let my sorrow now atone.

It were worse than death to see thee,
  With thy proud and piercing eye,

Longer coldly look upon me,
 Or unheeded pass me by
As if I were but a stranger,
 Or of slight acquaint at best,
I, who once was all thou wishedst,
 Who each thought to thee confest.
Oh, if all the earth possessest
 Were mine own, yet life were woe
From thy heart to be thus banished,
 Thy fond love no more to know.

" Woman," say'st thou true, " is faulty,"
 Angels dwell not on the earth,
And should one chance here to linger,
 She were not of mortal birth ;
And should man, however noble,
 To an angel wedded be,
'Twould not be a perfect union,
 Heaven and earth so disagree.
Then, again love smile upon me,
 Mortals should their kind forgive,
And though I may have offended,
 In thy bosom let me live.

A HINT TO HUSBANDS.

My thoughts will wander, how can they be true
   To one with such a cold and callous heart!
How can I school each pulse to throb for you,
   When no return is made me on your part!
Oh, I so long to feel myself beloved,
   And hear low, tender words breathed in mine ear!
To know that one whose constancy is proved
   Holds me of all the things of earth most dear,
That I am tempted, when one prized of old
   Essays again his deathless love to speak,
To listen to the slighted tale, erst told,
   Ere I was bound by bands so strong, yet weak!
Strong for the law has made them iron bands;
Weak, for your iceberg heart no love commands!

Oh, save me, Alfred! Let your bosom cold
   Warm with fond tenderness toward your wife;
Were you but kind, one little thread would hold
   Me faithful to you, till the last of life—
But now my heart, formed but to throb in love,
   Yearns to send forth its tendrils, and to cling
Unto some answering heart, or freely rove
   To sip the nectar from each lovely thing.
I scarce have power to curb its longing throes
   And teach it with schooled apathy to beat;
Its gushing fountain almost overflows
   Its iron bounds, its kindred throb to greet.
Oh, 'tis a piteous thing to waste on air
The heart's deep feelings, that with none must share.

My Alfred, save me! be to me more kind,
　　Give me some tender token of your love;
Oh, do you wish my heart to you to bind,
　　Let not harsh negligence your troth disprove;
I should not sin to drink in *your* fond words,
　　If such you deign to breathe within mine ear—
Let there be in your breast respensive chords,
　　And my inconstancy you should not fear.
But chill me as you now doth chill, each day,
　　And we may both be brought to curse the hour
When lawful wedlock bound our hands for aye,
　　But o'er our hearts estranged had no such power.
Husband, beware!　If you would hold for life
Me constant to you treat me as your wife.

Address me as you did in days gone by,
　　When you so tremblingly your love professed—
When fond entreaty plead from your dark eye,
　　And I so blushingly my own confessed.
Press now, as then, my hand within your own,
　　And to your breast, impulsive, clasp again
The being frail who gladly would atone
　　For every faithless thought to you since then.
For I can vouch my longing soul to brook
　　No longer coldness such as you now give;
My heart must wither 'neath that icy look,
　　Or its fidelity at length outlive:
The yearning reachings of its tendrils forth,
Must find some clinging spot in Heaven or earth.
　　　　　　　　　　　　1855.

TO A BIRD IN CENTRAL PARK.

Dear pretty, sweet pretty, bright pretty bird,
   Perching low in the juniper tree,
The loveliest songster that ever I heard,
   Did you sing that sweet song, dear, to me ?

Let Jenny Lind graceful and Nilsson the fair
   Trill their finest artistical note,
Their songs, to my mind, can never compare
   With warblings from tiny bird's throat.

Dear pretty, sweet pretty, bright pretty bird,
   Don't fly away now from the tree ;
The loveliest songster that ever I heard !
   Sing that song again, dear one, for me.

The songs of these wood-glades are caroled for all,
   The pretty birds enravish the ear;
The richest, the poorest, the great and the small,
   Without fee, nature's warblers may hear.

Come, then, to these wood-haunts ye sad ones and gay,
   Where thousands of harmonists sing,
Giving finest of concerts this lovely June day,
   As sweet as first flowrets in spring.

                          1871.

LINES WRITTEN UPON HEARING THE REPORT THAT ENGLAND WAS COMING OVER TO AID THE NORTH IN SUBJUGATING THE SLAVE STATES.

Back to old England ; back where ye belong,
Ye tyrant hordes, where force of arms is strong
To quell a people's might and guard a Throne ;
Back despots, back ; leave Freedom's soil alone.

Ye Democrats, erst pillars of our Land,
Are ye all powerless to War's rule withstand ?
Where all your giant minds whose counsels wise
Made tyrants quail, and myriads lift their eyes
With new-born hope as spied they from afar
The beaming glories of earth's Polar-star ?

My lov'd, my native Land ! How fall'n thou !
Freedom and Peace have spread their wings, and now
Are fleeing thy broad shores with sorrowing cry,
And War's red pennon floats along the sky.
How fall'n ! thankless that our fathers bled,
And broke the tyrant's yoke that we might tread,
With form uplift, our proud and native soil,
No more beneath a tyrant's power to moil.

O Shades of Liberty's brave champions, Come,
Return and strike War's clamorous chieftains dumb
As ye were wont. With words of wisdom quell
The warring passions that among us dwell,
Let your blest spirits heavenly dews impart,
Till Love and Peace again fill every heart.

'TIS PAST.

'Tis past!   O God, 'tis past!
  Our prayers for peace were vain ;
Confusion sweeps our native shores,
  And War doth o'er us reign.
Upon our own proud land
  He stalks with giant tread,
And Liberty—our goddess lov'd—
  Afar has weeping fled.

The din of arms is heard ;
  The martial fife and drum—
Each mountain, hill, and vale is stirr'd—
  From north and south they come,
With fratricidal hand
  To spill a brother's blood—
I hear, methinks, the dying groans,
  I see the crimson flood !

Aye, to my vision comes
  The blood-drench'd battle-plain—
Husbands and fathers in their gore—
  Brothers and lovers slain—
I list the widow's wail,
  I mark the orphan's tears,
I see the maiden's cheek turn pale,
  Blanch'd for the coming years.

Homes fall before my sight,
  Where erst around each hearth
Parents and children happy clasp'd
Their best belov'd of earth ;
And altars where they met
  To worship in God's name
Have sunk to ashes.   War's red torch
  Lit the destroying flame.

O God ! and must it be ?
  Is such our country's doom ?
Have Peace and Love join'd hands and fled
  To give dire Carnage room ?
Must War, by thee uncheck'd,
  Scourge us with fire and sword—
Make hearths and cities desolate
And Freedom's name abhorr'd ?

O Christian, let us bow
  Humbly beneath the rod—
We have deserved the scourge and shame
  Our sins have reach'd to God ;
Let us confess and turn
  From every wicked way,
That He may bend Him down to hear,
  And heed us when we pray.

TWO BROTHERS.

Two youthful brothers fired by Mars
Enlisted in their country's wars ;
One for the North—one for the South
Went forth to face the cannon's mouth.
A widow's pride and prop were they ;
She tried with prayers and tears to stay
Them from the fratricidal strife,
Lest one should take the other's life.
But vain her pleadings with each son—
Each felt that he was called upon
To battle in a righteous cause—
One for his " Home "—one for the " Laws."
Two great contending armies met—
The battle-plain with gore was wet,
For thick the wounded and the kill'd
Fell fast upon the murderous field.
Wilder, more dreadful grew the fray
From morning till the close of day ;
When lo ! the Northern army fled,
Leaving their dying and their dead.
Next morn, upon the crimson ground
Lying side by side two youths were found.
Two stripling youths with foreheads bold,
And ghastly faces icy cold—
With many a gash and wound to tell
Each bravely fought and bravely fell—
Lay bleaching in the sun's hot ray,
No more to see the light of day.
Sad news goes fast—the direful word
" Her sons were slain " the widow heard.
Her noble sons belov'd and brave
" Both sleeping in one gory grave."
Then, Oh the agony ! the woe !
Frenzied she cried, " Who dealt the blow
That spilt the life-blood of each son ?
Was't by his brother's hand 'twas done ? "

And night and day this widow's prayer
Is constant borne upon the air—
"O Thou who lookest from afar
On this vile, fratricidal war ?
Thou who didst give my brave sons breath,
And seest them now lie cold in death,
Smite him with thine avenging hand
Who brought this curse upon our Land ;
And bid the angels whisper low
(For surely, Heaven, thou must know)
If by a brother's hand was slain
My boys upon the battle-plain.
One for the 'North'—one for the 'South'
They faced the belching cannon's mouth ;
And each was taught the art to send
The deadly ball some life to end.
O God ! O angels ! whisper low,
Who gave my boys the fatal blow.
O tell me, Heaven ! O tell me, God !
Did either shed his brother's blood,
And enter with the mark of Cain
The dreary realms of Death's domain ? "
Grief-wild, will not this widow's cries,
With others, reach beyond the skies
Till the Avenger's mighty hand
Shall purge and purify our Land,
And send sweet Peace to reign once more
Upon our own fair, native shore ?
Sisters, who love the " Prince of Peace "
Plead in His name till war shall cease.

A CALL TO DEMOCRATS.

Sweet Liberty ! late goddess of our land,
Where hast thou fled ? Where wavest now thy wand ?
On what far hill—or fairer, wiser shore
Dost thou now smile ?   Hast gone forevermore ?

Ye Democrats, who erst the ship of state
Did safely guide to port o'er dangers great,
Where are ye now while plunging is the bark
Through wildly raging billows deep and dark ?
Sleep ye ? or has death sealed in bliss your eyes
To all your bleeding country's agonies ?
Or are ye palsied by the breath of Mars,
And helpless bow to these ungodly wars ?
Wake from your lethargy—reach forth a hand
To save, ere tis too late, your sinking land !
Speak ye in thunder tones till far and near
Your words of wisdom every ear shall hear,
And war, abashed, be banished from our shore,
And Peace and Freedom bless our land once more.
 AUGUST, 1861.

AN APPEAL TO FREEMEN.

Ye votaries of Liberty,
  Let not your country call in vain ;
Shake off your soulless lethargy—
  Plead ye her cause on land and main.
Speak, freemen, from each hill and vale,
  From town and hamlet far and near,
Until your counsels wise prevail,
  And Peace return our hearts to cheer.

'Tis time to do—'tis time to dare—
  Rise, freemen, rise to save our land ;
Let Wisdom's voice ring on the air
  From one united giant band,
Till the destroying, ruthless foe,
  By Freedom's glad and mighty tread
Prone on the dust is trampled low,
  And war, for aye, our shores hath fled.

Rise ye, who have the souls of men,
  'Tis now no time to shrink or wait ;
Your country calls—from hill and glen
  A wail goes up to Heaven's gate.
In trumpet tones, in Heaven's name,
  Dare in the face of tyranny
To shout till freemen's hearts aflame
  Burn fierce again for Liberty.

Rise ! make the base usurper quail
  Beneath your words of mighty power.
Your country's wounds make haste to heal
  Ere dark despair doth o'er her lower,
And Freedom's star goes down in night
  No more to beam with gladdening ray ;
Rise ye, 'tis time that wisdom's might
  Our native land again should sway.
        AUGUST, 1861.

A CRY FOR PEACE.

The air is filled with wailings o'er the dead ;
   And tears of sorrow flood our land like rain ;
While leagues on leagues of Southern soil are red,
   Stained by the hand of Abolition Cain.

And God, Almighty God, has seen the deed,
   And heard the cry of horror and of woe ;
And Heaven itself has donned the mourning weed
   While tears of pity in its precincts flow.

And yet—and yet the horrid work goes on,
   And men called " ministers " still shriek for blood,
And fain the gore they call " the nation's wine "
   Would quaff with smacking lip, in face of God.

And women, too, there are of high degree,
   With burning thirst for gore not yet allayed
Who cry, beseeching, on the bended knee,
   " Prosper our arms, nor let the war be stayed

Till o'er each Southern hearth our hordes have poured
   The reeking cup of Abolition hate—
Till every Southern man has felt the sword
   That goeth forth his land to desolate."

Alas ! we too can plead, and day by day,
   Ascends our soulful, agonizing prayer.
" O God of Power ! O God of pity ! stay
   The slaughtering hand that doth Thy vengeance dare :

O Christ of God, speak 'Peace, be still !' once more
   Assuage these billows that have surged in wrath ;
And from our precious Country's either shore
   Bid Peace speed o'er the warriors ruddy path."

Peace doth Prosperity and Love beget ;
   But war breeds hate, then ruin follows fast ;
O brothers wise, let no more eyes be wet
   Nor hearts be cleft as in the dark days past.

O sisters dear, bid kindly feelings rise
   Within your breasts erst gentle and humane ;
Pray, pray for Peace till Heaven heeds your cries
   And sends the balm to heal our Nation's pain.

And ye, who have besmeared with brother's blood
   Your sacerdotal robe once spotless white,
Throw off the garb—'tis an offense to God,
   Close your stained lips, polluted in His sight.

GOVERNOR SEYMOUR.

If pleasant sunrises and cloudless skies,
　Are Nature's auguries of good to men,
Last New Year's morn brought blessed auspices,
　Bright, golden-footed, to our State.　'Twas then
One firm in Right, who danger dared to face—
　A nobleman in heart and soul did stand
Within our Capitol, and "with God's grace"
　Vowed to protect a part of this our land
In all its lawful rights.　And he will keep
　His sacred oath, though wrathful foes assail,
And threaten him with dungeons dark and deep.
　Nor slacken will his arm, nor eye will quail
Though thousands point at him the leveled spear.
　One strong with God within him cannot fear.

And we have seen this man of noble worth,
　Of lofty brow, and fearless, stainless soul.
'Twas when the waves of sorrow round our hearth,
　Sent by a vengeful foe, did darkly roll,
That he did speak to us in hopeful words,
　And stirred anew the Faith we cherished dear,
That kept within our breasts the tender chords
　From severing ; though frequent gushed the tear
At thought of One who from his home was torn,
　And without stain of crime, imprisoned far
Upon a lonely isle by sea-waves worn,
　In granite walls, which long did him debar
Of the sweet home-light that around him flowed
　When Freedom in our peaceful realms abode.

Aye, we have seen him—and our faith is strong
　That he will aid to raise the sinking bark,
That 'mid huge shoals and quicksands, hath so long
　Been dashing pilotless and in the dark,
Far from its native haven.　He will steer
　It safely o'er the turbid, troubled sea

Now rolling wildly, and with wisdom veer
  Its course, until 'tis anchored by the lea
Where no rough winds nor raging waves again
  Shall have the power to dash its rock-ribbed sides
Over the billows of the angry main
  Where tyrant Neptune as a god presides.
Aye, God will help him in the path of Right,
  Peace, soon, will smile a sun where now is night.

Yes, God will help him, though black surges roll
  Over our saddened land as mountains high.
Though enemies to public weal control
  Our Nation *now*, as with an evil eye—
Though mad fanatics rave in frantic rage
  To bury deep in seas of human gore
Our noble ship of state—help him assuage
  The rushing tempest—still the thunder's roar,
Till stars again look forth from cloudless skies,
  Till sunbeams float upon their azure folds,
Till Liberty, our Goddess, shall arise
  And sway again the sceptre, that she holds
Over a country purified by fire,
  And purged, for aye, of abolition ire.

Yet though God help him thus—the thousands slain,
  Half buried, and unburied, that did fall
Upon our vast, vast Southern battle-plain,
  No god-like power will aid him to recall.
Nor can he dry the countless streaming eyes,
  Nor heal the countless breaking hearts that mourn
Of those who waited long, 'mid hopes and sighs,
  Their brave, their noble best belov'ds' return.
But he can say—and myriads hope he will,
  That vain increase of blood from brother's veins
Shall no more trickle down a Southern hill,
  Nor darkly flow along the Southern plains.
Would that such voice could *now* have potent sway,
  And hideous War "in hot haste" flee away.
    1863.

RAPPAHANNOCK.

Darkness shrouds our every mountain,
  Mantles every hill and glen,
Broods o'er sea and lake and river,
  Reaches every haunt of men.
For the sons who went to battle
  With a proud and martial tread,
Will never, never more return
  "From the cities of the dead."

Every city, town and village,
  Every hamlet of Northland,
Sent from them with waving banners
  A fearless, gallant band.
To battle for the Union,
  "Constitution and the laws"
By abolition "traitors" vile
  Deceived as to the cause.

They heard the musket's rattle,
  The cannon's deafening roar,
The sabre's clash and clangor,
  On Rappahannock's shore.
But they boldly faced the missiles,
  Rushed to their certain doom,
And were mowed down like blades of grass
  In summer's ripening bloom.

Yet quiet flows the river,
  As ever on its way,
Though crimsoned were its waters
  By the slaughter of that day.
The sun shines out as brightly,
  And the moon and stars at even
Are mirrored on the river's face
  From calm blue skies of Heaven.

But the death groans of the dying,
  The shrieks of mangled men,
From the banks of Rappahannock,
  Echo thick o'er hill and glen.
And many a tender mother,
  And many a loving bride,
And many a gentle sister knows
  Her brave belov'd has died.

No more in hut or palace
  Shall they hear the dear one's tread.
Deceived, they went to *conquer*,
  But they sleep amid the dead.
And the name of Rappahannock,
  For many a dreary year,
Will bring the pain to breaking hearts—
  To darkened eyes the tear.

O guileless Rappahannock !
  'Twas not thy gentle flow
That shrouded many a household
  With the sable pall of woe.
'Twas not the crystal waters,
  From thy narrow, pebbly bed,
That quenched the sunlight in our homes
  And heaped thy shores with dead.

'Twas done by Northern teachers,
  A Phillips, Beecher, Stowe,
They spilt our brave ones' life-blood,
  And laid our dear ones low.
Who, all self righteous, glory
  Over that dreadful fray,
While spirits of the slaughtered dead
  Call for a reck'ning day.

And certain as the sunlight,
  And as the evening dew—
As certain as the silver stars
  Shine in the ether blue—
As certain as there's *justice*
  In the balances of Heaven,
So certain to those guilty souls
  Will due reward be given.

Ye publishers and preachers
  With valiant *tongue* and *pen*—
Who have, so far, deluded
  More brave and honest men—
How soon will your own heart's blood
  The full cup overflow
Of the red " wine " the nation now
  Is drinking to its woe ?

JOSEPH AND F. D. FLANDERS.

Where are those noble brothers twain ?
    Those freeborn men—with freemen's right ?
Their place is vacant at the board ;
    ·Their presence glads not now our sight.
Their babes look up through falling tears,
    And ask, " Will father come to-day ?
What made them take my father off?
    How *long* must father stay away ?"

"If father can't come back, mamma,
    He'll want his ' little darling' there ;
He might be all alone and sick—
    Who then of father would take care ?
Perhaps the jailor-men would let
    Me go and see my father dear ;
I'd run and climb upon his knee
    And never cry a single tear.
I'd kiss him for you all, mamma,
    And do so very, very right,
I'm sure that *they* would let me stay
    If *you* would only say I might."

'Tis thus his youngest, " black-eyed one,"
    His little namesake, oft doth plead.
Sweet innocence ! she does not know
    What wicked hearts did prompt the deed,
What cruel hands usurped the power,
    Without the shadow of a right,
To tear her father from his home,
    And hide him from her longing sight.

Poor little child ! she does not know
  In that black prison in the sea
He's guarded by the bayonet—
  Nor given air nor sunlight free.
She does not know no loving kiss
  Can now be his, nor loving care—
But I will teach our child to pray,
   " *Forgive them, Lord, who put him there.*"
   1861.

A LEADER OF THE REPUBLICAN PARTY.

[Respectfully Dedicated to the Republican Party, by one who feels herself and family particularly honored by one of its leaders.]

Is his bed a bed of roses?
Is his conscience quite at ease?
Does he feel to say " Our Father,"
Praying on his bended knees?
Has he done his Christian duty?
Is his country's cause maintained?
Does he triumph in his laurels—
In the glory he has gained?

Mark how placid, now, his visage!
How benignant beams his eye
Through the patriotic fires
That enroll his name on high!
See how gracious are his manners!
How majestic is his gait!
Made a very god among you
By his soul so good and great!

Well, he's worthy of your worship!
He's accomplish'd the great end!
Your country safe, no arm now needs
Its bulwarks to defend!
Disband your grand battalions!
Hang up the sword and gun!
"The Boys" are sent to the "Bastile,"
The glorious victory's won!

Ah ! little did *we* know before
  They held such giant power !
We knew they sought their country's weal
  In this dark, trying hour !
We knew they fought, with 'conscience clear,
  For Liberty and Right !
But little did we dream how quailed
  The Tyrant at their might.

"Robespierre and the Bastile !" Good God !
  Has Freedom come to this ?
How do the nations looking on,
  At Liberty now hiss !
Blot out the page from Christendom—
  Hide ! hide the deep disgrace !
Ye patriots true, gird on your strength
  And Liberty replace !

"The Boys" are sent to Lafayette—
  How nobly did they go,
Leaving their homes and little ones—
  Bid by their country's foe.
They neither cringed nor faltered ;
  But trusted in the Right,
Believing that a reckoning day
  Would come with crushing might.

They're gone ! and we are proud to boast
  . Their manliness and worth.
Nor shackles, nor imprisonment
  Shall bow their souls to earth.
A holy faith, a perfect trust
  Their spirits will sustain,
Till they shall see their country free
  From War's inhuman reign.
    1861.

HOW CANST THOU, SUN!

How canst thou, Sun, illuminate a land
Where Christian against Christian lifts the hand
To spill a brother's blood, and send the wail
Of widowed wives and orphans on the gale,
And drench anew our country's blood-bought sod,
Made sacred to true hearts by Freedom's God!

April, thou month of coming birds and flowers,
How canst thou smile upon the frensied Powers !*
Methinks the clouds and storms of March should still
Hang heavy o'er our every vale and hill.
Trees should not bud, nor blossoms lift the head,
But weep their life's juice out in shame and dread ;
Weep o'er our country as a falling star
Whose beacon-light is dimmed by shameful war,
And hide their bending heads, lest justice lower
And smite our land with God-avenging power.

Shame to our nation ! shame to every soul
Who yields a heart or hand to War's control
In *Christian land*—do we deserve the name
While o'er our hearts is kindling War's red flame ?
Wisdom should hand in hand with love be joined,
And Charity have place in every mind,
Till he who finds no " beam " in his own eye
May to his brother's " mote " the knife apply.

Wives, mothers, daughters have *ye* naught to say ?
No voice to raise War's direful hand to stay ?
Think of the horrors that will o'er you burst
If still stalks on the bloody fiend accurst ?

   * Legislators.

Think of your homes, your altars, and your fires !
Think of your children, husbands, lovers, sires !
And pierce heavens concave with your prayers for peace
Till God shall bid the raging billows cease.
 1861.

A PRAYER.

O God ! O God ! in pity haste, look down,
Thy flaming sword withdraw—cease Thou to frown
Upon us sorely sinful.   Turn to Thee
Our smitten hearts, and make us bend the knee
In humble penitence and grief for sin,
Till we forgiveness from thy spirit win.

Pity ! O pity Thou ! the suffering souls
Upon our Southern land where Battle rolls
Its horrors, like the drenching, drowning flood
That devastated earth when none served God
Save Noah and his little household band.
Are there not *many* Noah's in our land ?
"If, peradventure, there be righteous *five*,"
Turn from thine anger—let our country live—
And bid those "righteous" preach Thy Truth in love,
Till they to serve Thee erring hearts shall move,
And Hate be banished—nevermore to come
And desolate a North or Southern home—
Till from *all* nations War shall driven be,
And every soul bend, true to Thee, the knee ;
Each prizing other as themselves they prize,
Making this earth again a Paradise.

Pity ! O pity, God ! our country dear—
We fain would make all Heaven our prayer to hear,
And with our cries persuade the angel bands
To come and dash the sword from brother's hands,
And plant the Olive Branch on hill and lea,
And nourish it till over land and sea
Its branches interlace like brooding wing,
And Peace o'er earth in jubilates ring.
O God ! O God ! pity the mourners here,
And homeless ones, and take them in Thy care,
Who 'neath a Southern sun have felt the blow
Of vengeful War, and drank its dregs of woe.

  1862.

WHERE ARE THEY ?

The Northern sun, with warmer, genial ray,
    Dissolves the snow—
The trees and shrubs shoot forth their living green,
    While soft winds blow ;
The birds returned from Southern, sunny climes,
    Flit to and fro,
And sing the same sweet, cheerful songs they sang
    Twelve months ago.

But where are they—the friends ye prized so dear ?
    A year ago
Ye waited not, as now, their coming feet
    With heart-beat slow ;
Will *they* return from pillaged Southern lands,
    Where *red* waves flow,
With hands as spotless of a brother's blood
    As unstained snow ?

Or do their loved forms sleep upon the plain
    Where clarions peal—
Their breasts laid open by the ghastly wounds
    Of warrior's steel—
With spirits freed, awaiting Heaven's doom ?
    For God is just—
Away ! away ! dark thoughts—our senses reel.
    Poor mourners—*Trust !*

A SINGLE INSTANCE OF McNEIL'S INHUMAN-ITY RELATED IN VERSE.

[McNeil, a general in the Federal Army, 1862-'63, shot ten men in his anger because a man by the name of Alleman had run away from his power.]

A noble, manly boy was he,
　　Some nine or ten years old—
An only child—who pleading went
　　Brave, earnest, yet not bold—
To one with heart of adamant,
　　His father's life to spare—
His father—one of those ten doomed
　　Death-punishment to bear
For one who voluntary strayed ·
　　From far Missouri State.
One Alleman, safely since returned,
　　Alas ! indeed, too late
To save those guiltless men, condemned
　　Like felons, to be shot,
By that inhuman murderer
　　Whose very *name* is fraught
With everything of evil kind
　　That brings a curse to earth.
Whose soul, if such he do possess,
　　In lower realms had birth.
That little, noble, manly boy,
　　Entreated, begged, implored,
"My father ! Oh my father spare !
　　We'll give our sacred word—
Mother and I—that father ne'er
　　For one whole month or more,
Had been from home the night when came
　　Your soldiers to our door,
And took my father off by force
　　And bore him to your jail ;
And left dear mother sick in bed

So sad, and weak, and pale ;
Oh, if you do my father kill
    What shall we ever do ?
I am too young to earn our bread—
    And we'll be lonely, too.
My father is so very kind,
    He never did one harm—
And he had worked so long and hard
    To buy our little farm—
And he was going to build a house,
    Our own to always be.
Oh, please do let my father live
    For mother dear and me.
O sir, do let my father live
    Till I am grown a man,
Then I will work and earn our bread—
    Dear mother says I can.
We have no friends to help us, sir,
    No kindred, near have we ;
They all are poor, or far away
    Beyond the distant sea.
Oh, if you do my father kill,
    My mother's heart will break.
O sir, *do* let my father live
    For my *poor mother's sake.*"
Thus plead the manly, tearful boy,
    But plead and plead in vain.
"Beside his father he might ride,
    In the funereal train—
Upon his coffin to the place
    Where those ten men must die "
The monster deigned consent to give.
    And he went riding by
Clasped in his father's loving arms
    Which did so close enfold
That when the doomed " were formed in line "
    'Twere hard to loose their hold.
And when his father's loved remains

Within the coffin lay,
That little boy with breaking heart
Rode from the scene away,
Upon the rough-hewn burial box,
That hid from his young eyes
The form he never more would see
This side the weeping skies.
Sad tale of War, but thousands worse,
Ne'er sung by mortal lyre,
Recorded are in Heaven's Archives
By Angel's pen of fire.

VALLANDIGHAM.

[It will not appear singular to many that I sympathised with Mr. Vallandigham, since Mr. Flanders, my husband, had been previously sent to Forts Lafayette and Warren. Written immediately after hearing of Vallandigham's wicked arrest, under Abraham Lincoln, on the fourth or fifth of May, 1863.]

They came, like cowards as they were, at night,
   And stole the father from his precious fold—
The people's Champion of Truth and Right—
   Vallandigham, the honest and the bold.

They dare not venture on a deed so base
   When men were wakeful—'neath the sun's bright eye,
But shrank with guilty fear the hosts to face,
   Who ready stood to shield their Chief or die.

But they were seen—the stars in heaven's height
   Espied the lawless, miscreant, hireling crowd,
And grieved and shamed they hastened from the sight,
   And hid their shining faces 'neath a shroud.

And the fair, queenly moon that sailed on high,
   As she looked down upon that fiendish crew
Paled at the sight, and veiled her silvery eye
   Behind the clouds that darkened at the view.

Yes, they were seen—above, afar, beyond,
   Sat one with portent brow, that woful night.
Nor distance, nor did darkness prove a bond
   To shut *His* vision from that shameful sight.

Vallandigham! the God whom thou dost serve,
   For every ill the tyrant heaps on thee,
"*His* red right arm" with vengeance dire will nerve,
   To smite the foes of Right and Liberty!

Vallandigham, wise, noble, brave and good,
   Honored of all whose hearts round Freedom twine
We'd sooner make thy garb, unstained by blood,
   Our God, than yield one nod at Lincoln's shrine.

True Friends of Liberty ! how long will ye,
   Supine, be trampled 'neath the tyrant's heel ?
Freeborn ! Freebred ! why bend the servile knee ?
   Up ! gird your loins with the avenging steel !

The People's favorite son from home is torn,
   Because, forsooth, he sought his country's good ;
And to some secret prison vilely borne ;
   Rescue your chief, ye patriot brotherhood !

PEACE.

———

"Peace !" "Hist !"
  "Whisper it low."
"Peace !" "Peace !"
  "Beware of the foe,
For war He is shrieking,
  For blood and for death."
"Peace !" "Peace !"
  "Friend, stifle your breath—
Bastiles are wide yawning
  And spies prowl anear—
To some of earth's noblest
  That word has proved dear.
'Tis ' treason ' to speak it,
  On Freedom's proud sod ;
' Peace' you must whisper
  In your closet to God."

But "Peace !" blessed "Peace !"
  I will cry thee aloud
Though "bastiles are yawning"—
  Or though in Death's shroud
I should pay such temerity.
  Would on hill-top, in vale
I could tell to the people
  Half of War's bloody tale,
For then would a cry
  Like a wild surging main
Sweep over our land—
  "Peace" would be the refrain.

"Peace !" "Hist !" "whisper low,"
  Never, no never,
I'll not bow to the foe.
  'Tis a word come from Heaven—

Sweeter far to my lips
 Than the nectarine draught
One from Helicon sips.
 Sing it ye zephyrs,
Waft it winds, near and far ;
 Shout it ye people,
Till the spirits of war
 Flee back to their dens—
Hades gates are ajar.

" Peace ! " precious word that our lov'd Savior breathed,
"Peace ! " never War to His saints He bequeathed—
On our white Christian banner be the golden word
 wreathed.
 1863.

VALLANDIGHAM, AFTER HAVING BEEN EXILED.

Exiled from his home, but with soul pure and high,
His step is as firm, and the glance of his eye
As keen as when erst a proud freeman he trod
On Liberty's soil in the smile of his God.

But Liberty wounded and bleeding lies low,
And freemen now bow at the beck of her foe,
Or if they dare breathe e'en with low, bated breath
A word in her favor—Prison ! Exile ! or Death !

Thus he who fought bravest and best in her cause,
Whose tongue wisest plead for the "Union and laws,"
Swerving never from right, uncondemned of a wrong,
Is banished his state by a ribaldrous throng.

But Liberty soon will be healed of her smarts,
And again rear her throne in the people's warm hearts,
And the exile returned, on his loved soil shall stand,
With new honors crowned by her liberal hand.

For Liberty knows how her martyrs to pay,
Who strove for her weal in the heat of the fray,
When her foemen came forth, like an avalanche hurled,
Her bulwarks to break—once the hope of the world.

Ohio ! Ohio ! proud Star of the West,
Come out from the clouds in your late splendor drest,
If manhood and might still inherit your sod,
Never kneel, never bow but to Right and to God.

Recall the lone exile, Ohio—e'en now
You've a laurel that waits to encircle his brow.
Betray not your trust—be strong in your might,
On your ensign be blazoned " My God and my Right."

Delay not, Ohio, but speed to restore
To her own sacred temple your Goddess of yore.
And never again let your ensign be trailed
Or torn by the foe who your rights have assailed.

Be constant on guard with an eye eagle-like,
With an arm bared in Liberty's honor to strike.
And level to earth the base, impious breast,
Who shall dare in the future her peace to molest.

Dimmed Star of the West, make haste to reclaim
From cowardice' stigma your once honored name—
This covenant bind you—*come woe or come weal,*
To never a tyrant til death will we kneel.
  June, 1863.

LINES REFERRING TO MRS. VALLANDIGHAM.

[Having been reported insane on account of the severe imprisonment
of her husband, and in her insanity raved of him dead.]

———

Take back the words ! Take back the words !
  Too sad, too dire to be believed.
I sicken at the woful tale—
  My brain near reels—my soul is grieved
So deeply that by day and night
  A woman pale, and worn, and wild
Haunts all my mind, and makes me weep
  Till I am weak as any child.

Take back the words ! Take back the words !
  They blind, they burn my eyes, to read.
One loving, beautiful and good
  To suffer thus—Oh wretched deed !
Sweet clinging vine torn from her prop,
  Insane to wail and droop and die.
O God ! O God ! upon whose soul
  Must such great guilt forever lie ?

Take back the words ! Take back the words !
  That *she, his* lov'd is maniac.
The news will rend his strong heart's chords
  More torturing they than sorest rack
That blackest despot did invent—
  Than wildest fancy can portray—
If true, Oh hide from him the fact,
  Till reason's light resumes its sway.

Take back the words ! Take back the words !
  Tell us the tale is all untrue—
Or if she *were* of reason reft—
  That she's regained her reason now.

I wait and watch and pray to read
   "The story false" that sears my brain.
Oh, say she knows *he* is *not* dead
   But looks to meet him soon again.

Take back the words ! Take back the words !
   They tell too true " what might have been,"
Had soldiers in the calm of night
   Stole on *us* with the frightful din
Of horrid implements of Death
   When he, *our* stay, by lawless hand
Was rudely torn from home and friends,
   And freedom in his native land.
     1863.

MY COUNTRY.

My Country ! My Country ! though humble and sore,
Though now thou art bleeding at each vein and pore,
There is joy for thee yet—for thy brow a bright crown,
And nations shall envy thy future renown.

My Country, My Country, thou pride of my soul,
Though storm-winds have raged with no hand to control,
And have rocked thee, as rock they the ship on the main,
Thy travail in sorrow shall not prove in vain.

Behind darkest of clouds shine the brightest of suns—
And deep shadows fall on the streamlet that runs
In the greenest, the loveliest, sunniest dell,
Where summer birds warble, and mortal men dwell.

But the clouds disappear, and the earth smiles again,
More fragrant and fresh from the torrents of rain,
And the shadows that darkened the streamlet are gone—
And the birds' songs are sweet as their matins at dawn.

My Country, My Country, there is One reigneth still,
Whom "He loveth He chastens" as He wisely doth will,
And thou from the furnace, like gold that is tried,
Shall brighter beam forth from thy dross purified.

Freedom's fires shall again burn in fane, hall and cot—
As erst they were wont in thy happier lot,
When the people were sovereigns, when by no despot hand
A sceptre was swayed o'er our Heaven-blest land.

My Country, My Country, thou art loved next to God—
Though man's blood has reddened thy Emerald sod,
'Till faith has been palsied, we'll wake from the spell,
And hope till thy watchmen shall cry, "All is well."

My Country; My Country, there is joy for thee yet,
Thy sun with its glory now dimmed is not set—
And the kingdoms of earth that rejoice o'er thy woe,
Shall bow at thy feet when *their* pride is laid low.
     JUNE, 1863.

ONE OF THE FRUITS OF BATTLE.

The war came on, and thousands left the plow
And anvil for the Southern tented field—
Willie, my manly boy, my bright brow'd one
To join them sought of me consent to yield.

Vainly he plead—I thought no duty called
My child to wander from my side away—
And to my simple mind no glory sprang
From man essaying brother man to slay.

But martial music stirred the young heart's blood,
And crafty men allured him from my side ;
Nor parting word nor parting kiss he gave—
Alas ! 'twere best my darling boy had died.

Days, weeks and months passed by—no tidings came
Of Willie, to his mother's longing ears ;
Days, weeks and months rose hopes of his return,
As oft dispelled by agonizing fears.

Fall, Winter and a part of Spring were gone—
Lonely I sat, when hark ! methought a sound
Of dear, familiar voice ! but laggard step !
I could not stir—my limbs seemed fetter-bound.

A hand was on the latch—'twas not his hand—
Another led my Willie to the door ;
They entered—pitying Heaven ! my senses fled
And swooning, prostrate fell I on the floor.

I woke—but Oh, 'twas agony to wake—
My bright-eyed Willie blind, lame, scarred, and wan,
His manly form bent as by weight of years—
Such, War returned the widow's only son.

And now with shattered mind, and blasted frame,
Life is to him a blank—a darkling night,
The pleasant sun and all it smiles upon,
No more can cheer his soul or bless his sight.

And I, his mother ! Mothers of our land,
How many anguish know, so darkly given,
Not in God's works your light of life put out,
But on the blood-red field where men have striven.

PESTILENCE.

Come on ye men, with pick and spade,
Thousands of graves 'tis time were made,
For thousands 'neath a Southern sky
Of brothers slain in battle lie.

Haste ye, dig quick, no time to spare—
Decaying bodies scent the air—
Lest Pestilence shall soon walk forth,
And other thousands fell to earth.

Throw in a corpse ! more haste—another—
Heap high the dirt on friend and brother—
Here ! there ! with bodies fill the trench.
Too slow ! too late ! The poisonous stench
Has filled the atmosphere with death—
Corruption taints our every breath.
Disease outvies the sword and ball,
Smites with its power both great and small.
The rich, the poor, the simple, wise,
The sinful, sinless, by it dies.
Speed faster, then, with spade and pick.
More graves we need—dig deep, dig quick,
Throw in the corpse of sister, brother,
Of husband, wife, of father, mother,
And nestling babe with prattling tongue ;
The plague respects ne'er old nor young,
But follows in the war-god's train,
And more by it than Mars are slain.
Scoop then the mould, throw in the dead.
Not on the battle-field these bled,

But Pestilence from gory sod
Walked forth a scourge from Christians' God
Who looks in anger from the skies
Upon War's bestial sacrifice !
Alas ! alas ! at what dire cost
Is victory gained or victory lost
When men with brothers warring go ?
The very heavens are palled in woe ;
For wails from hearts by anguish rent
In volumes pierce the firmament,
And pitying angels hear and weep
That Death such carnival should keep.

THE OLD NEGRO'S LAMENT.

Before this dreadful war I'd a pleasant, happy home
  On the banks of a clear, shining river,
Where no wintry winds did blow, and fell no chilling
   snow
  To make these rag-clad limbs ache and shiver.

Before this dreadful war I'd a pleasant, happy home
  In a cottage, with a wife and children near me,
With a master ever kind, I'd no word of fault to find,
  For want nor sorrow ever entered near me.

Now, since this dreadful war I've no place to rest my
   head,
  And sorrow has my health and reason shattered,
My wife of want has died, and my children far and wide
  Over the earth, I know not where, are scattered.

Now, since this dreadful war I no more can happy live
  In a cottage by the clear and shining river ;
Driven by a vandal band from my sunny Southern land,
  My bed the chilling snow, I shake and quiver.

Now, since this dreadful war I've a master kind no more,
  From my wife and children parted here forever,
I, impatient, wait to go where no wintry winds do blow,
  And war, and want, and sorrow enter never.

Aye, but this dreadful war made me freeman while I
   live,
  Free to wander, free to starve and ache and shiver,
Free to die without a friend, and moan till life shall end,
  And curse—no, Heaven forgive my freedom giver.

LINES SUGGESTED BY READING THE PETITION
OF THE LADIES OF THE SHENANDOAH
VALLEY, ASKING PARDON FOR JEFFERSON
DAVIS.

———

Pardon for *him?* What sinning hath he done?
  He of the lofty brow and soulful eye?
This wise, this noble, much-loved Southron son?
  Pardon for him you ask? in sooth, for why?

Was't wrong to take the Northman at his word?
  To heed the taunts flung in his manly face?
The dire "expense," the "ignorant, uncouth herd"? *
  The "blot" that brought his ensign to disgrace?

Was't wrong to side 'gainst Wrong though "Right" might
    fail?
  Wrong, when the tyrant's minions southward pour'd,
To use his utmost powers—might they avail—
  Backward to drive th' invading, hireling horde?

Was't wrong to worship at sweet Freedom's shrine?
  To cling to memories of her Washington?
Within his heart his teachings to entwine,
  And do as did our Country's sainted one?

Pardon for *him?* kind Heaven, stoop down and show
  The Christian tenet teaching us to pray
The Injurer's pardon for the Injured, who
  Sinned only that he could not "win the day."

Dear sisters of the stricken Southern land,
　　Our hearts in sympathy with yours do bleed ;
Hope lured us with her fair and beckoning hand
　　'Till Fortune fled you in your greatest need.

But for *his* pardon we were loth to sue—
　　Justice alone should set the prisoner free !
Demanding justice we would join with you,
　　Each State a sovereignty—all sovereigns we.

But hist ! we did forget us—times are changed !
　　Our birthright, too, is trampled deep in dust ;
For we are ruled *per force* by minds deranged,
·　　Who've trait'rous proved to Liberty's fair trust.

And on her pedestal have placed a god
　　For us to worship—woe betide the soul,
When his black " curls " he " shakes and gives the nod,"
　　Who dares ignore His Mightiness' control !

But shall we bow ? or as our fathers, serve
　　Right, Reason, Justice, Liberty and Law ?
And like good Daniel, ne'er a hair-breadth swerve
　　Though " lions " face us with a ravenous maw !

Alas ! the quivering flesh by torturing rack,
　　From agony will oft be forced to yield,
And Wrong will trample Truth and Right, alack !
　　'Till Heaven comes down and holds her vanquished
　　　field.

　　　　　　　* Words flung at the Southern people.

JANUARY, 1866.

TO THEE, HIBERNIA.

Fair Islet, enclasped by the ocean,
  More marked by a tyrannous power
Than thy shores by the lashing commotion
  Of waves since Creation's first hour—
I'm longing to hear the glad tidings,
  "Erin's burst the oppressors' hard chains,"
As an unweaned child yearns for its mother—
  For Irish blood runs in my veins.

Fair Islet, enclasped by the ocean,
  Would the day of thy bondage were o'er,
And Liberty's pinions in motion,
  Did rest on thy surf-beaten shore ;
Did brood o'er thy lakelets and rivers,
  Thy hills and sweet emerald plains ;
Then with rapture I'd shout at thy triumph—
  For Irish blood runs in my veins.

Fair Islet, enclasped by the ocean,
  Of heroes and orators sage,
Who loved thee with purest devotion
  Enstoried on history's page—
I'll pray with thy patriot daughters,
  And join in the lyrical strains
Of Erin, the gem of the waters—
  For Irish blood runs in my veins.

Fair Islet, thou brightest and dearest,
  With thy "Sunburst" just out of the sea—
May thy "Harp" be re-tuned to sweet music,
  And sing of the peaceful and free !
May thy beauteous flag float in glory,
  Where Virtue with Liberty reigns ;
And *I* live to tell the proud story—
  For Irish blood runs in my veins.

O Erin, mavourneen, forever !
  Would the shades of thy martyrs might rise,
And lead on thy warriors to conquer,
  'Till victory's shouts rend the skies !
Till back o'er the sea thy despoiler,
  All vanquished has fled in dismay,
Like a storm-driven wreck on the billows,
  When hurricanes revel at play.

O Erin, mavourneen, forever !
  May thy time of redemption be near,
And the sunlight of freedom smile on thee,
  Till mountains and vales disappear —
May now at thy bosom be nursing
  The heroes who'll win thee a crown —
And the evergreen laurel be growing
  For poets who'll hymn thy renown.

O Erin, mavourneen, forever !
  Warm friends here, low kneeling for thee,
Daily cry to the Power Supernal
  To set loved Hibernia free.
May the clank of thy chains long unriven,
  The wails of thy children in woe,
- Ere long, move a pitying Heaven,
  The guerdon thus sought to bestow.
        SPRING OF 186-.

TO ENGLAND.

Does Britain's Lion lash his sides
  In wrath, and shake his mane,
When he hears the Eagle's shrilly voice
  Come o'er the watery plain ?
And does he strive with angry growl
  The glorious bird to fright,
Lest on the soil of Ireland
  Ere long 'twill dare alight.

And does he, rampant, seek to catch
  This bird with wings full spread,
And crush her 'neath his heavy paw
  Till Freedom's hopes lie dead ?
Till England's slaves in all things else
  "Except in name" and spirit,
Shall no more dare to strive for Rights
  Which Freedom's sons inherit ?

Is he so greedy of his prey
  Ill gotten and ill held ?
And does he fear the hastening day
  When Erin, as of eld,
From every nook beneath her skies,
  From mountain, dell and river,
Shall start to arms in martial mood
  His galling bonds to shiver ?

Oh, England ! England ! well thou ken'st
  Thy Lion hates the Eagle,
And gladlier would hunt her down
  Than timid hare the beagle—
Had he but power to break her wing
  And wring her neck, she, never,
O'er any soil thy thought has trod
  Would soar again, forever.

Yet as we gaze on Albion proud
  Far over the great water,
We think we see her pale and quake
  With fear of coming slaughter ;
For Christian palm she will not wave,
  But dares, in dread the fury
Of marshaled hosts in righteous cause,
  With Heaven as Judge and Jury.

Oh, England ! England ! feel'st thou not
  Thy throne begin to tremble ?
"The writing on the wall" methinks
  Thy pride cannot dissemble—
For "in the balance thou art weighed,"
  And " Wanting" is the sentence
In all things save self-righteousness,
  Which keeps thee from repentance.

Oh, England ! England ! had'st thou seer—
  Would'st heed the darkling vision ?
Or would'st thou, like the proud Lochiel,
  But scorn it with derision ?
Beware ! beware ! lest soon thou find'st
  Some prophet truth hast spoken—
By Erin's arms, by Erin's sons,
  Thy sceptre shall lie broken.
    FEBRUARY, 1866.

MY COUNTRY.

[After the Veto—February, 1866.]

My Country, take heart ! for a day-beam is shining,
Through a rift in the blackness that shroudeth thee o'er ;
Perchance the dark clouds have a silvery lining,
And bright as of erst are thy days yet in store—
My Country, take heart ! though each city and hamlet
Has yielded her sons to the Demon of War—
Though thousands of widows and orphans are wailing,
Sore-crushed by the roll of the Juggernaut car ;
And though other thousands still smart from oppression,
That closely has followed red Mars' bloody wake ;
And wildfire fanatics have prospered in treason,
Till we feel the last vestige of Freedom at stake—
Up beyond the thick pall, a clear sun may be shedding
Its rays to dispel the thick gloom o'er thee cast,
Until Liberty, Peace and Prosperity bless thee,
It may be, as long as God's footstool shall last—
My Country, take heart ! for there *seems* at the helm now
One powerful to steer thy ship safe into port.
It must be a task for the boldest of seamen,
So long has it been of rude tempests the sport ;
But if, as he swore to, he follows the compass,
And swerves not a line from the course it points out,
He'll surely pass soon all the dangerous quicksands,
Charybdis and Scylla leaving far in the route.
Then will thy proud eagle come again from her eyrie,
On the far mountain crag, where she fled in disgust,
That her broad wings may shelter forever a people
Whose vigilant watch is the price of their trust.
Aye, then will thy Washington's spirit, returning
To the land of his birth, of his love and his toils,
Be a guardian saint with the sages whose teachings
Thy mad rulers spurned for impolitic broils.

Aye, then will thy shore be again the glad refuge
Of children oppressed in the lands o'er the sea ;
A Beacon, a Day-star, an Edenland envied,
Of peoples and kingdoms—the land of the Free!
My Country, take heart ! for a greater than mortal,
Who chastens, betimes all the world for its good
May yet look in love down from Heaven's far portal,
And crown with His blessings thy famishing brood.
Thou hast sinned, greatly sinned, and thy record is written
Too deeply in blood for long years to efface—
But Pardon, the offspring of Mercy and Heaven,
Gives sinners, repentant, beneficent grace.

ANOTHER NOTE OF JOY !

[Occasioned by the President's speech, February 22, 1866.]

———

Good God ! be thanked that we can breathe once more
One breath of freedom on our native shore !
Dear native shore, that with despotic sway
Hath for so long been ruled, there's joy to-day !

Oh, 'tis a joy to draw in such sweet breath,
After so long respiring fumes of death !
To see *one* shining star in skies of night,
After such darkness as has vailed their light !

'Tis an Aurora to the sin-sick eye
That weeps our country's woes of deepest dye—
An almost daybreak to the longing heart
That sighed and prayed for night-time to depart.

It is—it is a beam which does remind
Of other days, when Fortune served us kind—
Ere guiltless souls thick prison walls did vex—
When hangman's ropes were kept for felon's necks.

Good God ! be thanked. One dares the tempests brave,
That round his head in rolling thunders rave—
One dares to raise his hand to Heaven and swear
That Right shall rule, and our loved country spare.

Then let me strike my joyous lyre again,
For so my spirit sings the glad refrain—
Though fierce the howling storm, the murky scope,
Spanned by a sheening rainbow gives sweet Hope !

TO FRANCE.

I pity thee, O France,
　　Thou hast led so wild a dance
O'er stormy seas, *sans* compass, sail and rudder ;
　　Death has opened wide her door,
　　Thou hast glutted it with gore,
And the horrid sight has made the nations shudder.

　　Of Prussia's King the jest,
　　Thou his bloody wit confest
(Such a lesson erst thou taught thy neighbor brother),
　　'Tis the worst of thy disgrace
　　That thy sons before thy face
Like maniacs fell and guillotine each other.

　　Poor, sunny, sullied France !
　　Too changing to advance,
One forward step, and then one backward ever—
　　"A monarch," then "The People"!
　　"Prince," "Serf"; then "Free and equal"!
In Reason's name wilt thou be constant never !

　　In science first of nations,
　　All render thee oblations,
In government unstable as the water :
　　To-day a "king" doth reign,
　　To-morrow fled or slain—
"The People" rule—'tis anarchy and slaughter.

　　I pity thee, O France !
　　Thou hast led so wild a daece
Through bloody seas that oft thy bosom cover,
　　Oh, hast thou yet to learn
　　That true liberty will spurn
The land o'er which no Christian graces hover ?
　　1871.

TO LITTLE EDITRESS NELLIE.

[Whose father was not able to support his family on account
of ill health, and who was motherless.]

A worthy lesson thou dost teach, sweet one,
　　That children's willing hands can much avail
To ease the burdens of a parent's life,
　　When manhood's health and strength begin to fail.

In useful work one ever happier is ;
　　And yet thy youthful heart must oft be sad,
With no dear mother's fond, approving smile,
　　Nor cheering word to make thy task more glad.

Or when friends fail thee in thy sorest need,
　　When all seems dark or with temptation rife,
To have no mother thy soul-cry to heed,
　　And soothe with gentle tones thy inward strife.

Or when disease has paled thy fair, young cheek,
　　Or crimsoned it with fever's burning glow,
To have no mother near to smoothe thy bed,
　　Nor bathe with cooling hand thy throbbing brow.

Ah ! Nellie darling, I can feel for thee.
　　Like thee was I bereft in childhood's years :
My mother heard her Savior call, and soared
　　Where there is never weariness nor tears.

But often when my heart is bruised and sore,
　　Or to my brow the aching hectic clings,
I seem to hear her soothing angel tones,
　　Or feel the fannings of her angel wings.

Thou precious one, *thy* mother may be near,
　　As near as when thy baby head did rest
In perfect trust, in infant innocence,
　　Upon her loving, pulsing, earthly breast.

And certain am I there is One who deigns
　　His praying, working, trusting child to bless ;
He aids thy willing hands, dries all thy tears.
　　Oh ! God does, pitying, shield the motherless.

WE SHALL MEET AGAIN.

We shall meet them again, but no more by the hearth
　　Where the days of our childhood were fleeting ;
We shall meet them again, but oh never on earth
　　Shall our warm lips press theirs in the greeting.

We shall meet them again, tho' they've paled from our
　　　　view
　　As the bright starlight pales in the morning ;
We shall meet them again, tho' they've passed through
　　　　the blue
　　To realms of sweet Mercy's adorning.

We shall meet them again, when we've sailed o'er the
    sea,
  Where sorrow's waves heave in commotion;
We shall meet them again, when we land on the lea
  That lighteth eternity's ocean.

We shall meet them again—what sweet joy fills the breast
  When we tell to our sad hearts the story!
We shall meet them again, where no graves must be
    prest—
  There are no buried hopes up in glory.

We shall meet them again—the blest day draweth near
  When our souls shall unite ne'er to sever;
We shall meet them again, where there's no parting tear,
  Forever, lorn weeper, forever.

We shall meet them again, face shall smile upon face,
  Rehearsing the joys that have crowned them;
We shall meet them and know them and fold in embrace
  The Eden-forms Jesus hath found them.

We shall meet them again, we shall meet them again—
  I could breathe my soul out in repeating
The only bright hope that to me doth remain—
  My life's beacon-star is that meeting.

A LITTLE PRAYER FOR A GREAT GOOD.

Lord! help me think of Thee—
   Look on me from above,
And guard me from the snares of earth,
   With thy undying love.

Lord! fill my heart with grace—
   Let gratitude inspire
My tongue and pen till thankless men
   Confess 'tis heavenly fire.

Lord! make me all thine own—
   Thy holy spirit give—
And fill my soul with thy delights
   E'en while on earth I live.

Lord! let me see and know
   Thou heed'st my earnest cries,
And make me feel a heavenly zeal
   Each day my soul supplies.

Our cherub child with blithesome feet
Now happy walks the "golden street."
But Oh, we miss, each day and hour,
Her winning ways, her soothing power.

Life is Love, and Love is Life,
And in that Life there must be Hope—
Or life is Death.

SUNDAY.

This is the Christian's day of rest.
   A holy calm descends from Heaven
And fills the Christian's thankful breast
   With quiet trust in sins forgiven.

This is the day for earth to raise
   Its sweetest incense to the Throne—
Its heartfelt prayers and songs of praise—
   For all our loving Lord hath done.

This is the day the sin-sick soul,
   Unwashed in Jesus' blood, should cry,
"Be merciful!" "Lord, make me whole!"
   Unto thy sheltering arms I fly.

A LITTLE WORD FOR WOMAN'S RIGHTS.

In this proud age most men believe
  Women have souls as well as they—
"Yet there's a difference" they perceive—
  "Just what it is," they cannot say.

But woman's is a female soul;
  Perforce inferior to the male—
Man's stature, larger, should control—
  For "Might makes Right" and must prevail.

"Nor male, nor female," Christ hath said—
  "We're one in Him," His word doth tell—
No sex of soul the sovereign head
  Doth recognize where angels dwell.

Since there's "nor male nor female soul,"
  What righteous claim does man possess
That he should hold o'er us control
  Simply because our size is less?

Civilization's Christian school
  Teaches wise lessons all should ken—
'Tis mind and mind alone should rule—
  Not stature large nor simply men.

How many women of our day
  Show powers of thought that far excel
Some of our rulers—yet they say
  "*Why should ye 'gainst your yoke rebel?*"

A Christian woman bow the heads,
  And bend to man the willing knee;
When Christ our wise Lawgiver said,
  "Stand fast wherewith He made us free." *

* Galatians 5, 1.

I'VE CHANGED MY MIND.

Few years ago, as some have seen,
  Of woman's Rights " I sought to make
A little fun—my pen was green "—
  I was not then, full wide awake.

Experiences sharpen wit—
  My eyes, since then, are opened quite,
Some deeds before my vision flit
  That let into my mind the light.

I,ve heard, and seen, and felt, and known
  That woman is the veriest slave
That man, poor brutal man can own,
  Until her footsteps reach the grave.

And such too, in a Christian land
  Where worthy men and wise we find,
Who take all other " wrongs " in hand,
  But yet to woman's wrongs are blind.

Therefore with tongue and pen 'tis meet
  That now our birthright we should claim.
Freedom to women's ears is sweet—
  There's Heaven-wrought music in the name.

He who from Freedom's hallow'd stream
  Doth drink his fill each day and hour—
How can he fully know or dream
  Of woman's thirst for Freedom's dower ?

Push on the work then with our might :
  The battle now is well begun—
Brothers may aid us in the fight—
  But *we* must *lead*, till we have won.

Yet not as worker in the throng
  Of this grand cause ought I to speak ;
Worse than a laggard for so long,
  A blush of shame distains my cheek.

But blесséd, brave, large-hearted band,
  I ask forgiveness of you all.
I give you now my willing hand
  "To do or die " at Freedom's call.
    OCTOBER, 1869.

A DIALOGUE IN A NUTSHELL.

He—You have a little property,
  And so must pay a tax.
The Law requires you to obey,
  You'll find it in the "Acts." *

She—I have a little property,
  But I'm a woman, sir,
I have no voice in making laws,
  To pay you I demur.

  'Tis wrong to tax a person whom
   You wont permit to vote.
  I from our "Constitution" plain
   Must be allowed to quote.

He—If to the "Constitution," ma'am,
  You go, you lose your case
Within that treasured scroll you'll find
  You have indeed no place.

  "All *men* are free and equal" there
   Of woman 'tis not writ—
  For you to claim equality
   With us is quite unfit.

She—"Know all men by these presents," so
  Your men-made laws do say ;
If "all men" means not women too,
  Why should we them obey ?

  If "all men" women do include,
   Why then, wise sir, you see,
  If law-abiding citizens,
   We're "equal" too, and "free."

* The law "Acts," not the Bible "Acts."

If on our property we're "taxed,"
   We should be "represented";
And if we wish to vote, by what
   Just law are we prevented ?

He—Well, madam, if you think 'tis so,
   The law why don't you test ;
Go to the polls with force enough
   To prove you're not "in jest."

Let him who challenges your vote
   His legal right essay ;
To show why you should have no voice
   In laws you must obey.

She—Man makes the laws—enforces them
   His selfish aims to suit.
His brutal powers superior
   Few women would dispute.

On earth 'tis not the righteous cause
   That always wins the day ;
The "strongest arm" too often is
   Victorious in the fray.

In this proud land which boasts so loud
   Of Liberty and Reason,
For woman to assert her Rights
   Men think is worse than treason.

Yet soon we'll follow your advice,
   And, sir, please note the sequel—
We'll try the virtue of the law
   "All men are free and equal."
OCTOBER, 1869.

SUNDAY MUSINGS.

Is death a long, untroubled sleep,
  To last while ages pass away ?
To last till earth and waters deep
  Are summoned to give up our " clay " ?

It may be that these frames shall find
  A dreamless rest in earth's deep womb.
But where is the immortal mind
  While ages roll ?   Is sleep *its* doom ?

'Tis " dust to dust " when forms are laid
  Within the dark and silent grave ;
But the ethereal part is " weighed,"
  And sinks—or flies to God who gave.

Dear Lord, when in the earth's cold breast
  This senseless form must one day lie,
Let my " freed soul " in Thee find rest,
  And peace and joy while time rolls by.

And when the last, loud trump shall sound,
  And all of time hath pass'd away,
May I be with the righteous found,
  Thine own, through Heaven's eternal day.

And there, dear Savior, may I meet
  And join with friends I've loved so dear
In singing round thy mercy-seat
  Songs angels' ears will love to hear.

Songs of thy great redemption, Lord,
  Of triumph through thy precious blood—
That 'twas for us "made flesh the Word"—
Jesus ! the Crucified ! our God !

Unequalled deed ! most glorious theme !
  O matchless grace of power divine !
The bliss of which I now may dream,
  Shall it, dear Savior, there be mine ?

Dear Lord, 'tis meet, too, here below
  We hymn thy praise in grateful lays ;
Here streams of mercy constant flow,
  Thy blessings crown us all our days.

THE POOR MAN'S GRAVE.

The poorest man on earth at last
  One spot of ground will own,
And few will covet him his soil
  With thistles overgrown.
And even should some loving friend
  Bedeck his land with flowers,
'Twould scarcely then so tempting be
  As make us wish 'twere ours.

GOD'S VOICE IN NATURE.

Is it not strange that we who think and see,
Do not more clearly read God's hieroglyphs—
His marvelous works about us everywhere !
Sun, moon and stars—earth's seas, and hills, and plains,
Its ledgéd rocks of dark and shining ore,
Snow, rain and hail, and the tempestuous storms,
Tree, shrub and flower, and every breathing thing, ·
And feel the winter's cold and summer's heat,
And hear of the great wonders that the mind
Of man, pent in so frail and small a scope
As is.the brain within its narrow skull,
Can seemingly invent and so perform,
Acted upon by spirits unseen here,
But ever near ! Is it not more than strange—
Surpassing strange that we forget
Or fail to know and own Him all in all ?
Forget, or dare disown, His watchful care
And long enduring love, shown by His works ?
Our minds were very pent and dull to need
Another book than the Creation's Book
Wherein to read of God's omniscient eye,
His omnipresence, and omnipotence,
And boundless love to those who serve Him here !
It is indeed because our minds are small
(A drop as 'twere in the immensity
Of the great whole of thought that filleth space—
The spiritual essence of the Deity),
And dull to take in such great truths
Unless brought down to our capacity ;
That they must written be within a Book
Whose compass is so small that we may take
And hold it in our hand and turn the leaves
And read, as is our need, to give us faith

In One Supreme ; and teach us all is best
To those of contrite hearts ; even though oft
In sorrow chastened sore, or humbled low.
Father of all ! Awake our minds ! enlarge
Our thinking souls, even while bound within
This little span that clips the wings of thought,
And make us wisely worship on bowed knee,
And soar in grateful praises to Thee, First
And Best ! Creator! Savior ! Sovereign! loving Lord !

THE TWO.

There are lights in the palace
  On the green embower'd hill.
There's a light in the cot
  By the stream near the mill.
The lights in the palace
  Nearly rival the sun—
So brilliant and many !
  While the cot has but one.

In the palace there 's music,
  And dancing, and plenty—
In the cot there is sorrow,
  And the cupboard is empty.
The miller has long
  On his sick-bed been lying—
Does the mill-owner know
  That his miller is dying ?

The mill-owner 's rich
  And the palace is his.
Why should he feel sad
  On a night such as this ?
The music's entrancing !
  The dancing is fine !
The banquet unrivalled
  In viands and wine.

Sweet flowers with fragrance
  Perfume the soft air—
From sunny climes gathered
  Exotics most rare.

And every thing round him
  On which his eyes rest
Is a gem of its kind—
  The richest and best.

Soft moonbeams are falling,
  With the stars' silvery light—
Without all is placid,
  Within all is bright.
And the kind words of friends,
  And the repartee gay,
Wine, music, and dance
  Charm the wing'd hours away.

But the miller owns never
  A place on the earth—
The cot is not his—
  He has no home and no hearth—
His candle is dim,
  His fire burns low,
And the eyes of his loved ones
  With tears overflow.

No kind friends are near
  To give aid, or to speak
The comforting word
  That gives strength to the weak.
The moon's gentle light,
  And the stars' brilliant train,
Bring no charm to his cot,
  And no ease to his pain.

But the poor miller soon
  In *his* palace will dwell.
And bask in the bliss
  Which all earth's joys excel.

And the mill-owner rich
  On his couch will be lying,
And friends now so gay
  Will hold watch o'er him dying.

And the mill-owner's soul
  When from earth's duties free,
And his body lies cold,
  To what home will it flee?
In a palace above,
  Or with spirits below—
There will it be weal?
  Or *there* will it be woe?

MARY—THE HOLY.

Mary ! Queen amid the angels !
  Once thy foot-fall pressed the earth.
Fresh in youth and fair in beauty,
  In thy breast sweet hopes had birth.

And when womanhood came to thee,
  Crowned by spirits from above—
Thou didst know a mother's travail,
  Thou didst learn a mother's love.

And like us poor, sinful mothers,
  Holding close thy first-born child—
What ecstatic joy came o'er thee,
  When thy babe first on thee smiled.

And like us, what rapture thrilled thee,
  When thou sawest each beauty new
In thy nursling babe unfolded
  As in infant charms He grew ?

And, like us, how oft thou pondered
  Would He grow to manhood's prime !
And a blessing prove, thou wondered,
  Living here a life sublime !

Yet the words by angels spoken
  (To thy vision like a dream)
Much thy meditations broke on—
  Was He more than did beseem ?

For thou sawest Him in childhood,
 " Wonderful " in deed and thought.
And thou knew that with His being
 Something mystic was inwrought.

Growing from thee ! unlike others—
 Sinless yet with sorrow marred !
And thou questioned more the Future,
 Praying Heaven thy son to guard.

But the end came, boding mother !
 And thy heart with anguish filled ;
On the cross on sad Mount Calvary
 There His breaking heart was stilled.

Blesséd Mary ! Holy Mother !
 Honored most of human kind ;
For the " sword that pierced thy soul " so
 Brought the light to sinners blind.

THE LITTLE PEARL-DROP.

A pretty little pearl-drop
  Within the Ocean lay—
A daring diver found it
  And bore it far away.
The Ocean never miss'd it—
  The precious little thing !
But a Queen was proud to wear it
  Set in a golden ring.

And so how many a trifle
  The rich doth kindly give
Unto his poorer brother,
  To give him strength to live,
Not miss'd from his abundance,
  Oft proves of value more
Than the proud Queen's pearl-drop
  From Ocean's hidden store.

And to the donor 'twill be
  As " bread on waters cast,"
And he shall find 'twill come again
  When " many days " are past,
Bringing a goodly interest,
  Worth more than pearls or gems
Set in Queen's golden circlets
  Or in their diadems.

THE BIRD'S SONG.

There came to me a messenger—
  A bird of plumage bright—
As all alone I sat me here
  A reading late at night.
'Twas in the pleasant summer time—
  The window high was raised—
But 'twas an unco' time to come !
  Methought the bird was dazed.

It winged its way straight o'er my head
  As in my room it came,
Without a single sign of fear,
  It seemed so very tame,
Then lit upon the mantle-piece
  And smoothed its brilliant crest,
And folded close each little wing
  As though it fain would rest.

Then "quick as thought" it raised its head
  Cocked up its little eyes,
And opened wide its little bill
  All to my great surprise,
And softly sang this little song,
  So pretty and so sweet—
"Love each, love all, love every one,
  Love makes our life complete."

And then it spread its little wings
  And quickly flew away,
And left me lone to ponder o'er
  The words its song did say,

"Love each, love all, love every one,
  Love makes our life complete."
Ah, well methought to *be beloved*
  Is very, very sweet!

"Love each, love all, love every one,"
  Thus said the simple strain,
To "*be beloved*" it did not add
  Unto the sweet refrain.
And then methought who truly loves
  Will meet a like return.
Who giveth much receiveth much
  How many fail to learn.

And then I woke, for o'er my book,
  Fatigued with cares of day,
I'd dropped to sleep—but sure enough
  A bird had lost its way.
And poised upon my windowsill
  With little quiv'ring throat
The timid wee thing softly chirped
  Its lovelorn, winsome note.

FIRST ROBIN OF THE SPRING.

To-day I hear a robin sing,
  How jubilant the tone ;
First robin of the early spring
  Returned from Southern zone.

Welcome ! thrice welcome, pretty guest !
  Sweet songster in the tree ;
Last year a bird there built her nest,
  And there sang merrily.

Trill out the merry roundelay,
  No harm shall here come nigh thee—
No wicked hunter rove this way
  Nor naughty boy shall spy thee.

Perhaps thou art the self-same bird
  That trilled before our door
The pretty songs we last year heard,
  Come back to sing us more !

If so, where are the fledglings five,
  Thou reared within that nest ?
Are still the chirping things alive
  Warbling their prettiest ?

Before some other cottage door
  Do now those wee things sing,
Their birdling melody outpour
  A free-will offering ?

These crumbs sweet robin-redbreast take,
　We scatter them for thee—
A poor return, indeed, they make
　For birdie's minstrelsy.

WE'VE WAKENED.

We've wakened from our lethargy—
　The sleep of ages gone ;
Our cries have pierced the Heavens,
　Our prayers have reached the Throne,
And we know our Father heeds them—
　Gone forth is His decree.
O'er Christian lands the morning breaks,
　And woman shall be free.

'Tis passing strange our heritage
　We yielded for so long,
And bow'd so low our patient necks
　Because man's arm was strong,
When there was one Omnipotent,
　If we had sought his aid
In earnestness, would long ago
　Have burst the bonds *Man* made.

Our dear and blessèd Saviour,
　Eighteen hundred years ago,
Owned woman as His mother,
　And her glory did foreshow.
To mortal man such honor
　Was never, never given—
To be a parent of the Lord
　Who reigns o'er earth and heaven.

So sisters, we'll be trustful—
   Our wails have pierced the skies.
Our prayers have reached the Heavenly Throne,
   Our Father heeds our cries.
The hour of our freedom
   He will not long delay—
The hour which hastes the coming
   Of Earth's great millennial day.

We will burnish bright our armor,
   And gird our lances on,
And our champing steed keep harnessed
   Ready for the glorious dawn.
And we'll march to martial music
   While our serried ranks increase;
And our watchword shall be Freedom,
   And with Freedom shall be Peace.

For when we've nobly conquered,
   And our liberty secured,
We'll right the very many wrongs
   We have so long endured.
We'll wave the fresh, green Olive Branch,
   And, "white-winged," sally forth:
And wars shall end and love increase,
   And Peace fill all the earth.

We'll wave the fresh, green Olive Branch,
   And send our Carrier-dove
To all the nations far and near
   With messages of love,
And show them that the waves that lash'd
   Our noble Ship of State
Have made it pure—safe ark for all
   Who on its blessings wait.

HEARTH AND HOME.

A SONG.

I mind me of a Hearth and Home
  In a valley by the hill,
Beneath the elm tree's cooling shade,
  Anear a rippling rill,
Where brothers dear and sisters
  Beguiled the fleeting hours
With hearts as joyous as the birds
  And careless as the flowers.
        Oh, 'twas a happy, happy band around
            the Hearth at Home,
        Where time flew by on golden wings,
            'ere Heaven whispered, Come !

In that sweet home a mother's lips
  Spake e'er the gentle word,
And there a loving father's voice
  In kindest tones was heard,
And there the agéd grandsire,
  Beside the hearth of yore,
Told wondrous tales of daring deeds,
  And dreamed life's battles o'er.
        Oh, 'twas a happy, happy band, etc.

How humble in that pleasant home
  The morn and evening prayer !
What heartfelt hymns of praise were sung
  Around the hearthstone there !
How innocent the prattle
  Around the parent's knee !
How soft the soothing lullaby
  That hush'd the infant glee !
        Oh, 'twas a happy, happy band, etc.

I've pass'd through many lands since then,
   I've sailed o'er many seas ;
I've sought 'mid charms of every clime
   My lonely heart to please ;
But of all the lovely places
   Through which I've chanced to roam
The sweetest to my memory
   Is the old Hearth and Home.
      Oh, 'twas a happy, happy band, etc.

I see thy low and time-stain'd roof,
   Blest home of childhood days !
Thy moss-grown eaves, thy ivied walls,
   Thy broad hearth's cheerful blaze,
Where gathered friends the dearest ;
   A loving, kindred throng,
Whose words were music to mine ear,
   Sweet as a seraph's song.
      Oh, 'twas a happy, happy band, etc.

Methinks the star-crown'd angels came
   From yonder viewless shore,
And pass'd with silent footsteps oft
   Athrough the old Home door
To woo away our lov'd ones
   Who early went to rest,
And left the Hearth all desolate
   My youthful feet had prest.
      Oh, 'twas a happy, happy band, etc.

My forehead now is wrinkled o'er,
   My hair is growing gray.
I feel my bark is nearing fast
   A land not far away,
But my heart beats young as ever,
   And my pulses sweetly thrill
When I recall the Hearth and Home
   In the valley by the hill.
      Oh, 'twas a happy, happy band, etc.

"FOOTPRINTS OF THE CREATOR."

Hugh Miller ! I have read thy wondrous book—
"Footprints of the Creator"—master-work ;
What wonder that thy brain was overwrought,
Thou student of the Ages ! what research,
Deciphering the language of the rocks—
Of eras upon eras passed away !
Showing that time has been almost etern,
And this now is God's " seventh day of rest,"
In which He lays aside creative power,
And gives to fallen man free agency
To conquer sin and free redemption claim.
Thou'st given to us convincing proof that life
Of fish, and beast, and bird, exceeding ours,
Breathed, moved and flourished till the sea upheaved
And earth convulsed—thus ending age on age—
So that a new creation might arise
From débris of the old, superior
If not in size, in grace and intellect.
And all gives witness to thee of unrest
In every period of advancing time.
And thou believ'st man never could exist
In such a state of chaos.   Yet methinks
Each great upheaval might have been, alas !
The resurrection morn for mould'ring forms
Which human beings like to us did wear,
Sinning and suff'ring ; some redeemed, some lost !
Some may be spirits of the nether world,
Which come like "lions seeking to devour,"
Some angels and archangels round the Throne.
The angels who stood guard at Paradise
May once have lived, and felt, and died like us,
And, too, like us, when earth gives up its dead,
In the dark chaos leave no stamp or form
For other coming ages to find trace.

For all these " works shall be burned up," and so
From out the fire a " Heaven new and earth"
Shall spring again from God's creative hand
Showing forth His glory.

MY FATHER, DR. ROSWELL BATES.

My Father ! God ! who ever thus ordains
    The flower most crushed shall sweetest perfume give,
Why should not my bruised soul breathe tender strains
    So sweetly sad they would this life outlive.

For from mine infancy I've felt the smart
    That sorrows deep can make the weak one feel,
And life still offers me the darker part
    And wounds me when I thought Thy hand would heal.

My father ! Oh, my father's breath'd his last,
    And angels met him as he passed away ;
But how it wrings my heart that in the past
    He suffered while I could not ease his stay.

He prayed ! O God ! he prayed an easy death—
    Knowing so well his parting day was near,
But to his last, his very last drawn breath
    Thou show'd'st no token that Thine ear could hear.

But when kind Heaven did give his soul release,
    E'en after death's mark stamped his marble brow,
I said "Dear father if thy soul's at peace,
    And thou art happy, smile upon me now."

He smiled ! thank God ! thank Heaven, he gave the sign,
   He smiled upon me as I said the word,
And then I knew 'twas wicked to repine,
   Or doubt the goodness of his Saviour-Lord.

He smiled though kind friends told me he was gone—
   Though he lay bound beneath death's icy chain,
Yet did God give him power to make known
   Our loss was for our father's greater gain.

For his long eighty years of work was done—
   That thinking, active, praying soul was free,
To " Paradise "* the angels led him on,
   His anguish now was turned to jubilee.

He'd search'd the Scriptures daily since his youth,
   He'd bow'd him daily at God's altar-fire,
He'd taught his children " God is Love " in truth,
   And Heaven and Wisdom were his chief desire.

And so we feel more, God doth give reward
   To all who seek Him—all who love His name—
And the poor, sorrowing, sinking soul will guard
   Though anguish rack this weak and wasting frame.

He smiled, that smile comes to my vision oft—
   'Tis stamp'd indelibly upon my brain ;
It helps to raise my thoughts and hopes aloft,
   And makes me know that we shall meet again.

My father ! O my father ! theme so dear,
   I knelt beside thy grave but yestereven,
And prayed, and whispered to thee, didst thou hear ?
   Scarce four feet from me, yet so far as Heaven.

    * His last word.

I told thee of my sorrows, of my cares,
  I asked thee of my brothers, sister, mother ;
I hush'd me for some answer to my prayers,
  Some token to assure, as did the other.

I sought to learn of "Sherdie," precious dove !
  Thy only grandson thence so early flown—
If thou dost see him in thy Home above;
  A white-wing'd cherub nestling near the Throne.

And other friends long dear unto thine heart,
  If they were with thee, how they sped the while—
If they did act in Heaven an angel's part,
  And joyed to greet thee in the "Blessed Isle."

Oh, if good spirits come from spirit-land,
  If thou canst come and tell an angel-story,
How gladly would I clasp thy spirit-hand,
  And list with eager ear thy tale of glory.

It does not seem that thou for aye art gone,
  Thy spirit oft I feel, anear me lingers—
Each thing thy hand hath touch'd, thine eye look'd on,
  Methinks doth feel thy press of spirit-fingers.

I do believe thou hear'st me when I call,
  That when I think of thee, thy shade is near me,
For thought is linked to thought, and soul to soul,
  And Heaven to all, good God! who, loving, fear Thee.

MY FATHER.

Didst thou, then, meet, my father dear,
  The loved ones gone before thee?
Or why was that ecstatic look
  That suddenly came o'er thee?
After the long death-struggle ceased,
  What meant that upward gaze,
As though an unexpected sight
  Of bliss did thee amaze?

'Twas something beautiful, I ween,
  It seemed a glad surprise—
That vision of the other world
  That met thy raptured eyes—
That look, that last, that parting look,
  Did something more express
Than mortal power can ever know,
  Than earth-clad souls can guess.

We may surmise 'twas friends belov'd
  Met thee in bright array,
To waft thee from the realms of death
  To everlasting day.
We may surmise 'twas angel-bands,
  With wings of radiant light,
And starry crowns, and golden lyres,
  That met thy raptured sight,
With loving Jesus at their head,
  Bright leader of the throng,
Who came to bear thy spirit Home,
  With joy and angel-song.

We may surmise the gold-paved streets,
  Within that "city new,"
And birds with plumage beautiful,
  And flowers of rainbow hue,
And trees that grew from golden sands
  Hard by the shining river,
Were opened to thy gladsome view,
  A sight of joy forever.

We may surmise thou saw'st the Throne,
  Of Him the great "I Am,"
Whose praises shining seraphs hymn
  And wave the jeweled palm,
Waiting His mandates to obey—
  His messages of love—
To all the ransomed ones of earth,
  Through all the courts above.

We may surmise the star-gemmed skies,
  Were to thy vision clear ;
That what we count as grander worlds
  Is each a seraph's sphere,
Or guardian angel looking down
  With loving, pitying eye,
On every sad and death-doomed child
  Who would to Jesus fly.

We may surmise, but ne'er can know,
  What meant that parting smile,
Until for us is raised the veil
  By angel-hands erewhile.
We may surmise, but all in vain,
  What met that upturned gaze,
Till spirit-free our eyes shall see
  What did his soul amaze.

Eye hath not seen, ear hath not heard,
  Nor can the heart conceive,
The joyousness awaiting those
  Who on the Lord believe.
To mansions in our Father's house
  Naught can on earth compare,
Lit by the Sun of Righteousness,
  No shadow enters there.

SWEET TWILIGHT STAR.

Thou heavenly star ! at day's decline
So sweetly calm thy silvery shine—
Art thou an Eden for the Blest
Where wearied ones of earth find rest ?

My cherub babe hath taken wings
And songs—the Sweet !—with angels sings.
But, Oh ! I miss my precious one,
A cloudlet dims my earthly sun.

I miss her—every star at even
Reminds me of the loved in heaven.
But thou, far lovelier than the rest,
Methinks her tiny feet have prest.

Methinks the music of thy sphere
Enhanced by Baby's tones so dear !
Methinks the sweetness of thy light
Enhanced by Baby's eyes so bright !

Sweet Twilight Star ! thy gentle beams
Send to my spirit soothing dreams—
Cast round my soul a soothing spell ;
I feel "He doeth all things well."

COMING AND GOING.

Coming and going, coming and going,
  Coming and going as each winged moment flies.
Sowing and reaping, waking and sleeping,
  The infant is born and the hoary man dies.

Coming and going, coming and going,
  No turning, no halting, no rest by the way.
Toiling and hoping, through the darksome path groping,
  To-morrow is garnered what blossoms to-day.

Coming and going, coming and going,
  Up and down the hard steeps of the journey of life.
The youth, once so cheery, growing old, weak and weary,
  Foot-sore and head bowed with the burden and strife.

Coming and going, coming and going,
  Like the ebbing and flowing of the deep's restless waves.
Living and dying, sinning and sighing,
  Till the "last trump" shall summon the dead from
    their graves.

Coming and going, coming and going,
  Till the angel shall stand on the sea and the shore,
" And by Him that liveth shall swear time now ceaseth,"
  And coming and going shall never be more.

THE OLD HOMESTEAD.

[Written after my father's death, and before leaving his house.]

———

These walls my father built in manhood's morn,
And here he lived, and thought, and worked, and died,
And all around is hallowed by his touch.
The house itself, each window, wall and door,
Each piece of furniture, each table, chair,
Each bureau, sofa, every household thing,
Was his so long it seems almost a part
Of his dear self. And when I look without
And see his office, barn and sheds—the well
Whose waters cool so oft he drew and drank
(And taught his children 'twas the drink God gave
To quench their thirst, and therefore should suffice);
The pleasant yards with all their treasured shrubs,
The garden, orchard, with their precious fruits,
Of which he took such care, with his own hand
Nursing each root and sprout, and pruning where
He saw 'twas needful to lop off or prop,
And then in harvest gathered all their store,
And safely garnered it for winter use.
I cannot help but feel he still is here
And cares for all as he was wont to do.
And when we part with aught, or take away
That which was his, I feel as though 'twere wrong,
And we were wrenching from his hand his own.
And then his books he pondered o'er so much !
His Bible first, then books professional
And those of science, history and lore,
With margin marked on almost every page

Where something struck his mind as worthy note,
Showing us where his eyes had looked, and so
Had deeply drank the thoughts therein expressed.
And then the lectures that he wrote, and maps
He drew, whereby to demonstrate his thought
More clear, as he delivered them before
Societies and schools, and otherwhere,
To benefit the minds of youth and age.
And when I call to mind his daily prayers
As bowed he, worshiping before God's Throne—
Oh, how all, then, doth doubly seem to speak,
And tell us how his eighty years of life,
With all their joys and sorrows, lights and shades,
Were spent in busy thought and worthy deeds,
Improving every moment as it passed
In the best way that wisdom did direct ;
And setting us, his children, left behind,
Example worth far more than shining gold
Or precious stones.

        And when at morning time
I go into his lonely room to plead
Forgiveness for my sins, and blessings crave
As he was wont, I think I feel him near,
And he doth almost seem to say, " Amen."
And now to know, O Heaven ! that I must leave
This hallowed spot for aye—that strangers here,
Beneath this roof, within these walls shall dwell,
And call what was my father's for so long
Their own.

        To give into their hands the keys
By which he held possession, now no more
To do his bidding, keeping all within
Safe from the spoiler, and admitting friends
As welcome guests, to social chat and treat
Of all the best his table could afford
And house did offer for so many years.
To think that other voices, glad or gay,

Shall ring through all these rooms, and ours no more !
To think that others not akin, and strange,
Shall sit beside what was my father's hearth
And work and talk, not caring for him gone !
And in *his* room by night shall rest, and sleep,
And pray, perchance, upon the self-same spot
Which his bent knee had marked, with head bowed low,
And eye in pleading supplication raised !
And it may be that in some future day
Shall there, like him, be chilled, and sink in death
While angels waft the spirit to its God.
Or, it may be, it will be occupied
By one forgetful of his dues to God,
Who ne'er will kneel repentant, and with tears
Confess before his Maker all his sins,
And pray for his redemption, and His aid
To help him to resist the tempter's wiles,
And strengthen him to do his part in life
In such a way as shall acceptance meet
With Him who is all power and perfectness.
And then this room, in which I now indite
My thoughts so sad, speaking my poor heart's grief—
This room, around whose board he thrice each day
Did sit with his whole household, and did crave
God's blessings on the bounty He supplied
(Of which with thankful heart each then partook) ;
And when was ended the repast, at morn,
He read to listening ears the sacred page ;
Then closing, bowed before the altar which
In days long past he reared and still kept bright
With heavenly fire until the sickness came
Which forced my father to yield up, alas !
That daily boon, and keep his bed till death.
And then the room adjoining, which we call
The sitting-room, athrough whose windows shines
The pleasant sunlight ! where so oft have met
Dear friends, with happy hearts, who daily held
Sweet converse round its cheerful, homelike hearth,

And yet wherein have on their couches lain
Four of our household band in sickness dire
(With but few years between each solemn call),
From whence the angels took them—sacred room !
Then there's the hall familiar, parlor, too,
Where many guests, invited, came and whiled
Away the hours in pleasant chat, or joined
In pleasures of the gayer, livelier sort ;
And, too, the chambers where we children slept—
So full of comforts.   Oh, how dear to me
Is each and every room and thing therein !
Most dear and sacred since they all were his.
And can I leave ye, never more to come
And see my father here, and hear his voice
In tones of welcome to me !   Can I say
Farewell to each—farewell to all ?   Farewell !
I must ! and pray, " God help me !" and Thou wilt,
For Thou dost see and pity.   Help me, God.

AUTUMN LEAVES.

———

Gorgeous leaves of Autumn,
  Falling thick as dew !
Carpeting the earth here
  With every brilliant hue !
For you the artist-painter
  Hides his feeble brush !
Beside your dyes his colors fade
  To such a sickly blush !

Gorgeous leaves of Autumn !
  All the wood's ablaze !
You shame earth's proudest painter
  To lay aside his bays !
Vieing with the rainbow
  And the sunset fire !
For the Hand that painted you
  Paints the Heavens Higher !

Gorgeous leaves of Autumn !
  When our Fall has come
May we be as lovely
  In our other Home !
There, in brightest clothing,
  May our spirits shine
As beautifully wrought upon
  By artist-hand Divine.

THANKLESSNESS.

How forgetful we are
  In our follies and prides,
To offer up thanks
  For the good God provides.
We take what our Father bestows
  As our right,
Leaving our worthlessness
  Quite out of sight.

Poor, puny creatures,
  With nothing our own—
Being and doing
  By His strength alone,
Walking as heedless
  And thankless each hour
As though were created
  All things by our power.

Oh, man should be humble,
  Excepting in this—
That Thou, Dearest Saviour,
  May be his if he wis.
The Christian may bow low,
  Then rise from his knee
Lamenting his sin so,
  But glorying in Thee.

Oh, thou Unrepentant!
  That *thou* shouldst be proud!
Hide, hide thee like Adam—
  Of the leaves weave a shroud

To veil thy pollution
　From eyes that can scan.
Save only the Christian
　Should be prized a true man.

Save only the Christian
　Should dare to arise
And walk on the earth
　With his head tow'rd the skies.
The soul that is filthy
　Will grovel in mire,
As like clings to like
　And the slave to his hire !

CREATION TEACHES WONDROUS SONGS.

From mountain grand
  To little hill,
From Ocean vast
  To rippling rill,
From largest tree
  To tiniest flower,
From sun to star,
  From dew to shower,
From frozen sea
  To snowy wreath,
From howling blast
  To zephyr breath,
From Summer heat
  And noonday light
To Winter cold
  And black midnight,
From thunder roll
  To insect hum,
From shout of joy
  To sorrow dumb,
From table-land
  To valley deep—
Beneath whose sand
  Old ages sleep,
From hugest rock to silicate,
  From thinking man to radiate,
From Heaven above, from earth below—
  All with poetic beauty glow,
And we with thankful lips should sing
  Sweet praise to the Creative King.

JESUS LOVING, ALL-FORGIVING.

Jesus Loving, all-forgiving,
    Zone me with protecting arm !
Guide my spirit upward striving,
    And my tempter, Doubt disarm.

Jesus Loving, hear my story !
    In this dark my courage dies,
And the glimpses of Thy Glory
    Fade before my spirit-eyes.

Reach I forward, blindly groping,
    Falt'ring, stumbling in the way.
Always praying, always hoping,
    Looking for the lighter day.

Reach I upward, vainly trying
    That thy vesture I may touch ;
And I weary of my crying,
    And my soul faints overmuch.

Reach I outward, hither, thither,
    Seeking Thy dear Hand to find,
But my hopes within me wither,
    And I seem to grow more blind.

Jesus Loving, all-forgiving,
    Let Thy Voice my spirit hear !
Gently hush my spirit grieving,
    Make my Better pathway clear.

Jesus Loving, all-forgiving,
  Lead me to the Brighter Clime !
With the choral angels living
  May I hymn Thy Love sublime.

Oh, I know I'm all unworthy,
  Clothed in garment of the dust !
But my pleadings, Lord, must stir Thee
  To renew my hope and trust.

Oh, I know I'm bold in striving
  E'er to join the angel-choir !
Jesus Loving, all-forgiving,
  Through Thee only I aspire !

Of myself I'm less than nothing,
  In Thy strength I all may do.
Jesus Loving, all-forgiving,
  Thou canst make *me* angel, too.

Thou canst wash me in a fountain
  That will make my spirit white !
Thou canst lift me to the mountain
  That Thy Glory maketh light !

Thou my palsied lips can open
  In a song of seraphim !
Jesus Loving, I will hope on,
  Singing here my feeble hymn !

THE CHICAGO FIRE.

Please here permit us to rehearse,
Or read a tale done up in verse,
Of the star-city—so confest—
Of the star-city of the West.
'Twas mostly written while she lay
In ruins, as 'twere her Judgment Day—
A smoking, smould'ring, blacken'd mass—
Hearing of which we wept, alas !
Over the startling, woful tale
That made each human face turn pale,
And in our pity did indite
Some thoughts we here present to-night.
If the word-picture prove too faint
Bethink you it was hard to paint
A scene so *awful*, *sad* and *grand*,
Except 'twere done by angel's hand.
Within the scroll that *then* we penned,
Fancy, perchance, with fact may blend.
But one short prayer therein seems willed,
To be a prophesy fulfilled,
For wondrous deeds are being wrought
Almost surpassing hope or thought ;
And old Aladdin's famous light,
Chicago *now* casts out of sight—
Making us almost think 'twas so—
That story of the "Long Ago."

Now, since you Grantites "have the day,"
In everything can have your way—
Since you our Country firm enfold
In your embrace with strength to hold,

You can afford that speech be free,
Though *one should* with you disagree.
At least, to woman you may yield
The flow of tongue—her rightful shield.
If, therefore, in our verse you find
Words which you deem unwise, unkind,
Please pardon give us, for we've known
Some sorrows that have made us moan.
Our countrymen's sharp lash we've felt,
All undeserved, severely dealt.
The gash it cut was deep and sore—
The wound is not yet quite healed o'er,
For painful mem'ries, sad bequest
Of that dark time, oft fill our breast,
While unforgiving feelings rise
And bitter tear-drops dim our eyes.
In eighteen hundred sixty-one,
Clouds dimmed the sky, the air was dun,
For o'er our land War's tocsin rang
And warriors from the earth upsprang,
Till brother spilled his brother's blood
Cain-like before the face of God.
Opposed to War—" States' Rights " his creed—
Our husband saw his Country bleed ;
And in the name of " Liberty,"
Thinking expression still was free,
He dared some protests wise to make—
They did not " burn him at the stake,"
But for this crime long months was barred
In prison walls our lawful lord,
And we were racked with dreadful fear
He'd come no more our home to cheer.
With bleeding heart we wielded then
Our captive husband's guileless pen.
For we were left with children three,
Weeping around our parent knee
With mouths in want of daily bread
Which by our labors must be fed.

An editress we thus became
Forced by our need to earn the name,
Though angry threat and jeering word
Cast on us thick, the while, we heard.
Yet *some* there were who cheered us on
With blessings till our task was done.
Rememb'ring which, for each kind friend
A daily prayer to Heaven we send.
To "Woman's Rights" committed then,
To use her "talents," "one" or "ten,"
The which God gave her—we have quite,
At last, become its Neophyte.
And now with head, and heart, and hand,
Aspire to *join* that noble band
Which *since* has multiplied so fast
Some men among you look aghast,
Lest *woman yet* should turn the *tide*
And hold the reins while *they* must ride.
In other words, lest *she* should rule,
And *they* be taught in woman's school
To drudge in kitchens, cook and scrub,
And sweat for hours before the "tub,"
Teach for half-pay—or stitch till death—
Till pale consumption saps the breath—
Or deck their persons debonair,
Weak slaves to fashion—false as fair,
While she will vote, or strut at ease,
Or do whatever else she please.
Indeed, we think *some* are afraid
She'll turn the scales so, *they'll* be made
To bear *her* curse since Eden's hour,
And *motherhood* will be *their* dower.
But of *this last* there seems a doubt
If things *can* be *so* turned about.
Should such befall them, sure it is,
They'd shirk "responsibilities,"
Until a baby's darling face
Our lonely homes would seldom grace,

And earth become a desert wild
With only here and there a child.

Fire ! Fire ! hark that cry
As the wind goes rushing by—
Fire ! Fire ! It comes nearer !
Fire ! Fire ! It comes clearer !
Fire ! Fire ! Don't you hear, sir ?
And the gale is growing fiercer !
See ! that flame there, forking ! leaping !
And the storm-wind still increasing !
Fire ! Fire ! upward darting !
All the shadows skyward parting !
Forward shooting ! broader growing !
Like a heated furnace glowing.
Fire ! Fire ! myriad voices
Cry it ! shout it ! till the noise is
Deaf'ning ! stunning ! woful ! wierdful !
And the glare is growing fearful !
And the people ! hither ! thither !
Wand'ring wild—they know not whither
Like a host with leader dying
From a conquering army flying.
Fast, the fireman's engines playing—
Not a jot the broad flames staying.
Hasten friend ! let's aid our brother,
We perchance may help to smother
The destroyer fast advancing
Like a furious steed come prancing.
Fire ! Fire ! hither ! yonder !
How so many flames I wonder !
Are incendiaries round us lurking
With their lighted torches working ?
Thick as snow-flakes see the sparks fly !
Crackling ! striking 'gainst the dark sky.
Helpful men, alas ! are wanted
By the danger not yet daunted,

From the city's every quarter
To push on with hose and water
With a skilful hand, unflinching—
All the city thereby drenching.
So, to quench the fiery torrent
(To the creeping flesh abhorrent),
Leaping, flowing far and wide
Like the belching lava-tide.
Fire ! Fire ! hissing ! glistering !
All the air grows hot and blistering !
Speeding ! spreading ! fiercer rolling !
Hear the church bells faster tolling !
Wind and fire with might are waging
War against us in their raging.
Like huge Afric lion, *roaring*,
All his deadly wrath outpouring
On his enemy illfated,
Ere his blood his maw has sated.
Or Niagara's deaf'ning flood
Sounding like the voice of God.
Fire ! Fire ! Farther ! Nigher !
Sweeping with destruction dire,
And the tumult, and the blazing
Eye is dazing—brain is crazing,
Till the soul is sick and swounding
From the dangers thick surrounding.
As when burnished armor flashing
Of the soldiery fencing, clashing,
And the musketry's loud rattle,
And the shrieks and din of battle,
Make earth tremble with the jarring,
And skies sicken at the warring.
Fire ! Fire ! Fire ! Fire !
Comes the sharp cry louder, higher,
Cutting through the hot air quicker,
As the flames grow faster, thicker—
And the city's short of water !
Gracious God ! we fear the slaughter !

Men, to save their pelf, fast toiling
In the scorching flames are broiling !
Men, to save their lives are flying !
Women, children, shrieking, crying !
Pushing ! rushing here and there,
Seeking safety everywhere.
Roofs are caving—walls are falling—
Useless *now* man's toiling, moiling,
Hundreds 'mid the ruins lying !
Hundreds in the streets are dying !
And the blast is wilder blowing !
And the flames like floods are flowing,
Wreathing ! seething ! smelting ! burning !
Onward scathing, never turning—
And the shrieking, praying, groaning,
And the cursing, weeping, moaning,
Thieves and murderers join the melée,
Come from far and near to waylay,
(Of the people shaking, quaking,
Quick advantage thereby taking),
Jostling, trampling, killing, plundering,
While the earth seems rending, sundering,
With the swaying, creaking, crashing,
Of the rolling, leaping, lashing,
Flames that lick the earth and air,
Nothing from their wrath to spare.
Swiftly, o'er wire telegraphic,
From the East to the Pacific
(Than an eagle flying faster),
Wings the news of the disaster.
Calling friends to lend assistance
'Gainst the *foe* that *scorns* resistance.
And the calling so far-reaching,
Thousands hear the cry beseeching ;
And, with noble impulse thrilling,
Men with ready hands and willing,
With their implements of might,
Come the fiery fiend to fight.

But the efforts superhuman
Of a many a hurrying carman,
With his iron-footed horse,
Thundering o'er the short'ning course,
As 'twere with the whirlwind's speed,
Answering the call of need,
Are in vain—the city's sources
Of her numerous water-courses,
Which had erst her want supplied,
By the monster flames are dried.
So, from hours to days, the fire,
Like a besom, sweeps in ire,
As an army vast, victorious,
Sweeps the field of foe inglorious ;
All within its pathway blighting,
Hurling ! felling ! crushing ! smiting !
Ard as down from Alpine chain,
Hurtling o'er the peopled plain,
Comes the avalanche with power,
In the unsuspecting hour
Came it, and no mortal hand
The destroyer may withstand ;
And as molten lava glowing
From volcanic crater flowing,
Shooting upward in its streaming
Lights the far skies with its gleaming,
So the spreading flames, updriven,
Seem to reach the floor of Heaven,
And for miles from dangerous site
Night is brightened by their light,
And a gloom o'er hearts and faces
Casts in distant, skylit places.

Oh, our Saviour ! Father holy !
To Thine aid we look now solely.
Bend Thine ear Lord ! hear our prayer !
Are we not still in Thy care ?

Help us! shield us! to us proving
Thou art still our God the loving.
We have sinned and are not worthy,
But forgive us of Thy mercy;
On weak man, too long relying,
Now to Thee we lift our crying.
Our forgetfulness, transgressing—
All our littleness confessing.
Thee our *only* helper owning,
In our sin and sorrow moaning,
With our eyelids red with weeping.
Lord! we bow to *Thee*, entreating,
With Thy potent, outstretched hand,
Quell the wind and quench the brand.
With our faces in the dust
Thus we pray, and thus we trust,
Thus we pray, hist! God be praised
For our eyes look up amazed.
See! the wind its course is changing!
Backward now the fire is ranging
O'er the path it swept so cruel
Finding left but little fuel.
O'er the late gay streets, now covered
With the embers not yet smothered.
O'er the dead ones that departed,
Murdered, crazed and broke n-hearted.
And, good God! the rain is falling!
Heaven! sure, did heed us calling.
Thank Thee! Thank Thee! Thou all glorious
O'er all elements victorious.
Thou hast spoken, and Thy Word
Wind, and flame, and wrath have heard;
But, alas! what havoc dire
Here is wrought by wind and fire.
Palace homes and marble halls
Rich with frescoed, gilded walls—
Regal courts, and parks for pleasure,
Stores of varied, costly treasure—

Temples, spires magnificent,
And the poor man's tenement—
Operas, theaters, studios splendid,
In the mass of ashes blended !
Keepsake sacred, gold and jewel,
All commingled with the fuel.
Note, and bank, and bond are burned,
And to worthless dust are turned.
And the bones of beings human,
Women, children, rich and poor man,
Who to death were madly hurried,
Part consumed, part charr'd, part buried,
In the smould'ring heaps are lying,
Seen by eye the waste surveying,
Till the soul, faint, sickened, saddened
By such scenes of woe is maddened.

Dear Chicago ! bowed so lowly !
Ruin came to thee not slowly.
Like a lightning stroke it took thee,
Like a thunderbolt it shook thee.
As by sword from the Almighty,
Thrust by hand with anger weighty,
Thou art felled, and groan in dust,
Knowing still that God is just.
So each sister city shaking,
Fears the Powers above are waking
To chastise *their* woful sinning,
Money-worship, greed of winning—
Pride and self-love, God-forgetting—
Wallowing in sins besetting.
And to purge with fire-ablution
Stenching sinks of rank pollution,
Suffered in their midst to flourish—
Such iniquities they nourish.

Poor Chicago ! Fire-doomed city !
Others, guilty, give thee pity !

All their hearts for thee are broken—
All their purses for thee open,
While they weep the tear of sorrow,
Wishing thee a brighter morrow.
But nor pelf, nor tears dropped·for thee,
Thy dear dead ones will restore thee,
Nor make whole thy maimed ones living !
Heal *them*, *Jesu !* Thou forgiving !
And, *dear Jesu !* soothe the grieving !
Turn their hearts to Thee, believing !
Come ! with Thy sweet consolation,
Comfort those in desolation.
Bride and bridegroom, husband, wife,
Here untimely reft of life.
Parent reft of son, of daughter,
By the dreadful fiery slaughter.
Children reft of father, mother,
Reft of sister, reft of brother. .
And the poor man reft of shelter,
Shield from want in storms of winter.
And the orphan homeless, friendless,
And the widow let Thy hand bless.
And the brain with shattered reason,
Pray restore in happy season.
And again shed down Thy blessing
On the site to thought distressing,
Raising soon o'er these remains,
Rare in beauty, homes and fanes
(With sweet peace and love indwelling,
From glad, grateful hearts upwelling);
Halls of science, seats of pleasure,
Where mirth trips in guileless measure ;
Greening parks with grottoes, fountains,
Mimic lakes, and groves, and mountains,
Flowering squâres, like Eden's garden,
With the fairest blossoms laden.
And upon the waste terrific
Start again rich marts of traffic.

For yet countless generations,
The commingling of all nations,
With their footsteps coming, going
Like the ocean's tidal flowing.
All that makes a city's greatness
Gather here in its completeness,
Till the people gaze in wonder,
On the city's *second* splendor—
On the city's *second* rising,
Phœnix-like in haste surprising,
Till is told in truthful story,
That Chicago's second glory
Far exceeds its former height
As the moon the stars in light.
Sad Chicago ! thy dark hour,
Thick with fury, wrought with power,
Scarce is equaled in its horror,
Since Sodoma and Gomorrah
Helpless writhed in seas of fire
Sent by God's avenging ire—
Heedless erst of Heaven's anger,
Rushing careless into danger,
Warned in vain by God's evangel
Till he sent destroying angel
Forth to blast with flaming sword
Cities hated of the Lord.

Fated city ! molten lying !
In thy need and anguish crying !
Though not wholly lost, dejected,
Thy deep woes are far reflected !
All are more or less affected
By the sweeping, swirling, surging,
Fast consuming, blasting, purging,
Of the fire-god's furious urging.
Almost *all* within the Nation,
Friend had in thee or relation,

Suffering from the sea of flame,
That in heaving billows came,
Till sweet Mercy, far off hearing
Sounds tumultuous in their nearing.
Tones in agony beseeching,
Past the brazen vault up-reaching,
Looked adown from happy portal,
On such woes of beings mortal ;
And with humble mien, low bowing,
Came with saddened aspect, wooing
God to hear thy piercing prayer
And from darker terrors spare.
Heaven heeding Mercy pleading,
While with tender bosom bleeding,
Quick commanded, "Peace ! Be still !"
And His mandate did fulfil.

Fallen city ! in thy anguish
Hast thou thought how others languish,
By our Northern hordes invaded,
Which with men and pelf thou aided !
Sister cities of the South,
Felled by belching cannon's mouth !
Felled by fire and sword and plunder,
Till Heaven shrank aback in wonder,
That a Christian people could
So despoil a sisterhood ?
Christian ! Peace and good-will meaning !
Charity for others' sinning !
Loving as thyself thy neighbor !
Giving of thy goods and labor
In compassion—without hire,
As in need he doth require.
Nation no more wroth with nation,
Yielding war a dire oblation !
Swords to spears and plowshares turning—
Such the teachings for our learning—

Such with Christian deeds inwrought,
Is the gospel Christ hath taught.

Yes, Chicago ! each fair city,
Far from guiltless, yields thee pity,
For the " Good " espy from Heaven
Suffering souls to anguish driven.
And come down with spirits loving,
Noble hearts to blest deeds moving—
For *God gives* to them permission
To depart from realms elysian
On such errand pure and holy
To the needy, sad and lowly,
Till each hill-top, plain and valley,
From our North and West land rally,
To restore, in part, thy losses,
Feeling *such* a glorious cause is.
Men with riches in abundance
Send thee share of their redundance.
Poor men laboring send assistance
From their *scanty daily* pittance.
Fair-browed children thy name lisping
Ope their guileless hands assisting,
While the widow's sad heart yearning
To aid somewhat sends her earning.
And thy terrors far resounding
O'er Atlantic cable sounding,
Eastern nations haste to send thee
Kindly aid from smiling plenty,
Darksome days, mayhap, recalling
O'er their homes and altars falling,
When *their* stricken ones sad wailing,
Reached *thy* ear not unavailing—
And the *South*, so long bowed weeping,
On thee " coals of fire " is heaping,
Sorrow for thy throes now nursing,
Sending blessing for thy cursing—
Thy deep wrongs to her forgiving,

Thinking only of thy grieving—
Wishing she had greater power
To assist in thy sad hour.
In this blesséd truth believing
"Better giving than receiving."
"As she would be done by, doing."
This best, Christian way pursuing—
Taught in War's baptismal flood
Kindness is akin to God.
Though thy woes can but remind her
Of the dark days left behind her.

Chiefest Prairie city ! *lately*
In thy *wealth* and *power* so stately !
Grown with speed beyond compare
Up to giant height and " air,"
Looking down with queenly pride.
On the cities at thy side—
Mirror'd on the broad lake's waters,
Fairest of our Western daughters—
Standing *yesterweek* in splendor—
Crowned " Queen City " in thy grandeur,
Of thy throne secure *then* seeming,
Of thy doom *then* little dreaming ;
" *All* is well," thy watchmen crying
In back lanes and byways spying.
Now by devastation dire
Thou look'st one vast funeral pyre !
Or a monster holocaust
Scattered o'er the dismal waste,
Where, with sacrilegious tread
Men survey thy ashy bed.
Wond'ring at the conflagration
That could bring *such* desolation.

City ! clad in mourning vesture,
Shrunken, shrivelled in thy stature—

Fallen like a meteor spent—
While we o'er thy fate lament
In thy sorrow and thy need—
This the writing that we read.
Heed the lesson then we pray us,
God needs not *War's* hand to slay us.
When *His* brow is bent in ire
Then His chariot rolls in fire !
When *He* seeks earth's wrongs to right them,
Or in vengeance He would smite them—
He is able to accomplish
All His purposes, and vanquish
All man's striving and upbraiding,
Though the Powers below were aiding
To oppose His mighty arm
Which such wonders doth perform.
He alone can still the blowing
Of the wind in wild wrath going !
He alone can stem the rising
Of the flames in anger hissing ;
He alone can send the water
That shall stay the burning slaughter ;
He alone is God the chastening,
In our anguish comfort hastening ;
He alone is God the loving,
By our sorrow, our faith-proving ;
He alone, with scarce a breathing
Life to senseless clay bequeathing,
With His watchful eye surveying,
Rolling spheres His word obeying,
Needeth never strength to borrow
From this puny world of sorrow ;
He alone is God through all—
God is great, and *man* is small.
And though often He pursueth
Sinners, and by force subdueth
Whom nor love nor warning moveth,

Yet, since God and Christ are one
(In the Father dwells the Son),
"Mercy" in the eternal scales
"Justice" lifts, and "Love" prevails.
So of Love we'll speak awhile,
Craving Heaven's approving smile.
Love! the nectar of the chalice
Or in hut, or hall, or palace;
Love! the everflowing fountain,
Issued forth from Calvary's mountain.
Love! the manna at the board,
Where we feed on Christ the Lord.
Love! pure Love! and not the passion
Falsely so called by world fashion
(Not the sensual, sordid feeling
Proved by jealousy, revealing
Rivalries and *hates*, endangering
Life from bold or secret chambering,
Many to perdition leading,
Wisdom's cry to "turn" unheeding);
But Love perfect, undefiled,
Which o'er Eden's garden smiled
Ere the serpent *Eve* beguiled,
And *she*, clev'rest, Adam wiled
(Life from lowest type ascending,
Woman last and highest ending),
Wrath of Love upon them bringing,
For their primal, wanton sinning,
So that the cherubic warden
Drove them out from Eden's garden.
Love! for thought the loftiest theme!
Love! the guileless' purest dream!
Love! the poet's sweetest song!
Love! round which *all virtues* throng!
Love! the beautiful in feature!
Earth's and Heaven's fairest creature!
Love! "the Christian charity,"
With us "such a rarity."

Love ! the source of *every* blessing,
Holding *all* that's worth possessing—
Giving help all bountiful,
From the storehouse plentiful,
To God's children in their need,
Never questioning their creed ;
Giving money, food and raiment,
Suing ne'er for note or payment ;
Giving sympathy and pity
To a stricken, sorrowing city
By the flames so devastated—
That we call her the " Ill-fated,"
Until Mercy, Love's handmaiden,
To her rescue comes full laden
With a largess from each nation,
That to Love doth yield oblation ;
To us *doubting sinners* telling
There is much of God indwelling
In the hearts of many mortals
In these mammon-loving portals.
Love ! thou Purest ! Highest ! Holiest !
Oftentimes in garb the lowliest,
Thou dost bring the Heav'ns so near
That they touch this fallen sphere,
Dropping here and there some kisses
(Yielding earth some little blisses)
Through the clouds with silver lining,
Like the sun, perennial shining,
Till from out her ill-starred bosom
Springeth many a blessed blossom,
Something like the " Ròse of Sharon,"
Or the budding " Rod of Aaron "
Flinging its sweet incense up
From its golden-petaled cup—
On the air around it leaving
Perfume meet for angels' breathing—
Tempting saints to round us gather,
Linking Heaven and earth together—

For if *pure* Love in us dwell
We're far nearer Heaven than Hell.
"God is love," and where Love reigneth
Mercy for us Heaven obtaineth.
If pure love doth permeate us
It doth with the angels mate us,
For the soul from its imprison
To the Hights shall then have risen,
And the grand millennial morn
Of its blisses shall be born.
Love, thou Pearl! thou Priceless Treasure!
Richest Boon, surpassing measure!
Love! thou Noblest, Tenderest, Dearest!
Thy embrace all good inspherest!
As Immensity, thou'rt boundless!
As Eternity, thou'rt endless!
'Tis Infinity alone
Can Thy heighth and depth enzone;
Love! of Thee the seraphim
Weave their grandest, sweetest hymn,
And the music-strain enthrills
All the Empyrean Hills.
'Twas of Thee the "stars of morning"
Sang when earth and skies were forming,
Keeping time in circling motion
To the chant in their devotion;
And the whirling spheres through ether
Chime in song of Thee together;
And through the Eternal Days
Ransomed souls will sound Thy praise,
For Thou cam'st in fleshly guise
Down to bleed—man's sacrifice.
Love! thou sunburst of the soul
Where loud hallelujahs roll!
Love! Thou Sun of Righteousness,
Worlds on worlds *Thee* God, confess,
And 'tis Thy effulgence bright
Orbs the countless·stars with light;

While the loftiest hights etern
With Thy radiant glory burn,
And where Thou dost shed no beam
Darkest hell doth reign supreme.
Love ! we love Thee, Thou Divine !
Low we bow before Thy shrine,
Humbly, thankfully adoring,
All our soul to Thee outporing,
Praying that Thy spirit-teaching
Be not so beyond our reaching,
That Thou give us soulful measure
Of Thee, Peerless, Priceless Treasure !
Love ! the sunshine of Thy Being
Is the smile of the All-Seeing,
And the ecstacy of bliss
Is the rapture of thy kiss.
Love ! the Perfect—Father, Son,
Holy Spirit—Three in One—
May we *ever*, *ever* sing
Of Thy Glory, Gracious King,
Sing of it in gardens vernal
While we roam through realms eternal.

Oh, there will ever, ever roll,
Resounding o'er each starry pole,
Growing in sweeter, grander strain
The gladsome song that love doth reign.
And souls will ever, ever trace
Throughout the realms of boundless space
The sparks of Love's ecstatic fire
Emitted by th' enraptured choir
That sings the song and waves the palm
Before the loving, great " I Am."

Chicago ! in thy burning flood
'Twas Love wept o'er thee tears of blood,
And then sent forth a kindly power
To aid thee in thy darkened hour ;

Assisting so that now we gaze
On marvels that our eyes amaze,
Till we, like Sheba's queen of old,
Exclaim, "The half hath not been told."
And if to-night we bring to mind
The time when Love appeared unkind,
Remember Mercy still keeps troth
With Love's beloved, tho' Heaven seemed wroth.
And though dire chast'nings have been given
To thee, as by offended Heaven,
Look up—thy wondrous power behold !
The will, ability, and gold,
Poured out of Love's o'erflowing trust
To raise thy city from the dust,
Till in new beauty now she glows,
Like blushing bride or new-blown rose ;
Till adamantine walls arise,
Like Babel's, towering to the skies ;
And gilded domes, and burnished spires,
Glitt'ring as with electric fires,
Seeming almost to reach the stars
And pierce beyon l High Heaven's bars,
Astound us much that man could rear
Such architraves in one short year !
While, tireless still, with railroad speed,
From blackened earth new walls proceed
Each day, more lofty and more grand,
As if 'twere done by magic wand—
Soon leaving not a trace to tell
What fate Chicago late befell.
Let then thy thanks an incense meet
Reach daily to Love's mercy-seat,
And humble, fervent prayers arise
Like morn and evening sacrifice.
So, guarded by Love's shelt'ring wing,
Thou shalt move forward prospering,
And growing greater on through ages,
Leave written on historic pages

Proud records of thy glorious days
Encrowned by Song's immortal lays ; .
While other cities, far and near,
Catch at thy watchword, and revere
Thy guardian Power from above,
Acknowledging that " God is Love."

A few more words, friends, in your ear,
If you have patience still to hear.
Scarce has Chicago's tale been wrote
Ere comes another wailing note,
Flying along the quivering air
Like the shriekings of despair—
The Athens of America
In part in ashes lies to-day.
Her songs of joy are now unsung,
Her " harp is on the willows hung."
Her sacred fanes and ancient spires
Lie molten by the liquid fires ;
Burned are her richest marts of trade ;
Her merchant princes have been made
To sit in sackcloth, humbled, dumb,
Where the Destroyer's feet have come.
Again the tear of sorrow flows
Over a stricken city's woes.
And we are made to read again
Hieroglyphic signs more plain
Than was the writing on the walls
Of proud Belshazzar's palace halls—
Telling the world man's impotence
When God let's loose the elements.
Again kind hearts are made to bleed,
And with our Heavenly Father plead
To pity show, and haste to bless
Another city in distress ;
Her pleasant walls once more to raise
Surpassing those of other days ;

While *she*, in heartfelt thankfulness,
Her Chast'ner's goodness shall confess
And show the world in lines of light
How Justice bends in Mercy's sight. ⹁
Alas ! the flames *have* cast their sombre palls
Over two splendid cities, but there falls
A darker shadow on our Western shore—
The wise philanthropist is here no more ;
His spirit has ascended to the van
Of those who worked and died from love of man.
And, shame ! the men he wrought for drove the dart
That clave the tendrils of his broken heart.
Greeley "the Good" will stand a shining name
Written in gold high on the scroll of fame.
For though in former years he erred (we thought),
His noble deeds can never be forgot.
His "clasping hands across the bloody chasm"
Anointed him with Love's eternal chrism.
And South and North, and East and West will mourn
The palsied tongue and frame in Death's cold bourne,
While monumental iron, bronze or stone,
For perpetuity, *he* needeth none.

THE DYING PAUPER.

Hark ye, the night-wind !
  Low sighing, sighing
Over the lone couch
  Of a poor creature dying !
No one to mourn for her
  Or wipe the tear starting—
None but the night-wind
  To kiss her at parting.

Long time the life-blood
  In her young breast was drying ;
Heart-sick—with coldness chilled—
  Worn out with crying.
No one to comfort her
  With the milk of love flowing—
None but the night-wind
  To sigh for her, going.

Hush ye ! the last breath
  From the frail one is fleeing—
Life hath forsaken
  The poor blighted being.
No one to softly press
  The eyelids' last closing—
None but the night-wind
  To watch her reposing.

Soon in the church-yard
  Her form will lie sleeping—
No one will care to know
  Of her soul's keeping.

None but the night-wind saw
  Her angel-wing'd spirit
Soar through the ether blue,
  Bliss to inherit.

So those despised of us
  Short-sighted mortals
May reach beyond us, up
  Through heaven's portals.
Christ judgeth not like man—
  He sees their sinning,
All their temptations, too,
  From the beginning.

He sifts the chaff from wheat,
  Knows how they've suffered—
Striving for work or aid,
  No kindness proffered.
His blood can cleanse from filth
  That here has stained them—
Trials, temptations may
  Heaven have gained them.

Oh, earth has many sad,
  Weary and wasting,
Struggling for breath of life,
  Naught of joy tasting;
But there's a Home for them
  Over the River—
There the freed soul shall fly
  Back to its Giver.

AUTUMN'S SOUGHING WINDS.

The soughing winds of Autumn,
　How saddening is their wail!
As if cries of weeping mourners
　Came on the sighing gale!

As if the groans of millions,
　In passion and despair,
Through the other seasons gathered,
　Freighted the Autumn air!

As if the shadowy armies
　Of souls of the unblest
Were rushing wild through ether
　In the burden of unrest!

As if a myriad voices
　Pierced through the glowering skies,
Plainting of deeper ills to man
　Than earth's lost Paradise!

As if all things in Nature
　Send forth a woful moan,
Feeling dire retribution
　Falls not on flesh alone!

As if lost spirits wailing
　In Purgatorial fires
Had somehow made these doleful blasts
　Their telegraphic wires!

As if the conscience writing
  With sense of guilt and shame
Was shrieking to the frenzied brain
  Its crimes in words of flame !

As if a world of warriors,
  With battle-conflict red,
Were tramping nearer, nearer,
  O'er the bodies of the dead !

The soughing winds of Autumn,
  With suicidal breath,
How to the sensate mind they speak
  Of sorrow, sin, and death !

THE ADIRONDACKS.

I've seen the "Glory of the hills," the Adirondack chain,
I floated by them on the lake, our beautiful Champlain;
'Twas in this fair autumnal time of rich prismatic dyes,
And never such a sight before of beauty met my eyes!

Point after point in light and shade along the mountain
    range,
Hill after hill with colors flecked, in size and shape a
    change!
Such warp and woof of regal garb wove by the Al-
    mighty's Hand
No beauteous queen hath e'er enrobed this side of Eden-
    land!

The leafy crowns that deck their brows all kingly crowns
    surpass,
With ruby, emerald, amethyst, and topaz hues.   Alas!
Why thus do I attempt to paint their more than marvel-
    ous sheen?
The "Glory of the hills," dear Lord, I thank thee I have
    seen!
        October 23, 1871.

WHAT ARE THE OCEAN WAVES DOING.

What ! oh, what are the ocean waves doing—
Fretting and fuming, or tenderly wooing ?
Are they raging, or sportively playing—
Hither and thither swinging and swaying ?
Or are they praising in rolling numbers—
Waking the sea-god from dreamy slumbers ?
Or are they wafting their incense prayer
To the Throne round which crowned angels are ?
Or are they chanting a requiem grand
O'er the loved who have joined the seraphim band !
Or do they raise sad voices weeping
O'er the early dead in their bosom sleeping ?
Or are they sighing for wrecks ashore
That shall never dance o'er their surges more ?
Or do they o'er sinners sorrowing moan
Who die unrepentant with none to atone ?
Or are they wailing 'neath the wild wind's fierce lashing,
Roaring and surging, with thunderbolts clashing,
Till the seaman's strength fails 'mid the fury and strife,
And the sailor bold quails at the scene with death rife,
And in the ship's wake horrid sea monsters follow
With ravenous jaws far open to swallow
The dying and dead from the creaking ship dashed,
By the mountainous billows that the proud vessel crashed.
Or are they striving against One who reigns,
Writhing and heaving to loosen their chains !
Boiling and foaming and cleaving the air,
Cursing their bounds with the strength of despair !
Or are the winds stilled, and their breasts softly heaving,

While the palace-like bark through their blue tips is
　　cleaving
(As safe as if sweet angels stood at the helm,
Letting a storm ne'er its fair deck o'erwhelm),
Gliding in peace o'er the beautiful sea,
Or dancing its waves as they frolic in glee;
While the rover a song from his glad heart is singing,
As o'er its glass smoothly his way he is winging,
To scenes that are new, or to home-scenes and places
Where his soul shall be charmed, and his eye see loved
　　faces.
Oh, what—tell me, what are the ocean waves doing?
To danger and death they are ever awooing!

THE OLD YEAR, 1872.

The old year has gasped out the last gasp of death,
The young year is breathing of life the first breath;
The old year has left us with heirship of hope
And strength in the battle with evil to cope.

The young year has brought what—kept in store until
　　now?
Whether promise fulfilled, or the heart's broken vow,
Whether life with its thorns intermingled with roses,
Or *death* shall be ours—who can tell till it closes?

TO COUSIN MAY C———N.

So, May, you are " thirty " and not married yet,
"An asthmatic, old banker you'd take, could you get;"
For the lawful name wife and a pretty long purse
You're willing, the while, to be sold for a nurse.

Ah, May, you are getting you 're pay for the crime
Of the cruel heart-breakings you've done in your time;
Your heart must have grown very sordid and cold,
Or you'd never be willing to marry for gold.

But then you are " thirty," you say, and you fear
You'll die a " forsooken " old maid; so, my dear,
An old, asthmatic husband you prefer to the sin
Of woful old maidenhood....then there's the " tin."

Oh, well, I can't blame you, for 't is a disgrace—
Though I really don't like so to say to your face—
But 't is a disgrace none can ever o'erlook
For a woman from nobody's ribs to be took.

Though if you're but thirty, you're foolish to fret,
To meet with you're Adam there's time enough yet;
I look for mine daily, I'm sure he's alive,
I'm in nowise discouraged, though I'm most thirty-
     five.

This and a greater part of the following pieces were written before the war.

SING ON, SWEET RILL.

Sing on, sweet rippling rill,   .
  Thou mind'st me of the hours
When, in a cot behind a hill,
By such another rippling rill,
  I strewed life's rosy flowers.

Flow on, sweet wavelet, flow;
  I bathe my brow in thee,
As I was wont to, long ago,
In such a wavelet that did flow
  When I from care was free.

Glide on, sweet streamlet, glide,
  Beneath pale moon and star;
Thou 'rt like a streamlet when a bride
I roved by, happy by his side,
  Now gone to realms afar.

THE LITTLE BEGGAR BOY.

" Lady, I am cold and hungry,
  Mother's sick and very poor,
And of bread there's not a mouthful,
  Nor of meat, inside our door.

" Two whole days we've tasted nothing,
  For we'd not a cent to buy,
And I hated to go begging,
  But I can't have mother die.

" Mother used to go out washing
  After father died, and leave
Me and sister, all so lonely,
  Through her absent hours to grieve.

" But she bought us food and clothing
  With the pittance that she earned;
Now, in pain, she lies a moaning,
  And the fagots lowly burned.

" Little sister sits a weeping,
  In the corner of the room—
I'm afraid she'll freeze and starve there,
  In our cold and scanty home!

" Please, kind lady, give us something,
  If 't is but a crust of bread,
And a sixpence to buy fuel,
  Or my mother will be dead.

' And my almost baby sister—
   Oh, she is so very dear;
I can never live to see her
   Stretched upon the funeral bier!

" True, I'm now a little beggar,
   But if God will let me live,
And my mother, and my sister,
   I'll repay the gifts you give.

" Father said when he was dying,
   God would guard us if we prayed;
And my mother has us, kneeling,
   Ask of Him ' our daily bread.'

" But I think He does not hear us,
   For he seems so far away—
And we've kept a growing poorer,
   And more hungry every day."

To these touching words I listened,
   Then I donned my cloak and hood,
And I followed the boy-pleader
   To the border of a wood.

There, within a leaky hovel,
   Scarce a mile from my own door,
Lived, or rather barely lingered,
   Those described so very poor.

True, but faint, was traced the picture
   Of those human beings' fare;
But God heard the boy's petition,
   And that suffering mother's prayer.

Food and clothing, quick, He sent them,
   And the fagot blazed once more

On their lonely hearth; for kind hearts
Lent a hand to aid the poor.

And with kindly care and nursing,
That boy's mother health regained;
And his little, loving sister
Weeps no more with hunger pained.

Ah, my friends, how little know we
Of the scenes of want so near;
List the beggar's plaintive story,
Ladies, with a pitying ear.

Let us as a band of sisters
Help to lighten their distress—
Woman in her sphere of kindness
Many wrongs may yet redress.

Soothing words and kind endeavors
Is the glory of her brow;
At the fireside, not the forum,
Woman's worth will fairest glow.

* * * *

Childless wives and maiden ladies,
Who have time and wealth to spare,
Earth has plenty of God's children
Worthy of your goods to share.

Little, hungry, barefoot beggars,
With hearts true and warm and brave,
Like this noble little fellow,
From destruction you might save.

And with teachings true and tender
Rear them to respect our cries,

For, perchance, our legislators
   From their ranks may yet arise.

So, that in the good time coming,
   We, for " rights," no more shall sue,
For, like men of worth and wisdom,
   They shall give us woman's due.

That poor boy, so lately starving,
   Shiv'ring with the cold intense,
As he stood upon our door-sill,
   Has a soul worth more than pence.

Money could not buy his spirit,
   Though his body it might feed,
For his mind was stamped with honor,
   Though his frame was shrunk with need.

So, my sisters, from the quarry
   Of the poor we yet may hew
Men to be our legislators,
   Who will give us woman's due.

'T IS SWEET.

'T is sweet to have some one to love thee;
   Through the oft-changing scenes of this life,
'T is bliss to know one loved would shield thee,
   Though darkness and dangers were rife.

'T is sweet to have some one to love thee;
   When pleasure-beams brighten the day,
'T is bliss to have one whom thou prizest
   Walk with thee the roseate way.

'T is sweet to have some one to love thee;
  When thy sorrow-brimmed cup overflows,
When thy head droopeth wearily downward,
  'Tis bliss on his breast to repose.

'T is sweet to have some one to love thee;
  Should evil report mar thy fame,
'T is bliss to know one would stand by thee,
  Though all others spurn thee and blame.

'T is sweet to have some one to love thee;
  When Death lays thee low on the bier,
'T is bliss to know one's lips will murmur
  Another were never so dear.

'T is sweet to have some one to love thee;
  When thy spirit has soared to the skies,
'T is bliss to know one heart will miss thee,
  And tears damp the grave from his eyes.

Nov., 1858.

THE ORPHAN BOY.

A Story in Verse.

The wind was very sharp and chill,
  And blowing with its might,
And every thing that shelter had
  Had sought it for the night,
When, shiv'ring, came unto our door,
  With feet all red and bare,
And tattered clothes, and drops of rain
  Thick frozen in his hair,
A little pale-faced, mild-eyed boy—
  He asked "please may I come
And warm me by your kitchen fire,
  I feel so cold and numb."

I led him to the blazing hearth—
  Tea was not cleared away—
He looked so wishful at the board
  I could not say him nay;
I bade him warm his little toes
  And fingers at his will,
Then take of supper that was left
  Till he had had his fill;
And by the fire I'd make a bed,
  I said, for him that night,
And then his hist'ry he might tell
  When came the morning light.

"Dear lady, you are very kind,"
  He cried, through choking sighs,
While grateful dews fell on his cheeks,
  That gathered in his eyes;

"But let me tell my story *now*,
　'T will add a little joy
To know, to-night, there's *one* to feel
　For a poor orphan boy.

"Father was kind, but long lay sick,
　Before he went to heaven;
And from that home where we had liv'd
　Mother and I were driven;
But mother found another home,
　Tho' not so large and warm,
Yet it was snug enough to keep
　Us sheltered from the storm;
And there she sought, with fingers worn,
　To earn our daily bread;
But overwork and racking cough
　Soon laid her with the dead.

"So I am now an orphan boy,
　With none to love me more,
And sometimes I am very cold
　And hunger very sore;
And then I wish that I had died
　That night when mother died;
I should not starve nor feel the cold
　When sleeping by her side.
I'd very gladly work and earn
　My food and clothing, too;
But when I seek they look so strange
　And ask, 'What can you do?'
Oh, if I live to be a man,
　I'll try and help the poor;
I never shall forget how much
　I've suffered, I am sure."

*　　*　　*　　*　　*　　*　　*

Long years had passed since I'd recalled
　To mind the orphan boy—

Changes had come, and with them I
  Had lost my earthly joy;
But he had left for my support
  A widow's bounteous share,
So that, a while, of poverty
  I had no thought or care:
But unjust men, with grasping hand,
  And law's unlawful power,
Essay'd, ere long, unblushingly,
  To rob me of my dower.

A distant judge, for wisdom fam'd,
  'Had heard the wicked deed,
And, all unask'd, one day he came
  And craved my cause to plead.
He had a noble, lofty brow,
  And form of godlike mien—
I little dreamed that ere before
  His visage I had seen;
He plead the widow's cause and won,
  No recompense he'd take:
" You shelter'd a poor orphan boy,
  I did it for his sake;
Behold in me that orphan boy:
  The bread on waters cast,
Though quite forgot," he smiling, said,
  " Shall be returned at last."

FOR THE FOURTH OF JULY, 1850.

Hark! hear our nation's welkin ring
   From broad Pacific's streams to Maine!
'T is Liberty, the song we sing,
   And millions swell the glad refrain.

No craven here quails 'neath the might
   Of Tyranny's relentless nod—
From vale and hill and mountain height,
   Our *thanks* go upward to our God!

We thank Him for this festal day—
   It is our nation's natal hour—
We thank Him that His hand did stay
   The Tyrant in his greedy power.

We thank Him for that patriot name,
   So dear to every freeman's heart!
Great Washington! shall sound thy fame,
   Till time and tide and earth depart!

We thank Him for this Heritage,
   For which our brave forefather's bled;
And that we live in this bless'd age,
   Where Liberty and Justice wed.

Then louder let the anthem roll!
   And wave our country's banner higher,
Till Right and Freedom win each soul
   To burn with patriotic fire.

Let our proud eagle flap her wing,
  Exulting in our nation's powers !
Let shouts of joy re-echoed ring
  O'er this vast continent of ours !

Spirits of seventy-six, come forth !
  Join in the grand, triumphal strain !
Sing, East and West, and South and North,
  Our Union firm, for aye, remain.

THE NOBLE FIREMAN.

The stately mansion was ablaze,
  The wreathing flames raged wild,
A piercing cry came on the wind
  " Oh, God, save my child!"

What did that shrieking mother care
  For mines of wealth then spoiled !
'T was not, " My gold and jewels spare !"
  'T was " God, save my child !"

The firemen did their engines ply,
  With " might and main" they toiled,
Yet still, above the din, rose high,
  " Oh, God, save my child !"

Say, mid the thousands gathered there,
  Drawn by that shriek so wild,
Was there no ear to heed the prayer,
  " Oh, God, save my child!"

Aye, *one* sprang from the gaping crowd
  Whose suit *she* once reviled;
Tho' poor in purse, with soul endow'd,
  He'd die to save her child.

Quick, quick as thought, the wall he scal'd
  Where hissing waters boil'd,
And while each gazer's visage pal'd,
  He sought the sleeping child.

Thro' fire and smoke and sash he dash'd,
  With effort seeming wild,
And snatch'd unto his breast the boy;
  God saved man and child.

But where was he whose name she bore,
  Whose *wealth* her heart beguil'd !
He raved, his losses brooding o'er,
  Heedless of wife or child.

THE WARM WEATHER IN THE COUNTRY.

The warm weather's coming,
  The brisk bee is humming,
The shrubs and the tall trees are budding to-day.
  The valleys are greening,
  And the hill-tops are sheening
In the dew and the sunshine that beckon sweet May.

All nature is singing;
  The wood-birds are winging
From woodland to woodland, from tree-top to brake.
  The wild fowl is soaring
  O'er the deep waters roaring,
And the swan and her young brood are skimming the lake.

The cattle are sunning
In the fields by the running
And laughing and leaping and frolicsome rill,
And the lambkins are playing,
And up and down straying,
On the soft, sunny side of the neighboring hill.

The wise man is raising
His full heart and praising
The Maker and Giver of all of life's worth;
He is plowing and hoeing,
And planting and sowing,
In due time to reap the good fruits of the earth.

The warm weather's coming,
The brisk bee is humming,
And the wild birds are winging from tree-top to brake;
The cattle are grazing
And the good man is praising
Him whom from its sleep doth the earth again wake.

THE WINTRY WINDS; OR, THE WIDOW'S LAST PRAYER.

Are ye angry, ye winds—
Or, why blow so wild ?
Cease—cease your loud raging,
Thin clad is my child;
And our hut here, so lonely,
Is leaky and old:
Blow softly, blow gently,
Or she'll die with the cold !

Oh ! why are ye angry,
  Ye winds, with my dove ?
She's pure as the snow-flake,
  That falls from above !
And she loved you, when warmly
  Ye blew o'er the wold:
Blow softly, blow gently,
  Or she'll die with the cold !

O God ! listen to me—
  Heed—heed my prayer;
She's all I have left me—
  Oh, spare her ! oh, spare !
Or if thou wilt take her,
  That hour, do I pray,
Free my sorrow-bowed soul
  From its fetters of clay.

She's dying ! The cold winds
  Still pitiless blow
Through the old, leaky hovel,
  And pile high the snow;
They care not for sorrow—
  They shrink not for dearth;
But wilder they blow
  O'er the dark, fireless hearth.

She's dead !—closely lock'd
  In the widow's embrace.
With hand clasped in hand,
  And face close to face,
The mother and child
  Have gone upward to God;
And, together, their bodies
  Will rest 'neath the sod !

Blow on, then, ye winds !
Ye can chill them no more—
Blow wildly, and bold,
Through the old hovel door: .
Ye may howl—ye may shriek—
Ye may freeze with your cold;
But the mother and babe
Are safe in Christ's hold !

OUR SAILOR-BOY, SHERIDAN.

Oh, tell me, ye waves of Atlantic's vast tide,
Where the form of our lost one lies sleeping !
Though long years have passed since our sailor-boy died,
Our eyes dry not yet of their weeping.

Oh, tell me ye winds, that have swept o'er the wave,
And have searched through the wild roaring billow,
Beneath what mild star, in what deep ocean-cave
Did our sailor-boy press his cold pillow!

Thou once pride of our household—lost joy of our
hearth,
Who far from thy kindred art sleeping,
Did thy cherished form lay 'neath some green mound of
earth,
Our eyes had long dried of their weeping.

But to know that the bones of our sailor-boy bleach
In some grave 'neath the deep waters' rolling,
Which no eye can discern, where no footstep can reach,
In our ears keeps the death-bell a tolling.

Oh! little ken they, who can stand by the stone
  That mark by the buried one keepeth,
Of the wailings of grief for the grave, all unknown,
  Of him who in ocean's bed sleepeth.

I hear, when I list, the wild dirge of the wave,
  Rolling forth in its sorrow-wreathed numbers,
And I chill as I think of the waters that lave
  Our sailor-boy in his last slumbers.

Dark, dark was the day, and it near crazed the brain,
  When we heard the sad tale of his dying;
And our poor bleeding hearts heal not yet of their pain,
  Nor our tear-bedimmed eyes of their crying.

For our lov'd one died far from the friends he held dear,
  With no kind hand to smooth his lone pillow,
No fond one to drop on his wan brow a tear,
  Ere they flung his pale corse in the billow.

They said that he died with home-thoughts round his
     heart,
  Calling " father," and " sister," and " brother,"
But the name on his lips when his soul did depart
  Was that dearest and sweetest name—" Mother."

He now hath slept years in the deep, our dear boy,
  But when earth by the last trump is shaken,
We that mourn him will fold in our arms our lost joy,
  For the dead of the sea shall awaken.

THE LOST ONE.

No likeness sketched by painter's art,
　Nor lock of hair from his fair brow;
Naught, save the memories in my heart,
　Is left of him to cherish now.

Oh, he was dear to me, my own !
　Earth seemed so bright when he was near;
But joy was fled when he was gone,
　And sunshine mocked the darkness here—

Here on my soul thick shadows fell,
　My heart became a withered thing,
For, from a foreign soil, the knell
　Of death left in its depths a sting.

Oh, when the light of love is fled,
　And hope lies crushed within the breast,
And the world-weary droops her head,
　And hourly pines to be at rest,

What earthly charm again can lure
　The eye to smile, the heart to leap!
What earthly medicine can cure,
　Or lull the pangs of grief to sleep!

I'M GROWING OLD.

I'm growing old, and I do weep at thought
  That the sweet freshness of my youth has fled;
That simple purity with youth inwrought
  Leaves no bright halo round my drooping head.

I'm growing old; my girlhood's days have flown,
  And on my matron brow are lines of care;
The sunny look of early times has gone;
  Amid my locks I find my first grey hair.

Unconscious thread! I'd pluck thee, if 't would wipe
  From mem'ry's page the wrongs of vanished years,
Or lop their number—and thou tiny stripe
  Would perish with these overflowing tears.

But here, or gone, thou canst not alter time,
  For Time and Care have had thee in their power;
Thou art the witness in this lower clime
  Of the sad changes of Life's fleeting hour.

But though Time marks me as it onward flies,
  Still doth the rainbow Hope oft clearer shine,
Athrough the waters of my tear-dimmed eyes,
  As nearer reach I to the Home divine.

And when the tempests of my soul surge high
  In sorrow's waves, over my saddened way,
I lift my eyes of Faith toward the sky,
  And feel there's joy for me in Heaven for aye.

WHEN SHALL I SEE THEE.

When shall I see thee! notest thou the hour
  When I shall leave this tenement of clay!
Hast thou, departed, the foreseeing power,
  That thou canst tell when comes the joyful day!

When will thy loving hand clasp mine once more,
  When shall I hear again thy voice so dear,
Oh, when shall we together tread that shore
  Of which we converse held when thou wert here!

Lov'd spirit! dost thou know how fondly oft
  My thoughts do turn to thee though thou art fled!
Canst thou look on me from thy home aloft,
  And markest thou the tears I for thee shed!

Yet not for thee, 't is for myself, blest shade,
  That I do mourn and weep thine absence here—
I miss thy earthly presence that erst made
  All things so beautiful when thou wert near.

I miss thy love-lit eye's soft, earnest gaze,
  Showing sweet pity when thou found'st me sad;
I miss thy well-timed counsels and thy praise—
  The one to make me wise, the other glad;

I miss those pleasant walks at twilight time,
  When all thy words were music to my ears;
When I forgot all woes 'neath starry clime,
  Till my dark locks were heavy with night's tears.

I miss thee, and I long to look again
  Upon thy face tho' 't is in Spirit Land;

When shall I feel no more the parting pain,
And take no more, for aye, the parting hand!

Once ever near thee, now forsaken, lone,
Up Heavenward I turn a wistful eye;
More keenly, day by day, I mourn thee gone,
And long beside thee in the grave to lie.

OUR SISTER.

We had a sister, days agone, young, beautiful, and
  sprightly;
She was the sunshine of our cot, wherein hearts once
  beat lightly.
Her form was lithesome as the fawn's; her skin of lily
  whiteness;
Her eyes were like the stars above, outrivaling their
  brightness;

Her shining hair was amber-hned, and on her neck lay
  braided;
And 'neath her eyelid's silken lash her rose-tinged cheek
  lay shaded;
Her voice was musical as birds that sing in woodland
  bowers;
Her ruby lips were sweet with dew, as nectar in the
  flowers;

Her breath, like fragrant perfume, came through pearly
  portals slipping;
Her footsteps, ready at each call, were ever gayly trip-
  ping;
And smiles played on her happy face, reflecting love's
  light round her;
And never did she cast a shade till Death's white robe
  had bound her.

Her mind was innocent and pure —a gem dropped down
    from Heaven—
And through the windows of her soul shone like the
    "Star of Even;"
No mortal ever lived, methinks, with slighter faults and
    fewer,
And with her many winsome ways she won all hearts
    unto her.

Oh, gentle as a dove was she and pleasant as the morn-
    ing,
Whose dancing sunbeams kiss the dew, each vale and
    hill adorning;
Her heart was like a laughing rill, with joyousness o'er-
    flowing,
Refreshing all within its reach, as on its pathway going.

But, ah, the day! this sister dear, when Autumn leaves
    were falling,
Too lovely for this nether sphere, did hear the angels
    calling;
And then, from out our earth-home paled the sunlight of
    our gladness,
And naught but mem'ries of her gone, cheer now our
    night of sadness

So wait we on the dismal shore, to cross· the dreaded
    river,
And listen for the dipping oars that in the dark waves
    quiver;
And bend the ear and hush the breath, to hear from
    shining portals
The Heaven-winged spirit calling us to join the blest
    immortals.

And there's another, more than friend, whose heart was
    buried with her,

He daily feels her presence near, his spirit wooing
    thither;
And not in vain her winning call, fast fading from our
    vision,
He soon will greet our angel one within the Land Ely-
    sian.

1850.

WE 'RE DREAMING.

We 're dreaming of a happier Land, far, far away,
With skies serene and zephyrs bland, where cooling
    fountains play;
We 're dreaming of its spicy groves, which scent the
    balmy air,
And of its shady, vine-clad bowers, laden with fruitage
    rare.

We 're dreaming of gay, starry birds, amid its olive
    trees,
Warbling their sweetest choral songs upon the perfumed
    breeze;
We 're dreaming of the beauteous flowers that gem its
    emerald dales,
Whose nectar gorgeous insects sip, ne'er seen in earthly
    vales.

We 're dreaming of its city, walled around with precious
    stone,
Emitting hues more brilliant than a burning rainbow
    zone;
With sunbright arches, pearly gates, and streets of
    golden pave,
And crystal streams and lakes wherein the white-winged
    angels lave.

We 're dreaming of a gracious King upon its sapphire
throne,
Swaying the countless, joyous hosts with words of gen-
tle tone;
Love beams beneath His star-gemmed crown, upon his
Godlike brow,
And dignity and purity on every feature glow.

Bright beings round Him worshiping, in rapture bend
the knee,
And sing glad songs of praise, and wave their palms of
victory.
We 're dreaming that we join the band that tread that
joyous shore,
Or spread their fleecy wings at will and roam creation
o'er;

Or swell, with voices silvery sweet, the anthem pealing
high,
Rolling along, in rapturous strains, through Heaven's
resplendent sky;
Or touch with skill the golden harps that softest music
make—
We 're dreaming—cease! we still tread earth—awake!
sad hearts, awake!

Nor vainly strive with mortal powers to picture heavenly
bliss,
" Eye hath not seen nor heart conceived " Heaven's
depths of happiness;
Then let us work while yet we may, to reach that un-
seen shore:
This life is our soul's trial-time, let's pass it bravely o'er.

OUR OWN DEAD.

Softly, softly, lay her body to rest!
Gently, gently cross her hands on her breast!
Tenderly, tenderly smooth her hair o'er her brow!
Lovingly, tearfully gaze on her now.

Oh, she was fairer than Spring-time's first flower!
Oh, she was dearer than light in our bower!
And she was lovely when life lit her eye
As the prettiest star in a Summer-eve sky.

When she's laid down in earth's bosom to rest,
Then we shall envy the turf o'er her breast;
With tears we will water the grass growing green,
When we stand by her grave in the moon's silver
    sheen.

But we'll believe that her spirit, betimes,
Comes back to see us from happier climes;
We'll list for her whisper when dew gems the
    flowers,
And talk with her sweetly in night's stilly hours.

Oft her white wings will enfold our sad hearts,
Oft her soft hand wipe the tear-drop that starts:
Bright angels will guard her up and down on the
    road
That leads from the earth to her blissful abode.

Softly, O softly, then lay her to rest!
Gently, O gently, cross her hands on her breast!
Lovingly, tenderly smooth her hair o'er her brow!
Hopefully, trustfully gaze on her now.

THE ANGELS CAME FOR HER.

The angels came for her—
  Our beautiful one!
In the light of her morning—
  At set of the sun;
And they wafted her upward
  On pinions of Love,
And she left us a weeping—
  Our darling, our dove.

Beloved of the angels,
  They could spare her no more,
Lest she'd struggle and faint
  On earth's wearisome shore;
So they wooed her and won her
  Away from our nest,
And her bird-notes are warbled
  On her good Savior's breast.

So gently they took her,
  She smiled as she passed
From our arms to the angels—
  That smile was the last
We shall evermore see
  On the face of her clay!
We shall sigh for its light
  Till we, too, pass away.

Yet often we'll picture
  Our bird in the skies,
Looking lovingly down
  With her star-beaming eyes;
And we'll think on the air
  Comes a sweet, child-like tone
From the lips of our angel—
  Our bright one, our own.

The angels came for her,
  The brightness grew dim,
And fainter and fainter
  The seraphim's hymn;
And we felt that the spell
  Of a withering blight
Enshrouded our hearts
  With the darkness of night.

Oh! thou sorrow-doomed earth,
  Where we meet but to part
With the loveliest blossoms
  That twine round the heart,
Methinks all the tears
  That thy mourners have shed
Would outnumber the grains
  Of the dust that we tread.

But the sighs and the tears
  And the prayers offered up,
Overflowing the brim
  Of life's bitter cup,
Will be turned into joys,
  Is the promise that 's giv'n,
If the incense ascends
  On Faith's wings up to Heav'n.

THEY TELL ME.

They tell me of " Death"
  Full too often I sing—
Too oft strike " sad " notes
  On my lyre's faltering string!
Yet though none, save the wind,
  Should list to my dole,
To breathe out one's plaint
  Brings relief to the soul.

PETITIONS.

Petitions are not vain—-God hears our cry
When we lift our hearts to Him—by and by
We'll learn that every pious tear and prayer
Doth shine a jewel in the crown we wear—
      Wear, by and by.

"Ask and ye shall receive," in the Good Book
We read, as on the precious page we look;
But we must wait till God sees fit to give—
It may not be till we in glory live—
      Live, by and by.

Then pray and pray and weep, if it needs be,
But strive for patience, since God heedeth thee;
The more we kneel and turn our thoughts to Heaven,
More freely will the boon we crave be given—
      Given, by and by.

Yet let us feel, in very truth, to say
" Thy will be done." *He* knoweth best the way
To work out for us our eternal weal;
He knows the balm that will our heart-wounds heal—
      Heal, by and by.

DESPAIR AND PRAYER.

O God, in mercy list my plaint, I pray;
  My feet within a darksome path now tread,
Not e'en one smiling heaven-beam gilds my way:
    Faith's light is fled.

Despair broods o'er my soul with darkling wing,
  My head droops low in weariness of life;
No note of Hope's sweet song my pale lips sing,
    Chilled in the strife.

Mine eyes, with wasting tears, fail me to ope;
  In my seared heart life's fount is almost dry;
Fainting and worn, all battle-stained, I grope,
    And wish to die.

Nor near, nor far, is there one kindly hand
  Ready to aid me in my sore distress;
Alone, uncared for, on the brink I stand,
    All pitiless.

Prone on the ground and broken is my lute,
  No answering chord vibrates within my ear;
Each string, o'erstrained by hapless hands, lies mute,
    Not now to cheer.

O God, in mercy, bend Thine ear I pray,
  Let *one* sweet heaven-beam cheer the path I tread;
Let Faith again, with a pellucid ray,
    Light on my head.

Reach forth Thy hand and mend my broken lyre,
   And let its soothing chords strike on my ear;
Fill my dark soul with light of heavenly fire!
      Kind Father, hear.

Warm these chilled lips, with living coals that burn
   Upon Thy altar of forgiving love;
To sing again sweet songs of Thee I yearn—
      Father above!....

Thank Heaven! despair has waved her leaden wing,
   A glimmering light beams on my darksome way;
A little song of Hope again I sing,
      The while I pray.

THE LAND BEYOND.

Thank God! there *is* a land beyond the grave,
   Where weary souls may find a blessed rest;
There *is* a pitying Hand stretch'd forth to save,
   And fold the longing spirit to His breast.

Oh, tell me, ye great hearts which beat on earth,
   Have e'er ye known an hour of perfect peace!
Was there not e'en in infancy a dearth
   Within your souls, a flutt'ring for release!

When brightest sunbeams light the hill and plain
   And dance upon the rivers and the rills,
Do ye not feel, like some dark, surging main,
   Mock'd by the sunlight that the green earth thrills!

Say! am I all alone in my unrest;
   Do things of Time suffice your hungry souls!
Does mortal's love—earth's sweetest gift and best—
   Leave no deep void as Life its page unrolls!

Oh, earth must needs be weary for our good;
    E'en to the dearest lov'd there must be times
When the soul yearns for purer brotherhood,
    And pants to fold its wings in happier climes.

But what to the *un*-loved must life be here!
    A dark, a dreary blank—a sunless wild—
Without one tender tone the breast to cheer—
    Kind Heaven! help the earth-neglected child.

I do believe there is within each heart
    An aching void which naught but Heaven can fill;
Oh, then, how doubly hard to bear his part
    Who shrinketh, too, beneath the cold world's chill.

     *   *   *

The tender bud here wakens to a flower,
    And satiates itself with sun and dew,
And glories in its fullness its short hour;
    But *man* has yet a nobler end in view.

A something higher, holier, beyond
    The temporal, he reaches to attain;
But the immortal part must burst its bond,
    And soar to unknown realms its goal to gain.

Thank God! there *is* a land we yet may win
    And satisfy the yearnings of the breast,
Through Jesus' love our souls may enter in
    And sweetly realize the Promised Rest.

TO THE GRIEVING SISTER.

Tried soul, bestir thee, lest thou sink
  Beneath the rod;
With clearer faith look upward—
  Lean on God.

Cease, cease thy vain repinings,
  Lest they dry
The springs of life within thee,
  And thou die.

Arouse thy sinking energies,
  Thou'st much to do—
What work thy hands shall find,
  With might pursue.

Let chast'nings teach thee wisdom,
  'T is their aim,
To save thee from *worse* sorrow,
  Guilt, and shame.

BE HAPPY.

Be happy! be happy!
  For the good, life is bright;
They have day-skies of sunshine
  And star-beams at night;
The music of nature
  Enchants their glad ear,
And its beauties entrance them,
  For the " good," life has cheer.

Be happy! be happy!
　'T is the grateful are blest,
By them the best joys
　Of the earth are possessed.
Lift your hearts in due thanks
　To the Giver above,
And you'll bask in the pure beams
　Of Hope, Faith, and Love.

Be happy! be happy!
　Shut the cloud-land from view,
And look where the sun
　Is, for aye, shining through;
- No grumbler can enter
　The gateway of Heaven,
To the thankfully happy
　Is the light of God given.

OH, WHERE ARE THEY, WHERE?

Oh, where are they, where? the friends that were dear;
We watch for their coming, but they come no more
　　here;
We list for their voices, but ever in vain—
Shall we see them and hear them, oh! never again!

Nay, here nevermore shall our longing eyes rest
On the faces of those we held dearest and best;
No more shall our glad ears drink in the fond words
That thrilled with delight our heart's tenderest chords.

But where are they, where? we ask earth and seas!
No answer is borne on the wings of the breeze!
Rocks, mountains and caves, in re-echo sigh, Where?
And our souls whisper to us, Not there, no, not there!

Oh, where are they, where? we ask of noonday!
No answer comes down on the sun's dazzling ray;
And in midnight's still hour we turn to the sky,
And ask moon and stars, but they deign no reply.

Oh, where are they, where? ye wise of earth tell
Where our dearly beloved who have " gone before "
     dwell!
In fancy ye picture the Home of the Blest,
But say, do ye *know* where our cherished ones rest?

Kind friends, who would lighten our grief, can ye say,
To what blessèd spot do our dead flee away?
Ye have stood where the forms of our buried ones lie,
Have ye traced out the shore where their winged spirits
     lie?

Oh, where are they, where? tried souls discern ye,
Earth's lost one's fair Isle on Eternity's sea?
Ye have heard of a far-away Happier Land—
Have ye looked upon *one* of its shadowy band?

Where are they, oh, where? ye sainted ones, come!
Return, for a while, to our desolate home!
Sing to us a song of your sanctified Rest....
We listen....and listen....how vain the request!

Where are they? oh, tell us, we plead with high Heaven,
At morning, at noon, and at darkling-browed even;
But the heavenly hosts from the bright vales look down,
And breathe to our spirits, *No trust, and no crown!*

Then let us with Hope's glowing eyes look above,
And "trust" in the mercy of Him who " is Love;"
So when to our Savior's bright Home we repair,
We shall see them and know them, for they 're There,
     yes, they 're There.

OH! CAN THEY FORGET?

Oh, do they e'er think, in their home in the skies
  Of the earth-home where dwelt they in childhood;
Of the cottage where first the light came to their eyes,
  On the brink of the stream near the wildwood?

Oh, do they e'er think of the pleasant playground,
  Just back of the neat little dwelling,
Where they frolicked so oft, all so joyful each sound,
  Save that of the ax the wood felling?

Oh, do they e'er think of the hearth where at eve
  They gathered when wild winds were chilling;
Where around its bright blaze they bright fancies did
    weave,
  Or over their school-tasks were drilling?

Oh, do they e'er think of the clear running brook,
  Where oft their light barque was seen dancing;
Where they angled for trout with the worm-baited hook,
  Through its waters so temptingly glancing!

Oh, do they e'er think of the time when they strayed
  On the side of the neighboring mountain,
Plucking wild flowers or fruit, or repaired to the shade
  Of its trees by the cool, crystal fountain?

Oh, do they e'er think of the little church near,
  Whose spire still points toward Heaven;
Where all met on Sundays the tidings to hear
  How a Savior to sinners was given?

Oh, do they e'er think of the friends they have left,
  Who still o'er their absence are sighing;
Can they look down upon us, so sadly bereft,
  From mansions where there is no dying?

What though, in the beautiful world where they are,
  Light-wing'd they may ever be soaring,
And roaming at will o'er each radiant star,
  And other new beauties exploring—

What though they now bask in the glorious light
  From the throne of the Deity shining,
Can they ever forget the dear faces, once bright,
  And the fond hearts still round them entwining?

I can but believe that they sometimes recall
  The scenes of their innocent childhood—
The mountain, the church, and the cottage and all,
  On the brink of the stream near the wildwood.

I can but believe though they strike the glad lyre,
  With seraphs rejoicing above us,
That sometimes they sing a sweet song mid the choir,
  Rehearsing how deeply they love us.

Oh, Heaven is nearer than many surmise;
  When we've safely passed over Death's river,
Its waves will have washed the thick scales from our
    eyes,
  And we'll look on all loved ones forever.

Perchance, could we peer through the mystical veil,
  Which now in its foldings hath bound us,
We might find ourselves nearer the friends we bewail
  Than when erst they were smiling around us.

There is something that tells us down deep in our hearts
 That no link of Love's chain is e'er broken;
Refined in the fire from all earth's drossy parts,
 It shineth Eternity's token.

How, then, can it be that the friends who have gone
 Think no more of the dear ones left grieving;
Love joins soul to soul, from the earth to God's Throne,
 Is the star of my spirit's believing.

DO THEY RETURN?

Do the beloved dead return to us, oh, nevermore!
Come not their spirits sometimes back from the eternal
 shore!
How oft when in my aching heart have sorrow's waves
 beat wild,
Have I thought I heard my mother's voice soothing her
 grieving child;

And then, again, my brother dear, the eldest of our
 band,
Doth visit me when I am sad from that fair Spirit-land,
And wipes with softest, gentlest touch the tear-drops
 from mine eyes,
And sweetly murmurs low of joys that wait me in the
 skies.

And then a younger brother comes, with seraph-harp
 and voice,
To raise my sinking spirit up and make it to rejoice;
Though faint the sounds fall on mine ear, I catch the
 loving words,
And my whole being seems to soar upon the heavenly
 chords.

And then the fairest flower that bloom'd upon our house-
    hold tree,
A darling angel-sister's song would bid all sorrow flee,
And waken my desponding thoughts to something holier,
    higher,
And elevate Faith's drooping wings above sin's altar-
    fire.

Alas! how far from Spirit-land must feel the soul bound
    here,
That never in the stilly hour, when anguish walketh
    near,
Dost hush the tumult in the breast, and breathless list
    the while,
To hear the well-remembered tones that would its woes
    beguile.

Far more than all the joys of earth I count this firm
    belief,
That the departed come to us to soothe away our grief;
That when our heartstrings almost break, soft voices
    from above
Breathe in our ears sweet seraph-strains, a hymning
    " God is Love."

THE LAND OF THE FOREVER.

There's the Land of the Forever
  On Jordan's further side,
Where mortal man may never
  Within its realms abide.
Imagination strives to paint
  The scenes within its walls,
And Fancy soars with outstretched wing
  To roam its princely Halls.

In the Land of the Forever
  We query, Are there flowers
And birds and trees, too beautiful
  To be compared to ours;
Are its brilliant skies more glorious
  Than Summer's sunset sea;
And are its hills and dales more green
  Than any earthly lea?

Are beings that inhabit it
  Fairer than mortals deem;
And is the music of their words
  Sweeter than poet's dream?
Do peace and love and unity
  Encircle all in one;
And is their spirits' purity
  Brighter than mid-day sun?

How look its streets, all paved with gold,
  Its walls of precious gems?
Who of our friends, soul-free, are there,
  Wearing their diadems;

Who that we loved are waving palms
  Before the great " I Am;"
What songs of gladness do they sing,
  Bowing before the Lamb?

Vain quest! the splendors of those courts
  No earth-clad soul can ken—
And Fancy, with her utmost wing,
  Availeth naught to men;
Fruitless while here to hope and strive
  To catch a glimpse of Heaven;
No shadow of its glories yet
  To mortals has been given.

Methinks that could we have a view,
  Though dim the vision were,
Of half the joys laid up for them
  Who yet shall enter there,
This earth would seem so dark, at best,
  And worthless in our sight,
That souls would too impatient wait
  To climb the God-lit Height.

Our mission here would 'scape our mind,
  Life's battle be unfought—
Too eager for the victor's crown,
  No victory be wrought.
In patience we must bear the cross,
  In Faith must fight our way,
Ere we can win the Promised Land
  Of Life's Eternal Day.

Then the soft splendors of those courts
  Shall cheer our spirit-eyes;
Proportionate unto our cross
  Shall be up There our prize;

To those with whom earth darkest deals
Shall Heaven brighter be,
If they but strive and trust and wait
For their soul's jubilee.

THE FAR COUNTRY.

In a Country far, there are joys untold,
Nor bought with silver, nor bought with gold,
Nor precious gems, like the diamond rare,
Will ever avail to bring us there—
'T is the tears we shed in sorrow for sin
And the blood of the Lamb will take us in.

In a Country far I have friends most dear,
They were chastened oft while they lingered here,
But the stripes were bathed with the drops that fell
In penitent grief from the crystal well,
And cleansed and healed in the crimson tide
That flowed from a Savior's bleeding side.

I long to go to that Country bland—
Weary and worn I waiting stand,
List'ning to catch from the shining shore
The sound of the ferryman's dipping oar;
The river is black and the waves are high,
But a Beacon Star illumes the sky.

'T is the Star of Bethlehem, ever in sight;
Should we raise our eyes in darkest night,
Over the river of Death 't will lead
Each mariner safe, if we give it heed;
And our ferriage o'er will cost us nought—
" For without money and price 't was bought."

In a Country far, o'er the billowy surge,
We shall hear no more the mariner's dirge,
Nor the solemn stroke of the splashing oar,
For we never shall cross the dark waves more—
The redeemed ones' song shall ravish the ear,
And the River of Life to our eyes appear.

In a Country far, in visions by night,
I see one watching to catch the sight
Of a sister dear, when her feet shall press
The shining shore, in an angel-dress—
And I know 't is *he* who will grasp her hand
And welcome her first on the golden strand.

In a Country far there are others I know
Who will greet her with joy where the bright waters
    flow.
Over emerald glades, by meandering streams,
Through amaranth bowers they lead her in dreams,
And I feel in my soul that shining ones wait
To lead her with songs through the wide pearl gate.

BE STILL, MY SOUL.

Be still, my soul, and list,
  The angels' whisperings!
I taste, methinks, their balmy breath,
  I feel their spirit wings,
  Unlike all earthly things!

Ye temples, cease your throbs,
  Quiet, thou feverish brain,
The wildering tumult of my thoughts!
  'T is a soft music strain
  To ease my sore heart's pain.

Hush! his the voice I hear....
  The noble-browed and brave;
He languished 'neath a southern sky
  And sank beneath the wave—
  His early, tombless grave!

Hush, thou, my soul, again!
  That sound is like the tone
Of him, our fair-haired, blue-eyed boy—
  The patient, gentle one,
  Whose bright sands quickly run.

Still hush! another sings
  A song within mine ear;
'T is like a song her young lips sang
  Which I was wont to hear,
  Whose notes were very dear.

And yet another joins
  The sweet angelic band!
That voice is like a mother's voice,
  Who passed to Spirit-land
  The first of all our band.

But, ah! my list'ning soul,
  Clogged by this mold of clay!
How soon the tones grow faint and far,
  And seem to pass away,
  Just like a sunset ray.

In vain thou tried to catch
  The silvery, loving words;
Although thou felt the soothing tones
  Outvied the warbling birds—
  Earth's sweetest, finest chords.

How quick, when loosed from earth,
   My spirit shall aspire
To soar beyond the upper skies,
   And tune a golden lyre,
   With that loved, kindred choir.

THE HILLS AND SEAS.

Ye everlasting hills of mammoth mold,
Could ye but speak, what tales ye could unfold!
What histories since the creation's birth
Of men and matter on the struggling earth!

And thou, vast sea! where myriads find a grave,
Thou could'st tell much that's passed upon thy wave;
Of many a wail and agonizing shriek,
And prayer, since ages rolled, could'st thou but speak.

But hills and seas tell not within our ears
The things they 've looked on during untold years,
Yet there's a language written on each face
Which we with mortal eyes may plainly trace.

It speaks a power divine! a mighty God,
Who makes and rules creation with a "nod!"
Who cleaves the hills in twain, makes boil the deep,
And rocks its caverns where proud nations sleep.

It speaks of One whose angry thunders roll
Athwart the lurid sky from pole to pole;
Who shakes the earth's foundations with his breath,
And dooms each sinful soul to taste of death.

Yet speaks it, too, the gentle power of love,
Wooing and winning, peaceful as a dove;

Soft quieting the elements in strife,
Restoring man repentant unto life.

Oh, volumes are writ out in Nature's book,
Upon the common things we daily look:
A page each spear of grass, each flower and tree,
Who reads or earth or skies, reads, God, of Thee.

WHAT IS FAME TO WOMAN!

Oh, what is fame to woman! Will it still all those yearnings of the heart, those cravings for pure love from noble souls, that it doth more than willingly go farther than half way to meet! Will it unsay the words of coldness and of harsh reproach uttered by him who swore before the altar matrimonial to love and cherish and protect the fragile, trusting one, who forsook all for him till death the bonds should sever! Will it return the child, exiled from home, to loving parents, brothers, sisters dear, whose every well-remembered word of kindness thrills the weeping heart, now from them cast as if it were a poisonous reptile, fit only for its own companionship! Will it bring faith and meekness to her soul and help her smile serenely, 'neath the sable wings of sorrow, at every shaft with which dark death has stilled the pulse and chilled the frame of each and all the loving hearts that once around her clung, in spite of trials and adversities! Will it at last waft her poor, tired soul to mansions in the Heavens! Oh, what is fame to woman!

LOST SOULS; OR, THE DRUNKARD'S DANCE.

In the whirligig of time,
Rushing on through shame and crime,
Hands besmeared and garments dabbled
By the filth through which we 've traveled;
Hast'ning to the gulf before us,
Every jarring note in chorus:
Riotous laughter, loud, o'erreaching
Angry passions in their screeching;
Drowning conscience' timid whimper,
Till 't is shamed beyond a simper,
In a Babeldom of voices
Which confusion's ear rejoices;
Elbowing by the way our betters,
Hurrying on to clasp our fetters:
Wild, delirious, eyelids blinking
From the poisons we are drinking;
While the blasting fumes and fire
Through our nostrils we respire;
And the craving, burning thirst
Makes us drench in drams accurst.
Whirling, twirling, out of breath,
Swirling in the dance of death!
Shrieking, howling, drunken, grinning,
Onward in our dizzy spinning,
As we reel and curse and wrangle
In the scorpion folds that tangle;
Till we reach the nether goal
Yawning for the poor, lost soul;
When the creaking, hell-gate 'wide

Opens for the rushing tide
Who the pandemonium enter
Where the fiery billows center.
Through that hell-gate never, never
To escape, while beats forever
The huge Pendulum Supernal
Keeping time to the Eternal!

AUTUMN WINDS.

In the wailing winds of Autumn,
  With golden sandaled feet,
A grieving for earth's sorrows,
  Methinks the angels meet.

I know I hear their tramping
  And their pitying lament,
Below the misty cloudland,
  For the woes that sin hath sent.

They would weep away our trespass,
  They would fain have us forgiven,
But the weeping of the angels
  Will not win our souls to heaven.

One, greater, wept our errings,
  More than bewailed our woes,
Yet we, forgetful, journey on,
  Nearing life's fitful close.

Oh, the wailing winds of Autumn,
  Who can divine their dole!
Like jarring death-bells ringing out,
  As sinks the passing soul!

THE LONE TREE.

SEEN IN THE STATE OF MAINE IN 1841.

Here I for ages long have stood,
Once the proud monarch of the wood;
But peoples came from o'er the sea
And from my side felled every tree,
And left me lone to mark the years
Of rolling time and rolling spheres,
And heed events swift passing by,
Some crowned with joy, some with a sigh.
The birds have in my branches sung,
Here built their nests and reared their young;
The squaw's papoose my branching arm
Hath rocked to sleep away from harm;
I've been the tryst for man and maid,
Children have round my body played;
I've seen the ground about me red
Stained by the blood in battle shed.
The generations come and go,
Like Summer's heat and Winter's snow:
The red man's little birch canoe
A giving place to ship and crew;
The red man's arrow, scalping blade,
To cannon ball and sword instead;
The red man's wigwam, "pipe of peace,"
To palace-halls and war's surcease;
His dusky bride, unkempt, untaught,
To faces fair, brows marked with thought;
His hunting-grounds to towns and schools

Where lore in place of nature rules;
The woodman's ax has passed me by
Unharmful, and the whirlwinds high,
The thunders peal and lightning's glare,
Have left me still to carp and care—
To listen to the angry storm,
As howls it round my aged form;
To green in Summer's fervid heat,
And yield to man a cool retreat;
To wave in Winter branches bare,
While whistles through my limbs the air;
And to bow down with heft of years,
My hoary head bleached with night's tears;
Without a friend or kin anear
To help me pass a pleasant year;
But in reflections of the past
To wither till I die at last,
Unless some hand forestalls the day,
And fells me ere all strength decay;
And hides the spot on which I fall,
'Neath palace, hut, or garden wall,
With none to mourn at missing me,
And drop a tear for the old tree.

THE MOTHER AND BABY.

Another soul an infant form has taken,
And come to earth a mother's love to waken.
A matron, but one year ago a bride,
Is sitting now in all a mother's pride,
Fondling her baby-boy with fond caresses
And thoughts in loving words she thus expresses:

Sweet eyes, so heavenly blue, just like thy father's,
And flossy hair that golden sunbeams gathers!
Sweet rosebud lips, and soft and silken skin,
And such a pretty, little, dimpled chin!
Oh, how I love you, darling, pretty creature,
Sweet as a cherub's is each tiny feature.

Such chubby hands and chubby little feet, too,
I hug you, kiss you, almost want to eat you!
And now to see my pretty baby laugh
Is sweeter than the nectar angels quaff!
Although to speak so is, I fear, transgression,
But oh, I love you so beyond expression!

My babe! my own! my precious, blessed treasure,
A mother's love who but herself can measure!
I know his father loves his baby-boy,
I see he smiles on him in pride and joy;
But his eyes see not half thy baby graces,
That every hour thy mother fondly traces.

So sat a youthful mother, talking, smiling,
Fondling her baby-boy, swift time beguiling,
When o'er her spirit came a saddened thought
Of what with baby's future might be fraught,
And quick she raised her heart to God in Heaven,
And prayed a blessing on the gift 'He'd given;

And thus from motion of her lips I read:
" My Father, shield from harm this precious head,
Save him from the impending curse of sin;
Now in his infant heart let good begin,
And guard him should he reach to boyhood's days;
Teach him to turn from all earth's slippery ways;
And should he ever climb to manhood's hight,
Guide still his footsteps in the way of right;
Make him a blessing to the suff'ring world,

Bearing Christ's banner o'er his brow unfurled,
Reaching a helping hand to sinful men,
Teaching the paths of love with tongue and pen;
Giving example of a noble life,
Soothing men's passions, quelling war and strife;
Of lightest vice, oh, let him bear no stain!
Or should he slip, help him his path regain,
And wash from him the filth in Thy pure blood,
And safer plant his feet in Thy straight road.
Dear Father, hear my prayer! Earth's pleasures
   hollow
Set his face firm against. Let him ne'er follow
In courses vain of wicked, thoughtless men;
Far rather take him back to Thee again,
Now in his infancy and guilelessness,
E'en though 't would break my heart to no more
   press
My mother-lips upon his precious face.
(O God! what e'er befalls us give us grace),
'T were better now in grief to beat my breast
Than mourn my boy a living man unblest.
Dear Father! should life's rugged path he tread,
Let no sin heavy sit upon his head,
But walking in the spirit of the Lord,
Let angel's pen his worthy deeds record;
So up through manhood make my darling boy
Be then, as now, his parents' blessed joy,
And when his honored head in death lies low
With spirit blest may he to glory go:
And with his parents in celestial clime
Thank God they erst had trod the shores of time,
And mid the ransomed sing triumphant song
In mansions where our Christ's redeemed belong."

'T was thus a youthful mother earnest prayed,
With face uplift to Heaven, craving aid;

I pray God bent to her His gracious ear,
For unto me that daughter's boy is dear.

1871.

A MORNING IN NOVEMBER, AFTER THE SNOW.

The earth appears robed in a pure, bridal garment,
    And many a leafless and snow-covered spray
Adds a wreath to her brow, like the bridal adornment,
    That crowns the fair bride on her glad wedding day.

Oh, garment the purest, Oh, garment the whitest,
    That e'er below Heaven hath covered a breast!
Methinks thou art fitter for seraph the brightest,
    Than this poor, fallen earth with its sin and unrest.

The angels looked down, Earth, from skies that glow
      o'er thee,
    And blushed as they saw thee in wintry undress,
And flung thee a robe of their own to throw o'er thee,
    To veil from their eyes thy brown, stark nakedness.

YE MAY PART!

Ye may part! ye may part! in anger may sever,
    But there 'll be a plaint that will never be still;
Ye may part! ye may part! may dissever forever,
    But a pang in each breast will all happiness kill.

Though hillside and valley, though moorland and
      mountain,
    Though rivers and oceans the broad hemisphere
      through
Divide ye, you'll find in each heart lives a fountain,
    Will ever gush forth to love's memories true.

WRITTEN AFTER THE DEATH OF MR. WIL-
LIAM CASSIDY, OF ALBANY, EDITOR
OF "THE ARGUS."

When God sees fit He calls His children Home,
And in Death's awful presence *lips* are dumb;
But grieving *hearts* will murmur "Why this one!"
Striving the while to say, "Thy will be done."

" Thy will be done." But there is none to fill
His place left vacant since his pulse is still;
With heart by sorrow touched, with talents rare,
His exit from us earth cannot repair.

When men in power, with passion anger-blind,
Their minions sent with manacles to bind
The father in our household; and did bear
Him to an ocean isle, a prisoner there,
For simply speaking truths a freeman might,
Without the least surpassing freeman's right,
He lent us kindly aid in our great need,.
And proved to us a noble friend in deed;
And for like Christian acts toward many here,
His name will e'er be linked with memories dear.

YE ARE GONE.

Ye are gone! ye are gone
 To the Beautiful Land,
Mother, brothers and sister,
 An angel-wing'd band;
Ye have crossed the dark valley,
 Have sailed o'er death's flood,
And have entered the gates
 Of the city of God.

Ye are gone! ye are gone,
 With your garments made white,
To the Beautiful Land,
 From our fond, longing sight;
And ye chant with the saints
 The redeemed one's glad song,
And wave shining palms
 Mid the bright spirit throng.

Ye are gone! ye are gone
 And are roaming at will,
Over emerald plains,
 Which the sweet dews distill;
And ye feed upon manna
 And cull the fair flowers
That blossom for aye
 In the Heavenly bowers.

Ye are gone! ye are gone
 To your blissful estate,
Where with angels and saints
 Around Jesus ye wait;

Where your golden harps' music
  Fills the ambient air:
Oh, there! my loved friends,
  Do ye think of me there!

Pray wing a soft zephyr
  From yon balmy sphere!
Waft on it a whisper
  For my soul's list'ning ear.
Tell me, wait ye my coming
  By the river that flows
Through the Beautiful Land,
Where the weary repose!

Oh, the Beautiful Land
  That I've thought of so long,
And talked of and dreamed of
  And wrote of in song!
Could'st thou here pierce the eyes
  Of our souls with thy light,
Would we find thou wert ne'er
  Very far from our sight?

Oh, thou Beautiful Land!
  Oh, thou Beautiful Land!
I have so longed to see thee
  I scarce could withstand
The wish Death would strip
  The thick film from my eyes,
So that I could look in
  Where the wing'd spirit hies.

Ye are gone! ye are gone
  To the Beautiful Land!
Do I ne'er feel the touch
  Of a soft, spirit-hand!

Do I ne'er hear a voice,
  So gentle and kind
That I think 't is the breath
  Of the cool, Summer wind!

Do I ne'er hear the stir
  Of a footfall so still
That I'm racked with the doubt
  Do ye come here at will!
Do I ne'er see a shadow
  Of angels so bright,
That I think 't is a sunbeam
  Astray in the night!

Ye are gone! ye are gone
  To the Beautiful Land—
Mother, brothers and sister,
  An angel-wing'd band!
But have ye not sometimes,
  When my heart was sore tried,
In sweet pity come back
  And sat down by my side!

Hath not Love wrought a chain,
  Though unseen by our eyes,
Linking soul unto soul
  From the earth to the skies!
A ladder on which
  The freed spirit can stand,
And sometimes return
  From the Beautiful Land!

Ye are gone! ye are gone!
  Does no barque near the shore,
That I may step in
  And be rowed safely o'er,

Where I'll look in the face
　Of the Lamb for us slain,
Who has passed on before us
　O'er Jordan's dark main!

Where I'll roam o'er the strand
　With its emerald dyes,
And gaze when I wish
　In your dear, loving eyes!
And join in your praises,
　With hand clasped in hand,
And part nevermore
　In the Beautiful Land!

Oh, thou Beautiful Land!
　I shall see thee I know
When I've passed o'er the vale
　Where the dark waters flow.
I shall raise my glad voice
　With the seraphim band,
That chant the sweet notes
　In the Beautiful Land.

For Faith is the bulwark
　And prayer is the stair
By which one repentant
　Shall rise through the air;
And my faith has been strong,
　I shall reach the far strand,
By the pure, crystal sea
　In the Beautiful Land.

THE WAY OF LIFE.

When morning skies are clearest,
Oft darkest cloud inspherest
   Before the setting sun.

When youth has prospects brightest,
Oft many a sorrow blightest
   Before life's work is done.

We roam mid works of beauty
And fail to do our duty
   Till needful chast'nings come,

In sorrow to remind us
Earth's pleasures must not bind us
   Upon our pathway home.

IF ALL THE PRAYERS, ETC.

If all the prayers that I have prayed
   Have reached my Savior's ear,
And all will yonder granted be
   That are not granted here,
I think that I in part divine
   The joys my soul await,
When I have fled the bounds of time
   And passed the pearly gate.

"Ask and ye shall receive," such is
   The word our Lord hath said,
And earnest for some longed-for boon
   Each day my heart hath plead;
But here the good I so desire
   He oft to me denies;
Oh, will he grant the gift refused
   In angels' Paradise!

BEFORE MYRA H——'S DEATH, IN TIME OF FEVER.

Turn back! turn back thy scythe, O Death!
It seems not meet to stop the breath
Of those so young, with promise fair!
Go turn thy steps some otherwhere—
To older ones now tired of life,
Its cares, its sorrows, and its strife,
Waiting with an impatient ear
Thy call to blissful rest to hear;
But leave to us our glad and gay
And come for them some other day.

Turn back! turn back thy scythe, O Death!
Nor breathe around thy poisonous breath!
There 's none anear we wish to lose,
None could we pick if bid to choose.
In other place some so forlorn
Thou mayest find, with none to mourn
If thou should'st take them, but not here—
We 've none to spare! oh, come not near;
With thy dark presence from us fly,
None with us now would wish to die.

Turn back! turn back thy scythe, O Death!
Haste from us with thy blasting breath.
Alas! we think we hear not far
The rolling of thy dreaded car,
And see the flashing of thy blade!
Must some friend pass through Death's cold shade!
Can no prayer stay thy onward course;
Can no words fright thy pallid horse!
Take from us, then, no tender flower,
No father's hope in life's staid hour.

AFTER HER DEATH.

To hear it said that " Myra's dead,"
  Our neighbor's precious daughter;
To pass so soon, ere verge of noon,
  Over death's turbid water!

So like a dream the thought doth seem,
  A troubled dream of sorrow,
That from our sight she's taken flight,
  Nor will return to-morrow!

To friends so dear who miss her here
  This solace sweet is given:
Her spirit soars o'er vernal shores
  In blessèd realms of Heaven.

Mid untold charms her mother's arms
  In ecstasy enfold her,
With angel-throngs she sings sweet songs,
  Death's bonds no more can hold her.

Could she come back along earth's track
  And speak to friends now weeping,
Her gladsome voice would say " Rejoice,"
  " I'm in my Savior's keeping."

By her pale lips, since Death's eclipse,
  Will no more words be spoken,
But o'er her soul he's no control,
  No link 'twixt souls is broken.

From in the Book where oft we look
  We drink this gracious teaching:
The chain of love enwrought above
  To earth from Heaven is reaching.

So sometimes here she may be near
  Their hearts within them burning,
Her footfalls still may come at will
  To soothe her sad friends' yearning.

But they will moan who miss her gone—
  Bereft ones left behind her—
Till beyond Time in other Clime
  Their soaring spirits find her

I LOVE TO BELIEVE.

I love to believe in the good Spirit-land
That is round and about me and ever at hand,
So that when I reach forth I can touch with my finger
Some unseen loving, fond one that near me doth linger.

And when I am sitting alone and forlorn,
And almost regretting that e'er I was born,

Then the glad thought uprises, With the spirits there's
    union;
That the good with the good spirits hold sweet com-
    munion.

And my soul lifts its wings, flings behind her despair,
Throws aside for a season each cankering care;
And talks with the friends now her Savior beholding,
And feels their kind arms round her spirit enfolding.

Oh, 't is blessèd, 't is sweet, to know, if not here,—
Some one who cares for thee is in Spirit-land near,
Who sees thee and hears thee and knows thy heart's
    bleeding, ·
And for thee face to face with thy Jesus is pleading.

A pleading to wash from thy spirit its sin,
And that good and good only its folds shall let in;
When thou art an hungered for His hand to feed thee,
When thou criest for faith in His mercy to heed thee.

Oh, comforting thought! oh, most glorious theme
To speak of and hear of and feel 't·is no dream—
This Spirit-land near us, just hid from our seeing
By this veil of frail flesh that gives form to our being.

Freed spirits of loved ones, kept so out of sight!
I wish I could hear your dear voices to-night
In the very same tones that I heard ere you left us,
Ere God of your dear earthly presence bereft us.

I wish to our eyes God would let you appear
In forms like to those that we knew you in here;
And that Jesus, our Jesus, our Savior so precious,
With His bright living presence just once here would
    bless us.

Yet I think could I once see Him smile, hear His
  voice,
My soul, too ecstatic, would fail to rejoice;
It would so long the bonds that here held it to sever,
And till 't was released 't would be sighing forever.

Dear Lord! what are others compared unto Thee!
We yearn much to see Thee as erst some did see;
Thou, the essence of love, sweetest, purest, and dear-
  est!   *
To our hearts and our souls be Thou ever the nearest.

I'M ALMOST THERE.

I'm almost There!
I've nearly reached the road
That leads me to my Father's blest abode.

I'm almost There!
My feet now press the shore
Of the dark waters I shall soon pass o'er.

I'm almost There!
A little longer, soul,
And thou wilt rest thee in thy Heavenly Goal.

A few days more!
Let patient trust record,
And I shall see the coming of the Lord.

OH, IF FOR ONLY ONE SHORT HOUR.

Oh, if for only one short hour
    We might beside our hearthstone greet
The loved ones who have passed away,
    And hold with them communion sweet!
Or could we leave our living clay
    And join them in yon blissful sphere,
And there a rapturous converse hold
    Of all that erst to them was dear;
And could they then permitted be
    To breathe some words of joys above,
To strengthen our weak, wavering faith
    Till rest we in that Land of Love;
And then could we return at will,
    Till Death resume our human form,
Mid those to whom our hearts here cling,
    What thrilling ecstasy would warm
    And shield our breasts 'gainst life's cold storm.

Oh, if for only one short hour!
    An hour will come, 't will not be short,
When we shall meet our " lost and gone "—
    Not " lost," but in some better port—
And then and There we'll hear and see
    And know all that we now desire;
Unclad of earth's foul drapery,
    Our souls, fleet-wing'd, may then aspire,
And not in vain, to converse hold
    With dear ones in a holier sphere,
Nor will we wish *then* to return,
    To mingle with bereft ones here;
Or if we do, my faith is strong,
    If to our happiness 't will add,
Our absence Christ will not prolong
    From presences that make us glad,
    For Heaven is not, when souls are sad.

MY SAVIOR DEAR.

My Savior dear, since " God is love,"
  And Thou art one with God,
It were not strange Thou camest down
  And spilt for man Thy blood.

Blind, erring, weak, repentant man,
  Groping his darksome way!
How canst Thou close Thy loving ear
  When sorrowing he doth pray!

When helpless man with hope looks up
  To find Thy loving face,
How canst thou, Lord, deny to Him
  Thy free and pard'ning grace!

When man for man so much will dare,
  If love his soul pervade,
Held in Thy greater love, dear Lord,
  Why should he be dismayed!

O Jesus, Savior, loving One,
  When my dark soul doth cry
To Thee unseen for living faith,
  Do not the gift deny.

And when I beg Thy present aid
  In weakness, sorrow, care,
Bow down Thy pitying ear, dear Lord,
  And grant my soulful prayer.

Help! Jesus, help! in my distress,
  I lift my hands and plead,
Oh, could I but " Thy garments touch,"
  My heart would cease to bleed.

WHY MAY NOT WOMEN PREACH!

How can we let them go!
Do we not see them, day by day,
Frittering their life away,
And yet reach forth no might of ours
To urge their use of better powers
    As on they go!

How can we let them go!
The young, the fair, the bright, the gay,
And older ones not long to stay;
Filled up with cares and joys of life,
Quenching within the conscience' strife
    As on they go!

How can we let them go!
Our friends so true, our friends so dear,
And others' friends, to them as near,
Without meet warning from our tongue,
E'en though our hearts are sorrow-wrung
    As on they go!

How can we let them go!
Must women's lips no good seed sow
Outside the doors which we look through!
Nor step beyond our walls to catch
Some dying souls within our reach
    As on they go!

How can we let them go!
'T was woman first and woman last
Before the Sepulcher stood fast
Until the Savior bade them then
" The Lord has risen " tell to men,
    Obeying so,

The blesséd Marys go,
The Lord's disciples telling first
That ". Christ the bonds of death had burst,"
And then to others whom they met—
And still the tale they 're telling yet,
Where e'er the Testament is read,
That " Christ is risen from the dead."
    Let us do so.

Why *should* we let them go!
No word hath Jesus left behind
That every one of womankind
Must be a Martha—Mary's choice
He most approved with gracious voice:
    So choose we, too.

Why *should* we let them go!
Huldah preached, and Miriam sang
A song that through the wide world rang,
All unrebuked, and to this day ·
Are honored by all those who pray:
    So would we do.

Why should we let them go!
Deborah—a prophetess—
When heathen hosts did sore oppress
" Her people Israel," led the van
To battle, for there was no man
In all the tribes anear or far
Who dared to lead their sex to war,
    So lead she on.

Why should we let them go!
If woman may to conquest lead
God's chosen people in their need,
Why may she not in public teach!

To wand'ring sinners kindly preach,
In pulpits where men often fail
To speak the word that doth avail
    To save.a soul!

    And we *will* preach!
Paul, the apostle and the sage,
The women of the present age
Forbade not, but as times were then,*
Where women were the slaves of men,
Uncultured in the wiser arts,
Scarce claiming souls and scarcely hearts—
He rightly deemed *they* should not tell,
Like Anna,† of Immanuel.

* In Pagan lands.
† Prophetess in the Temple at the time of the birth of Christ.

WHY AND BECAUSE.

Why do I plain for thee, dear one,
    When all thy sorrows now are o'er!
'T is that thou lovedst me as none
    So dear will ever love me more.
Thy love to me was like the sun
    That breaks the gloom when tempests roar,
And with its brightness sweetly thrills
The panting earth and plainting rills.

BUZZ.

Buzz! buzz! buzz! thou tiny being!
What about me art thou seeing
That offends thee, little lurker!
Fly away, thou busy worker!

Of thy sweets I've pilfered none, sir!
Nor thy Summer haunts have shorn, sir!
I would ne'er in garden bowers
Rob thee of the sweetest flowers.

I've ne'er been anear their hive, sir,
Where thy wee bees live and thrive, sir;
Nor thy queen have I molested,
Nor her realms with ills infested.

Fly away, then, lest I harm thee,
For thy buzzing does not charm me;
Go and sip in weather sunny
From the flowers that give thee honey.

I no more can risk thy stinging,
From my ears be quickly winging
To thy wee ones, not yet flying—
For their " bee bread " meal a crying.

Fly away, thou noisy fellow,
For thy music is not mellow;
Lest I hurt thy little pate, sir,
Fly away, ere 't is too late, sir.

Oh, I did not mean to crush thee,
But to brush away and hush thee!
Have I marred each tiny feature,
Have I killed thee, little creature!

WHEN HE COMES.

Were our dear Jesus to appear,
As read we in the Book most dear,
" Like as from earth He now doth rise,
He shall descend before our eyes,"
On whom would His kind glance first fall?—
On rich and grand or poor and small,
On those with intellect broad and deep,
Or on the ones in sorrow's steep—
In lowly station, childlike, dumb,
When they within the presence come
Of those the gifted and the wise,
Who vault their knowledge to the skies!
The grand expounder of "The Faith"
Will doubtless feel that right *he* hath
To the first notice of the Lord,
Who'd taught the thousands from "His Word!"
Should not *he* first be called to meet
The Lord in air, and have the seat
Most honor'd by his side, when He
Shall rest His feet on earthly lea!
The poor and ignorant herd must know
Their place before the Lord is low;
Their minds' capacities are small
And dull and weak—the unlearn'd all
Will have a place they can enjoy
Just suited to their minds' employ....
But, ah! me simple, dost bethink
Those who did most of sorrow drink
Will meet His loving gaze before
The king or priest most learn'd in lore;
For He has said, "Father to Thee
I thanks do give that Thou for me
Hast from the prudent and the wise
Hidden these meanings—dimm'd their eyes,

And unto babes hast them revealed;"
The humble, helpless, sick, hast healed;
And also for Thy just decree,
"Here many last, *there* first shall be.

AN UP TELEGRAM.

Ye Heavens be propitious, send us rain
    •To cool the air;
'T is filled with fiery shafts King Sol shoots on us
    From his lair.

Methinks he sends his fiercest darts in haste
    To conquer Spring.
July is come in May, and all too soon
    We're sweltering.

The months are out of tune—all tangled up—
    "Hot August" days,
If August comes again, belike will be
    As cool as Mays—

As cool as Mays before the " weather man "
    So mixed together
Our Summer and our Spring, and quite upset
    Our other weather.

Ye Heavens, be propitious; send us rain:
    Be quick, or truly
The " Millerites," this time, will have their way—
    We'll burn up, surely.

                      May 20, 1877.

WILLIAM CULLEN BRYANT.

This day I saw him titled President
Unveil the new bronze statue in the park,
In honor and commemoration of
Our poet Halleck.   T'was to me a sight
·I was unused to in my country home,
And I was thankful for such privilege.
But quicker leapt my pulse with joy when saw
I him with head made hoary by the years,
And countenance thought-marked, and kingly eye,
Arise and speak.   The noisy crowd, so dense,
Chopped in my ears the polished sentence
Of this wise father of our country's bards.
But when he left the stand, so close he pass'd
I caught his hand—as other weak ones caught
Another's—and I said, "I rather far
Shake hands with thee than with a President—
A thousand times! oh, yes, ten thousand ·imes,
Would I prefer so could I take my choice."·
He stopped, and with a very pleasant smile,
Grasping my hand with kindly clasp, he asked
Me if he knew me; and if not, my name.
I, answering, said, " You do not know me, sir,
But since my first remembrance I have known
Of you, for I have read your thoughts in books,
And loved them;" then my name carelessly gave,
For he would not remember it, I thought,
Nor ever after bring to mind my face.
But, oh, to me it was a holy touch—
That handshake with the poet-god, and I
Shall not forget it in the by-and-by.

                                   May 15, 1877.

A CENTENNIAL ODE.

A hundred years ago was sown
  A seed of value rare,
In soil enriched by heroes' blood,
  And nurtured by their care.
And from that precious seed has grown
  A grand, far-spreading tree,
Where millions, now, of freeborn men
  Are holding jubilee.

The blossoms of this fruitful tree
  Send forth a perfume sweet,
And peoples, scenting it afar,
  Have come with weary feet
To rest within its favoring shade,
  And view, with wondering eye,
Its rapid growth—its happy realms
  That in its shelter lie.

Beneath its boughs they find a home
  Where Peace and Plenty reign ;
Where education's richest lore
  The poorest may obtain.
And so they learn to love the soil
  That healthful breezes fan,
Where all are sovereigns—each is peer
  To every brother-man.

And now from Europe, Asia far,
  And from a sister land—
America—mid Southern seas—
  A treasure-laden band
Are come to vie with us in Art
  And join our jubilee,
And taste the nectar of our vines,
  Beneath our Century Tree.

And here, beside our " stripes and stars,"
  Their pennons are unfurled,
Which have, a score of centuries, waved
  Over an older world.
The drapery floats in " standards " brave
  Which gentle zephyrs fill ;
Speaking, in symbols, gracious words,
  "To this New World 'Good-Will.' "

Hail ye ! a hearty welcome then,
  Nations of other clime.
If in our youth *ye* bear the palm,
  In arts of olden-time,
Ye still must marvel at our strides
  Beneath our own loved Tree,
And, with us, honor those who sowed
  The seed of Liberty.

Ring out, then, ring, ye countless bells !
  Ye heavy cannon, roar !
Let myriad voices pœans shout,
  Swelling from shore to shore ;
Let every hearth, and every haunt,
  Roll forth the anthem grand,
In thanks to Him who guards, in love,
  Our free, our happy land.

LINES FOR THE "FOURTH," 1876.

None, none who fought on Bunker Hill,
  At Trenton, or on Monmouth plain,
And none who signed our charter bold,
  In human form with us remain;
But millions feel those spirits brave
  Down from their heights have found their
    way,
And with us jubilates keep
  On this our grand Centennial day.

Loved Washington! the scene is changed
  Since by the tree in Cambridge thou
Of our brave yeomen took command,
  Who in the furrow left the plow;
In homespun garb, untrained in war,
  But girded with a righteous shield,
Each spirit bold, and proud to bare
  His bosom on the bloody field.

And ye brave souls who dared to sign
  The charter of our Liberty,
Can ye conceive this country now
  That bondland that ye sought to free?
Did ye with far prophetic gaze,
  Through the long vista of the years,
Behold the upgrowth of the seed,
  Sown by your hands in blood and tears?

Welcome, ye heaven-clad spirits, then,
  Who join us in our jubilee;
You laid our country's corner-stone,
  And gave to us our birthright free.
Your bodies sleep amid the dust
  On which we tread our gladsome way;
But well we know your spirits keep,
  With us, this grand centennial day.

THE CRY FOR LIBERTY.

Down the long roll of centuries,
   O'er graves of buried years,
Has come the cry for " Liberty,"
   Through bondmen's wail and tears.
Were our forefathers wiser men
   And of a nobler mold,
Than they who fought, and bled, and died
   Upon the ramparts old,
That they should plant a goodlier tree
   Within this Western soil,
Than e'er was in the Orient laid
   By bondmen's sweat and moil?
Or is it that a kinder God,
   With a more pitying eye,
Was moved to mercy's farthest verge
   To heed the people's cry?

A HYMN OF PRAISE.

We do rejoice and praise Thee, God!
   For 'tis Thy hand
Has led us through a hundred years
   To this fair land.
No war's alarms affright us now,
   For by Thy grace
The plowshare and the pruning-hook
   The sword replace.
The school bells peal, and Sabbath chimes,
   And love's refrain,
Resound, in peace' melodious notes
   O'er our domain.

Erst prairies vast the grains have made
    A waving field ;
Erst howling wilds and rocky soil
    Now blossoms yield.
And towns and villages begirt
    Each dale and hill;
The vine-clad cot and mansion broad
    Our country fill.
The fiery horse with iron hoof
    Flies o'er our land.
With wafting sails our streams are white—
    Our lakes are spanned.

Our mountains yield their precious ore,
    Our vales their gems ;
And Commerce brings us treasures rare—
    Peace' diadems !
Science and Art have opened wide
    Their entrance-door,
Till of their wealth each freeborn man
    Hath golden store.
And for all this we praise Thee, God !
    For 'tis thy hand
Has led us through a hundred years
    To this fair land.

WORLD WONDERS.

CENTENNIAL YEAR—1876.

Kentucky's Cave! Niagara!
And Montmorenci's Falls!
Wild Watkins' Glen! with awe and bliss
Each marvelous work enthralls
The mind that has the privilege
This glorious page to see
In Nature's Book, telling in part
God's Power's Immensity!

'T were sacrilege for one to strive,
With mortal's finite power,
To picture ye....Such gift divine
Were more than angel's dower.
So wild! so weird! grand! beautiful!
Such heights and depths sublime!
Such shifting scenes magnificent,
God-wrought through countless time!

Such rocks, God-hewn! ravines, cascades,
And cataracts' boiling flood!
Such chasms deep and dark and dread,
Where never foot hath trod!
Such caverns curious with their suites
Of roofs and floors and walls,
Bedecked with forms grand, fanciful,
Færies' ancestral halls!

The simplest mind in scenes like these
　　Is forced a power to own
Who works with skill omnipotent
　　Throughout the vast Unknown;
For here the while his soul is raised
　　Above the low routine,
Wherein it takes its daily rounds,
　　And glimpses the Unseen.

Go all the world, strike hands and go,
　　These master works to view!
The soul needs change, as flesh needs bread,
　　As plants need sun and dew.
This hemisphere is dotted thick
　　With sights for wond'ring eyes,
Such visions rarely can be seen
　　Beneath far, foreign skies.

Mosaics, sculpture, carvings fine,
　　And painting's highest art,
Can never move, like Nature's works,
　　And thrill the human heart.
Our great " Centennial " marvels showed
　　From lands beyond the sea;
But would you view earth's grandest scenes
　　Range o'er our country free.

FURL THE FLAG—1877.

The clouds are thick, the skies are dark,
　The winds are sobbing, sighing,
The tempest lulls awhile its breath
　For Liberty lies dying....

Toll the sad knell! furl, furl the flag!
　For Liberty is dead;
Fold from our sight forevermore,
　The " blue " and " white " and " red."
Let our broad banner now be black,
　That floats from sea to sea;
We mourn a country brought to scorn,
　That late was " brave and free."

Toll the sad knell! furl, furl the flag,
　Shred, trailing in the dust!
Our plotting foes have recreant proved
　Unto their sacred trust
Which our forefathers left for us
　To die for or to shield;
Dishonor triumphs in our sight
　Upon their blood-bought field.

Fraud, treachery and trickery,
　Unstinted, wily, bold,
Inclosed our sacred goddess fast,
　Within their vilest hold.
O'erwhelmed she sank beneath their ire,
　And, blasted by their breath,
She sleeps, our Country's martyr'd maid,
　Within the clasp of death.

Toll the sad knell! furl, furl the flag!
  Our first Centennial year
Was born in joy, but dies in grief,
  O'er Freedom's funeral bier.
And each who once was Freedom's son
  Must hide with shame his face,
While nations proud are looking on,
  And mock at our disgrace.

Toll the sad knell! furl, furl the flag!
  Which nevermore may wave
Its "stars" and "stripes" in victory
  Above a tyrant's grave.
Its "colors" have been trampled low
  By foul and impious feet;
Furl it, and shroud its tattered folds
  Within Death's winding-sheet.

So lay it by—a memory dear
  Of happy days now past—
Of sunny years too glorious
  And brightly sweet to last.
And on fair Freedom's tomb we'll carve,
  For future times, this line:
Virtue and valor firm must stand,
  Life-guards round Freedom's shrine.

Toll the sad knell! furl the dear flag!
  But lift unceasing cries,
Till liberty shall, phenix-like,
  From its lov'd dust arise,
And plant her feet in deeper soil,
  Purged by Contrition's fires—
A greater boon to earth than when
  Won by our sacred sires.

                              Feb. 20-23.

CENTRAL PARK.

Am I in Paradise! bright, happy realm!
How few the moments that have wrought the change.
The skies are fleecy white and sapphire blue;
The atmosphere is like a breath of balm;
The leaveing trees and flow'ring shrubs and vines,
And smooth green velvet lawns skirt me around;
And charm my brimming gaze baldheaded rocks,
And rocks, with verdure crowned, of every shape
That's pleasing to the eye; and rippling rills,
And trickling rivulets, and waterfalls;
And lakes with dancing skiff and boats with sails,
Light curveting upon the gentle wave:
And goldfish sporting 'neath the glassy face,
And the white swans, so graceful, floating o'er
The little ocean, and the duckling broods,
And " classic " quacking geese, slow swimming by;
And pretty singing birds that cleave the air;
And clean and cosy paths that lead you on
To owlets' caves, and the brisk squirrel's nest,
And the proud, gorgeous peacocks' grassy glades;
And meadow-land for herds and bleating flocks,
And parks for deer, and timid rabbits' haunts;
And little hills and blooming glebes and dells;
And lovely fountains dashing feathery spray;
And grottoes cool, roofed with the ivy's blooms:
And everything in Nature, Nature's world
In miniature, surpassing Nature's self!
This seems indeed a taste of Heaven when
Compared with the close city's dingy walls
And filthy streets and noisome atmosphere,
And sounds uncouth and grating to the sense,
And sights that try the soul.   Oh, it were strange
If innocence and purity could live

And thrive, unstifled by the blasting breath
Of fest'ring bodies, and polluted minds,
Reared in such charnel-house—this city's mart.

New York, May, 1877.

LONGFELLOW.

We crossed the river Charles, daughter and I,
And to our minds recalled on passing by
His lines upon it.   Then, to Cambridge bound,
Soon pressed our willing feet on classic ground,
And saw the tree beneath whose branches stood
An earnest, worthy, solemn brotherhood
Of warriors: here our country's honored son
They first acknowledged chief—our Washington.
Then passed we on to Harvard's hallow'd walls,
And loitered through her consecrated halls,
Where students of Pierian waters quaff;
And saw so much, we disremember half
Of the small half we saw; and then we stroll'd
Along the pleasant streets; then, making bold,
Asked of a stranger, Tell us where to find
Longfellow's home; for we'd a goodly mind
To go and view the shrine wherein he dwelt
And kneel before it, for our hearts did melt
Within us when we found ourselves so near
The poet-soul we both did so revere.
The stranger kindly pointed us the way.
We only meant outside the wall to stray;
But when we stood beside the open gate,
The impulse came—why should we calmly wait
Outside Parnassus! we would venture more;
And though somewhat abashed we reached the door
And told our errand: 'T was to see his face

And hear his voice, so would he give us grace?
"Certainly, bid them enter;" and we did,
While our hearts' throbbing scarcely could be hid.
But when we saw him all our tremor still'd,
As if some sweet magnetic power so will'd.
His pleasant greeting and his easy ways
Soon made us feel we'd known him all our days.
He talked of books and travels; said 't was here
Our Washington and family lived the year
Before he girded on his sword to fight
And win from Britain's hands our country's right.
He showed us pictures he most valued hung
Upon the walls wherein he much had sung,
And one so like his book's fair frontispiece,
And asked if he had changed with Time's increase;
And told us tales of Browning, Tennyson,
With whom he was familiar; but the sun
With fiery coursers downward fled toward night,
And we had trespassed, with no claim of right,
Upon his golden moments, so we said
We thanked him for his kindness, and then bade
Good-by. Then slow repassed Parnassian gate,
Where singeth one whose songs are an estate
Cambridge will hold her highest honor while
The world is rolling and the heavens smile.

True poets' songs fling on the air a wealth of fragrant
      breath,
Sweet as the perfumes sweetest roses yield when
      crushed in death.

                    1872